Popular Mechanics Complete Step by Step Appliance Repair Manual

By Mort Schultz

Book Division, The Hearst Corporation,
New York, N.Y. 10019

Library of Congress catalog card number: 75-18652
ISBN 0-910990-60-3

Contents

Major appliances

Section 1
Small Motorized
Appliances

Chapter 1

Introduction

**The chapters which make up this section deal with small appliances
which use motors. Further on you will read about large motorized appliances.
Small? Large? For our purposes, a small appliance is one you can easily hold
or carry in your hand. A big one, like a washing machine, you can't**

EACH OF THE SMALL appliances we discuss in this section uses one of four kinds of motors. The following is a chapter-by-chapter rundown of the appliances, and the type of motor each uses:

Chapter 2. Electric Food Mixers—AC-DC universal motor

Chapter 3. Electric Food Blenders—AC-DC universal motor

Chapter 4. Vacuum Cleaners and Electric Brooms—AC-DC universal motor

Chapter 5. Floor Polishers—AC-DC universal motor

Chapter 6. Electric Knife—Direct current (DC) motor

Chapter 7. Electric Toothbrush—Direct current (DC) motor

Chapter 8. Electric Shaver—Direct current (DC) motor

Chapter 9. Electric Can Opener—Shaded-pole motor

Chapter 10. Hair Dryer—Shaded-pole motor

Chapter 11. Small Electric Fans—Shaded-pole motor or split-phase motor

Chapter 12. Home Workshop Motors—AC-DC universal motor

The job of any motor is to drive something that does work. This goes for the engine in your car—it goes for the motor in your food mixer. It is not our intention here to make you an expert on each of the four kinds of motors mentioned above, or to get too theoretical, but you should have some understanding of how they work. Without this understanding, troubleshooting and repairing small motorized appliances becomes difficult.

The remainder of this chapter gives brief descriptions of the AC-DC universal motor, direct-current (DC) motor, shaded-pole motor, and split-phase motor. Information contained in the chapters dealing with the appliances will fortify what is discussed here. Also contained in this introductory chapter are explanations of other terms that you will find in this section —terms you may or may not be familiar with. Let's not take chances. We'll explain them.

facts about motors

1. AC-DC UNIVERSAL MOTOR. This motor derives its name from the fact that it can run on either alternating current or direct current. Alternating current is current in which the direction of flow is reversed at regular intervals. Direct current *always* flows in the same direction.

The value of the universal motor

lies in its ability to provide an extremely high starting torque and to attain high speed quickly while under a fairly heavy load. Look again at the list of appliances mentioned above which use the universal motor, and you can see that each of them may require a high torque value and may be asked to operate under heavy loads.

Torque, incidentally, is the tendency of an object to rotate. It is a measure of turning or twisting effort imparted, for our purposes, by a motor.

The AC-DC universal motor consists of two major components: a rotor and stator. Let's talk about the rotor first.

The **rotor** is a part that rotates. It doesn't move up and down, in and out, side to side, or in any other direction than around.

In effect, the rotor of an AC-DC universal motor is made up of an **armature,** which is an iron core with coils of wire wrapped around it, and the **commutator.** The commutator and armature are together—that is, they comprise a single assembly (Figure 1).

The **commutator,** which is positioned on one end of the armature, consists of a series of copper bars laid out in circular fashion. They do not touch each other. Rather, they are insulated from each other by sheets of mica. The commutator is a switching mechanism—but more about that in a minute.

Passing right through the middle of the armature and commutator is a shaft that sticks out of both ends. The distance that the shaft extends from each end varies from appliance to appliance, or whatever, and is really not very important.

However, what is important is that one end of the shaft is normally attached to a bearing assembly so the rotor can rotate. (But it doesn't have to be. In some cases, for example, the shaft may have a small fan that cools the interior of the appliance.) The other end of the shaft is attached to the appliance's working device. In the case of a food blender, for example, the end of the shaft is attached to the cutting knives.

But that "working" end of the shaft may instead be attached to a gear train which, in turn, is attached to a working element. This is true with food mixers and floor polishers.

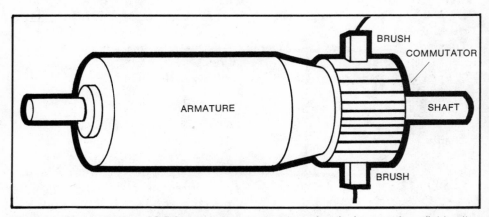

Figure 1. The rotor of an AC-DC universal motor receives electrical energy from field coil through one brush that touches commutator. Current passes through armature and out through another brush. This establishes magnetic field, causing armature to revolve.

Now, what about the **stator?** Well, that's the part of the motor in which the rotor is positioned, but keep in mind that it is positioned in this way so its movement cannot be impeded. The stator is a frame (iron, usually) containing coils (wires) called **field coils.**

Essentially, this is what happens: electricity enters one of the field coils through the appliance's line cord, which is plugged into a wall socket. Current passes from the field coil into one of two carbon segments, called **brushes,** which are positioned directly opposite one another on the commutator. The brushes are held in contact with the commutator by springs.

Okay, current flows through the brush to the one commutator bar the brush is touching, through the armature coil to which the armature is connected, out through another commutator bar that is in contact with the other brush, into another field coil, and back to its source (Figure 2). This means that the brushes and commutator bars, as indicated before, act as an automatic switching device that connects and disconnects each coil at

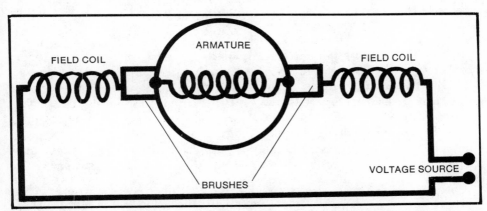

Figure 2. This drawing demonstrates the circuitry of a universal motor. Refer to Figure 1 and then to this drawing, and you will understand the way this versatile motor works.

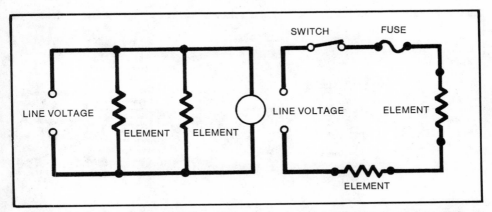

Figures 3 and 4. In a series circuit (right) all components are wired together so electricity flows throughout all components and back to the source with no "detours." In a parallel circuit (left) line voltage divides itself among many components as it flows along.

exactly the right moment as the armature revolves.

All components of a universal motor are wired together in tandem, and current at every point is the same. This arrangement is called a **series circuit** (Figure 3).

This differs from a **parallel circuit,** which is a term you'll run across again. In a parallel circuit (which is also called a multiple or shunt circuit), components are arranged so the current divides itself between them (Figure 4).

It is interesting to note that every universal motor is made the same way —the smallest and the biggest. Thus, the starter motor in your car, which is a universal motor, has the same configuration and parts as the universal motor in your vacuum cleaner.

2. Direct Current (DC) Motor. The direct current (DC) motor looks and acts almost like an AC-DC universal motor. It has an armature, commutator, and brushes. However, it can operate on direct current only—on current which flows always in the same direction.

One of the main differences between an AC-DC universal motor and a DC motor is that most DC motors have stators consisting of a series of permanent magnets rather than field coils. This creates a magnetic field, just as field coils do, so the rotor can revolve. However, the voltage needed to get the rotor of a DC motor revolving is much lower (5 to 7 volts) than that needed by an AC-DC universal motor (115 volts).

Consider the appliances in which a DC motor is used—electric knives, electric toothbrushes, and electric shavers. These are all units which do not need a great deal of power to do work. For this reason, a DC motor provides much less torque than a universal motor.

In addition, the fact that many electric knives, shavers, and toothbrushes are "cordless" demands that the units be capable of working on battery power (Figure 5). As you know, a battery pack provides relatively low voltage.

A direct-current (DC) motor may "work" on alternating current (AC). How can this be? Some models of electric knives, toothbrushes, and shavers can be plugged into an AC wall outlet and will operate. How-

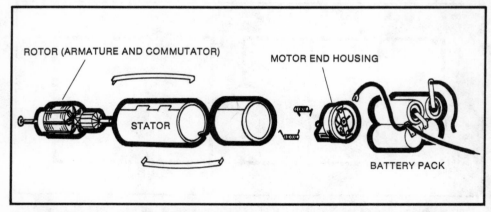

Figure 5. This drawing shows the relationship of the armature and commutator (rotor) to the frame (stator) of a direct-current motor. Magnets (not visible) are in the frame. Notice the battery power pack. (The example here is the motor part of a cordless electric knife).

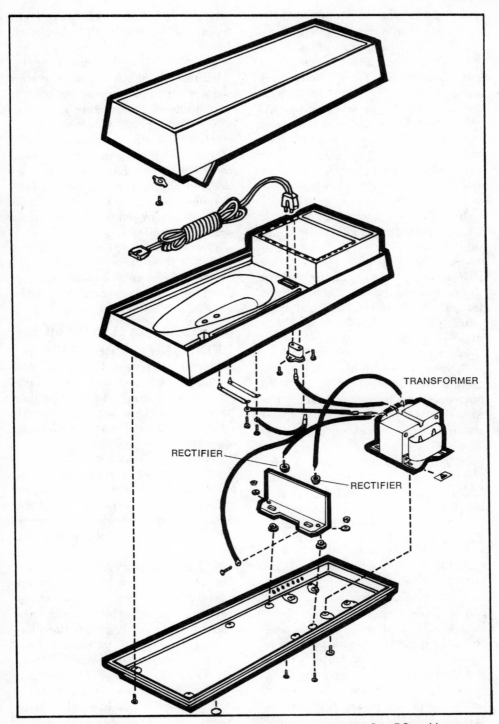

Figure 6. This drawing shows the essential parts needed to convert AC to DC and lower current to a usable level in the electric knife shown in Figure 5. The rectifiers convert AC to DC and the transformer reduces the voltage.

ever, the appliance is not actually functioning on alternating current.

The alternating current is being transformed into direct current by a part inside the appliance called a rectifier (Figure 6). The same thing happens in about the same way inside the alternator of your car. The alternator actually produces alternating current, but it is converted to direct current by mechanisms called diodes. The lights, radio, and all other accessories in your car need direct current to work.

Inside the DC motor of an electric knife, shaver, and toothbrush is another feature that works like a transformer operating in reverse. Rather than stepping up the voltage, voltage drops, so the appliance can operate at its normal energy level of 5 to 7 volts when plugged into the wall. At a greater voltage, the unit may be damaged.

3. **Shaded-Pole Motor.** Shaded-pole motors are small (1/100 to 1/20 horsepower) alternating-current motors that are used where very low starting torque is needed (Figure 7). There is little or no resistance (load) imposed on the motor when it tries to get going. With small electric fans and hair dryers, for example, the only resistance the motor encounters is air —and that's not much resistance at all.

A shaded-pole motor has no commutator on its armature and no brushes. The shaded-pole winding consists of solid copper rings on each pole tip. The rings set up a magnetic field which alternately aids and opposes the main field coil. The effect is a field that produces a turning force and starts the armature spinning.

4. **Split-Phase Motor.** This motor will be discussed again in the introduction to section 3 on major motorized appliances since it is primarily employed in large units, such as washing machines. However, you might encounter one in a large electric fan.

A split-phase motor consists of two windings (coils). One is used to start the armature turning, and the other is used to keep the armature turning at a constant speed. Once the motor starts and attains running speed, the starting coil is cut from the circuit and the running coil assumes the task of keeping the motor running. This is done by means, usually, of a centrifugal switch (or governor), that has a spring-controlled arm.

On the end of this arm is a contact point. When this contact point "breaks" away from a mating contact point, the circuit is broken and the starting coil shuts off.

the importance of continuity

"CONTINUITY" IS A WORD you will see more frequently in this book than any other technical word. Continuity refers simply to a continuous circuit—that is, to a circuit through which electricity flows without being interrupted.

When there is an interruption in electric flow, electricity can't reach the point it is supposed to reach, and the appliance won't work. The job of the home-appliance repairman, therefore, is to find the point of interruption and fix it.

A continuity test can be performed with one of several kinds of instruments. The most reliable is a multimeter that usually combines into one instrument a number of functions, including an AC/DC volt-meter, ammeter, ohmmeter, and leakage checker (Figure 8).

An instruction booklet accompanying a multitester you buy will explain exactly how to use it for the various functions the tester performs, and I must emphasize that a multitester can

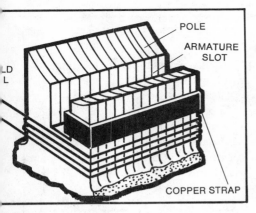

POLE

ARMATURE SLOT

COPPER STRAP

Figure 7. In shaded-pole motor, current is induced in copper strap, which sets up magnetic field across slot, moving armature.

Figure 8. The handyman who plans to do a lot of appliance repair should consider purchase of a multitester, which is very useful.

be employed for tasks other than checking continuity.

For example, you can measure current drawn by an appliance from a line, you can measure the power consumed by an appliance, you can check the value of a resistor, and so forth. It is an extremely versatile and useful instrument.

How you check continuity with a multitester depends on the appliance. If the appliance does not have resistance built into it, as does a food mixer, then continuity with a multitester is checked the same way as you would check it with a flashlight tester (we describe below). The "leakage" light serves as the continuity light. It will or it will not show continuity in the circuit.

However, when an appliance has resistance designed into it, as one possessing a heating element does, then continuity usually has to be tested using an ohmmeter. An ohmmeter tells you how much resistance is in the circuit. If the amount meets manufacturer specifications, then you conclude that the circuit is in proper working condition. If continuity is excessive, there is damage that has to be repaired.

Testing resistance is something that you cannot do with any testing instrument except an ohmmeter, or a multitester that has an ohmmeter function.

In any case, how does one check continuity? Let's take an example. Look at the schematic in Figure 9.

You want to check continuity. Start by attaching the tester to the prongs of the plugs (points A & B). If the ohmmeter needle records a reading, probably there is continuity. I say "probably," because a short circuit in the line cord can cause the meter to show continuity when there really isn't any. To test, simply switch the appliance off. If the meter goes

9

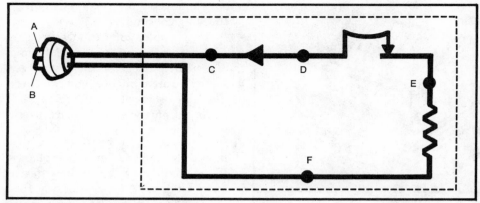

Figure 9. This drawing indicates the procedure to follow in making continuity tests of an appliance. If the appliance won't work, each segment of the appliance should be tested until the faulty component is located. It can then be repaired.

"dead," it means the line cord is okay. If the meter stays where it is, then the line cord is shorted. It should be replaced and continuity retested.

But suppose you get no "life" from the meter. There is a loss of continuity somewhere in the circuit. If you probe each segment, you can find the point of trouble.

For example, place the leads of the continuity meter across the switch (points C & D). Flip the switch on (if the switch is off—"open"—electricity can't flow, and no continuity will show). There should be a reading on the meter. If there isn't, the switch is bad. Replace it.

Now skip to points D & E—across the thermostat. The thermostat points have to be closed, too. Turn on the appliance. Lack of continuity indicates a bad thermostat. Get the idea?

There are two important facts to keep in mind regarding checking continuity:

1. During a continuity test, the appliance is *never, never, never* plugged into the wall outlet. The energy for the test comes from the continuity tester itself (Figure 10).

2. The switch of the appliance when testing most segments of a circuit

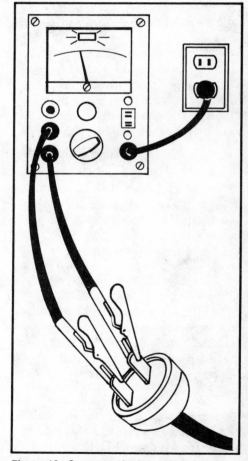

Figure 10. Some continuity testers operate on household current, but *never* plug appliance into wall during a continuity test.

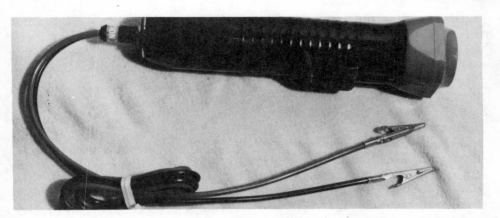

Figure 11. The flashlight continuity tester is the safest. However, it does not give a reading if an appliance has built-in resistance—even though the appliance is in perfect condition. In most cases, an ohmmeter is needed to check a circuit with built-in resistance.

must be turned on.

Another instrument you can use for making continuity tests is a simple flashlight-type testlight (Figure 11). It has two probes and is powered by ordinary dry cells. When there is continuity in a circuit the bulb will glow. When continuity has been disrupted, the bulb will not glow.

You use the flashlight continuity tester in tracing a circuit exactly as described above. Touch the leads across the segments you are testing—a switch, for example. If the bulb glows, there is continuity. If it doesn't glow, there is no continuity.

The flashlight tester is very safe to use. It works on dry cells. You can't get much of a shock from a flashlight battery—not even from three or four. But you could get one big bang if you accidentally touch a probe of a multitester.

You can also fabricate a continuity tester. How this is done is explained in the next chapter dealing with electric food mixers. There is nothing wrong with a makeshift continuity tester, but of the three kinds, the ones sold commercially are preferred.

caution . . . caution

YOU ARE DEALING with *electric* appliances, and electricity can kill. I don't want to preach or belabor the safety aspect of what you're about to embark on. Instead, let's just list a few precautions. The first is the most important—

1. *Think* about what you are doing *at all times.* Working with electricity safely is a matter of common sense.

2. Never touch a bare wire as long as there is chance that electricity is flowing through it. It could be the last bare wire you ever touch.

3. Never work on an appliance that is "live." Be sure the line cord is disconnected. A good habit to get into is to tape the cord to something so you *see* the plug as you work on the unit. The appliance switch being off (open) doesn't mean that the appliance is "dead." Electricity could be getting to a certain point, and that might just be the point where you have to work.

4. There are times, of course, when you have to plug a line-cord plug into the wall and turn on an appliance. For example, when you perform a continuity test using a multitester or makeshift tester, leads have to be connected to the circuit and the tester

must be plugged into the wall. The wrong way to do this is to plug the tester into the wall outlet and then connect tester probes to the circuit. The safe procedure is to make connections first, and then plug the tester in.

5. If you must replace an appliance's line cord because it is faulty, make certain you get a new cord of the same gauge as the original. If you are not sure of the gauge, take the old cord with you to the dealer. Undersized cords can lead to fire.

6. Always make sure an appliance you have repaired is not grounded (shorted). A wire inside the case, for example, may have accidentally shifted and is touching the case.

When the appliance is plugged into the wall and turned on, and the case is touched, the user of the appliance could go flying across the room.

Checking for a ground is very easy. Set the appliance on a table or workbench. Make sure the line cord is disconnected. Attach one lead of a testlight to a metal part of the appliance's frame. Attach the other lead of the testlight to a ground, such as a pipe. Plug the appliance's line cord into the wall and flip on the unit's switch.

If the testlight glows, the appliance is grounded. Disconnect everything, open up the appliance, find the short, and fix it.

Chapter 2

Food mixers

How's that? No more cakes or cookies until you repair your wife's food mixer? Well, there's no particular mystery. Determine the possible problems, then eliminate them one by one

THE MOST COMMON PROBLEMS afflicting electric food mixers are damaged beaters and failure of the motor to run at all. However, there are other malfunctions which can affect this useful kitchen appliance. The most common ones include the following:

- The motor runs too slowly and lacks pep
- The motor sparks as it runs
- The motor runs, but the beaters don't turn
- The motor overheats

Any one of these malfunctions can strike your mixer, whether it's a "sta-tionary" (upright) or portable unit. Larger and smaller mixers are basically the same although upright models possess as many as 12 different speeds. Generally, portable mixers have just three speeds—slow, medium and fast.

Upright and portable electric food mixers are equipped with universal motors (Figures 1 and 2). A universal motor is so called because it will work on both AC and DC current. In fact, frequently you will see this motor referred to as an "AC-DC universal motor," although as you probably

Figure 1. The electric food mixer is one of the most used kitchen appliances. Upright and hand-held models are basically same.

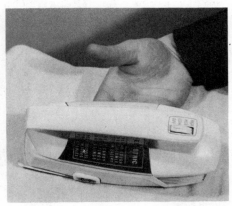

Figure 2. The portable electric food mixer normally has a three-speed switch. In this model, the switch is in the handle.

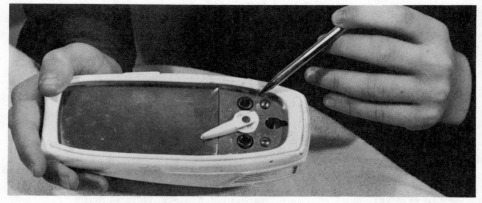

Figure 3. An AC-DC universal motor in a food mixer has the task of turning a set of gears which permit two chucks in the base of the appliance to revolve. The white switch-type device you see is the release mechanism which detaches the beaters from the chucks.

know direct current (DC) has virtually disappeared from the American scene in preference to alternating current (AC).

A universal motor provides an extremely high starting torque and high speed. Torque is turning power. For a given size and weight, in fact, the universal motor provides more power than any other type of motor. A universal motor, therefore, is used in appliances that have to start and work under relatively heavy loads. In addition to electric food mixers, these include electric food blenders, vacuum cleaners and floor polishers. In case you didn't know, the starter motor in your car is a universal motor.

The universal motor of an electric food mixer provides rotary motion to turn a set of gears. The gears rotate to turn two chucks which hold two beaters (Figure 3).

The rotating member of a universal motor is the armature, which consists essentially of coils of wire wound around an iron core. The armature is positioned between two field coils. A field is an area where magnetism can be created.

The armature and field coils are connected by carbon brushes. There are two—one directly opposite the other. The brushes are held by springs right against one end of the armature, which is called the commutator end. The commutator consists of a series of metal bars that are uncovered to permit free passage of current.

When the mixer is in operation, electricity is fed by the line cord from a wall outlet to one of the field coils. Current passes from the field coil through the armature by way of the brushes, and flows out the other field coil. This establishes a field of magnetism between armature and field coils, causing the armature to spin at a very high rate of speed.

However, high speed is not often desired. In an electric food mixer, for example, it is frequently desirable to have the beaters operate at slower speeds, according to the consistency of the food. Another characteristic of a universal motor that makes it ideal for use in mixers and some other appliances is that its speed can be varied.

variable speed

AN ELECTRIC FOOD MIXER employs one of three methods of speed control: centrifugal switch, tapped field control, or adjustable brushes.

The **centrifugal switch** is a governor that keeps the motor at the desired speed by alternately impeding and restoring current (Figure 4). When the motor is shut off and is at rest, with no load on it, a spring pulls a movable contact point against another contact point. When the motor is turned on, it starts up normally and begins speeding up. When it reaches a certain speed, centrifugal force overcomes the pull of the spring and causes the contact points to separate. This breaks the circuit.

With no voltage being applied, the motor slows down. Centrifugal force is reduced, and the spring is able to pull the contact points together again. The motor speeds up, and the process repeats itself.

Making and breaking a circuit occurs many times during one revolution of the motor, so that motor operation is hitchless and smooth. The actual speed at which the motor turns can be set by positioning the adjustable contact. When the contact is moved to the left (you do this by setting the speed switch), centrifugal force will break the circuit at a lower speed than when the contact is moved

to the right. In other words, the voltage will be "off" a greater part of the time, thus permitting a lower speed.

Contact points can be burned and ruined from the frequent making and breaking of a circuit. Off-on applications of current produce surges of electricity. To absorb these surges and keep them from burning points, a small capacitor generally is placed across the points. This capacitor, then, serves the same purpose as the condensor in your car's distributor—that is, it absorbs excess current created by the making and breaking of a circuit.

The **tapped field control** method of varying speed, in effect, shortens or lengthens the magnetic field. When this is done, less speed is created.

Let's suppose your mixer has a low-(L), medium-(M), and high-(H) speed switch. The setting of the switch taps one field coil. When the switch is on H, the entire coil is in the circuit, allowing maximum magnetism and, therefore, maximum speed. At M and L settings, the coil is progressively shortened, producing less magnetism and less speed (Figures 5 and 6). Incidentally, the number of taps does not have to be limited to three.

Use of **adjustable brushes** is no longer popular. There is one best position for the brushes, and that is right smack up against the commutator. Here, maximum torque is produced. Moving the brushes from this position will cause reduced speed, and also reduced torque. Less power is created. Furthermore, greater wear of the brushes and commutator takes place, because current is forced to jump a gap between the two. This arcing, as it is called, creates a burning that causes more wear than normal. However, if you have a very

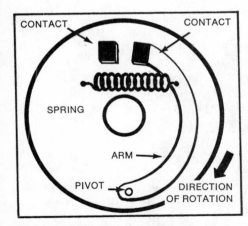

Figure 4. A centrifugal switch has contact points that "make" and "break" rapidly to keep food-mixer speed constant.

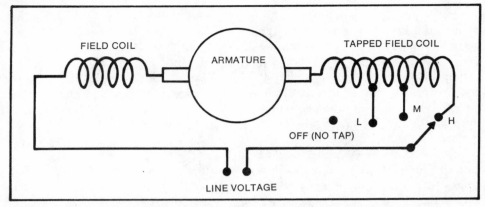

Figure 5. This line drawing of a tapped field-coil switch demonstrates that speed is controlled by the placement of the tap vis-a-vis the field coil.

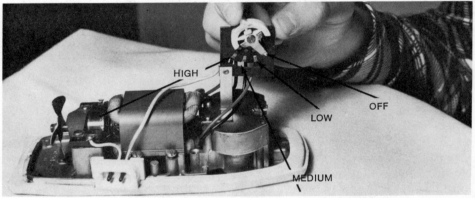

Figure 6. The tapped field-coil switch is often employed on portable food mixers. This photo of the switch when viewed with the drawing above will clarify the mechanism.

old mixer, you might find that it uses adjustable brushes.

let's repair your beater

DAMAGED BEATERS, as we mentioned, comprise one of the most common problems affecting electric food mixers. Carelessness is the chief reason that beaters are bent.

Beater blades are normally made of fairly soft metal. If you put them down on a hard surface before the motor has come to a complete stop, you can bend the beaters. Also, laying objects on top of beaters will bend them.

Often, if beater blades are bent, you can straighten them. However, if the shaft is bent, forget it. Buy a new beater (Figure 7). It is very difficult to true a bent shaft so it can be attached to its chuck without ramming it home, which may damage the chuck.

After years of use, beater shafts may wear to a point where they slip in their chucks. Replace the beaters. Keep in mind, too, that if beater shafts stick in their chucks, they can be lubricated to provide easier operation. Just squirt a few drops of penetrating oil into the sleeves (Figure 8).

Other common problems of electric

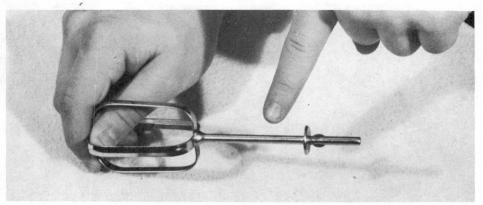

Figure 7. Beaters take a beating when used carelessly. Check the shaft. If bent, replace the beater. However, if only the beater blades are bent, you can usually straighten them.

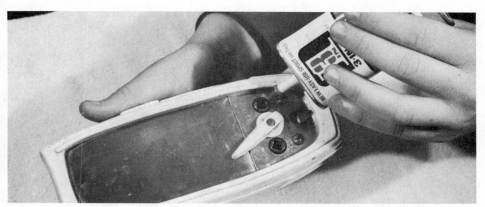

Figure 8. If the beaters stick in the chucks, a drop or two of oil will usually solve the problem. Just squirt penetrating oil into the sleeves.

food mixers usually require disassembly of the mixer for repairs. In the repair procedures given below, we proceed from the most likely cause for a problem to the least likely.

When you *must* take a food mixer apart for repairs you will notice that the case is held together by two or three large assembly screws. Do *not* force anything. If some part doesn't come out easily, search closely for a hidden fastener or wire. Do not pull. You may cause more damage than you already have.

As you take the unit apart to reach the troublesome part, as spelled out in the discussion below, keep track of your disassembly. Make notes and drawings if that will help. This will allow you to reverse the process to assemble the unit properly.

Caution: Make absolutely certain that the line cord is *not* plugged in.

when the motor won't run

1. **Start by checking** to see that electricity is reaching the unit. Plug the appliance into another wall outlet. Unless electricity is out all over the place (check fuses and circuit breakers), it is unlikely that two wall outlets will be dead.

Figure 9. One way of trying to determine if a break in the line cord is causing a failure is to plug the cord into a wall outlet, turn the unit on "low" and manipulate the cord.

2. **Check the line cord** for an internal break.

Plug the line cord into a wall outlet and manipulate the cord over its entire length, bending it back and forth (Figure 9). Do not bend the cord in half. All you want to do is bend it sufficiently to recontact wires if they are split at any one spot.

Caution: Before making this test, inspect the line cord carefully for frayed insulation. If insulation is frayed, replace the cord. Do not grasp the cord at any worn spot. You may get a kick you don't want.

If the motor whirrs as you manipulate the line cord, it's a tip-off that the cord is defective. Replace it with one of the *same* rating. Do not use an undersized replacement cord. It can burn up. Take the old cord with you when buying the new one to be sure you get the right size.

A defective line cord may not show itself with this test. Maybe wires are parted in more than one spot. Anyway, a more accurate way of testing line cords is with a continuity tester. This test requires that the cord be disconnected from the unit if the cord is an integral part of the unit, which means that on some models the case

has to be split open to reach the cord's terminals. You may not want to do this until you check for worn brushes, which you might be able to do without dismantling the case and which is a major reason for the motor not running. If the cord is the detachable kind, the easiest procedure is to test it on another appliance which you know works. In any event, let's discuss continuity testing here.

What is continuity all about? Continuity refers to the **non**interruption of electricity flowing through a circuit. As long as electricity is getting to and through each electrical part of an appliance, the appliance will function (unless there is something *mechanically* wrong).

Testing continuity doesn't require an elaborate test instrument. All you need is a test lamp which you can buy in a hardware store, or components that will allow you to make a test lamp yourself.

A test lamp (from now on we will refer to it as a continuity tester) is made by using a waterproof electric socket, two insulated alligator clips, a two-prong plug, and ordinary lamp wire. Be sure to use ample wire so you can reach large, stationary appliances from the nearest wall outlet. A continuity tester is used for checking all appliances—washing machines and dishwashers as well as food mixers and vacuum cleaners.

You can make a continuity tester in the following way:

a. **Strip the ends** of a length of wire. Connect one end to the waterproof socket. Connect the other end to the two-prong plug.

b. **Strip the ends from another length** of wire. Connect one end to the remaining terminal of the waterproof socket. Connect the other end to one of the insulated alligator clips.

c. **Strip the ends from a third length** of wire. Connect one end to the remaining terminal of the two-prong plug. Connect the other end to the other insulated alligator clip.

d. **Equip the waterproof socket** with a 7- or 10-watt bulb.

To use the continuity tester, you have to insert the tester's two-prong plug into a wall outlet. This means that the metal parts of *both* alligator clips are going to be alive.

Never touch the metal ends of the alligator clips when the two-prong plug is in a wall outlet. You will receive a severe shock. The reason you use alligator clips in the first place is to eliminate the need for you to touch metal ends when the continuity tester is activated.

Very, very important: Before you test a circuit for continuity, **before** plugging the tester's two-prong plug into a wall outlet, hook up the alligator clips. Then, and only then, insert the plug into the wall outlet. Before you disconnect the alligator clips, pull the two-prong plug from the wall.

As important: When checking continuity of any appliance part, the appliance must be disconnected from the wall outlet. Only the continuity tester

is connected. Failure to disconnect the appliance can result in serious injury and damage to the appliance.

The danger of a makeshift continuity tester appears when it is not used carefully. I advise that you purchase a tester, which must also be used with care. But there is less possibility for error with a manufactured unit.

Now, let's test a line cord for continuity. To determine if a cord has developed breaks, disconnect the cord from a wall outlet, open the case and remove the cord from the appliance (This discussion deals with internally attached line cords only). This leaves you with two bare wires on the non-plug end of the cord. Twist these two ends together.

Connect one of the continuity tester's alligator clips to one prong of the cord's plug. Connect the other alligator clip to the other prong. Connect the continuity tester to a wall outlet.

If the tester's bulb lights up, the appliance cord is in good shape, but flex the cord over its entire length anyway just to make sure that there is no break which has mated itself together temporarily. If the bulb flickers off and on as you flex the cord, there is a break in a wire. Get rid of the cord. Naturally, if the tester's bulb doesn't light up at all, replace the cord.

Detachable line cords (those that connect externally) are more easily checked. Just connect a similar cord to the appliance that you know is in good condition. If the appliance now runs, the old line cord is shot.

The primary reason for damaged line cords is careless use. Pulling on the cord when disconnecting it from a wall outlet will tear it apart inside. Grasp the plug instead and pull on that. That's the primary reason plugs

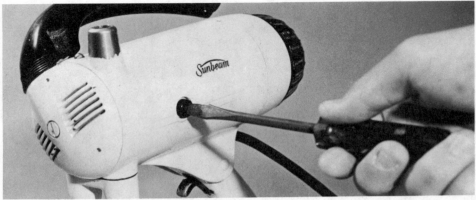

Figure 10. If you see two large slotted caps like this (one on each side of the mixer), the brushes can be removed without taking the mixer apart.

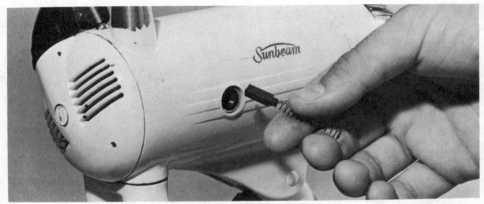

Figure 11. The carbon brush is an essential part of an AC-DC universal motor. It may be the cause of a problem if worn. Worn brushes may cause an appliance to "spark," to operate intermittently, or to cease operating entirely.

are fitted with such heavy thumb fixtures.

Okay, let's turn our attention once more to the list of things that stop food-mixer motors.

3. **Worn brushes** are the main reason electric food mixers fail to run. Brushes are blocks of carbon that are held firmly against the rotating commutator by springs. Eventually they wear out.

Replacing brushes in some cases is an easy job, because usually you do not have to dismantle the appliance.

On each side of the appliance housing you may find a fairly large slotted

cap (Figure 10). Remove both caps and take the brushes from the mixer (Figure 11). However, be careful not to lose or damage the brush springs. They may have to be reused if replacement brushes don't come equipped with new springs.

To determine if the brushes are worn, measure them with a ruler. A brush that is ¼ inch or less in length is worn and should be replaced.

If one brush of an appliance is worn, replace them both.

Parts for your electric food mixer may be purchased from a dealer who sells your make of appliance or from a

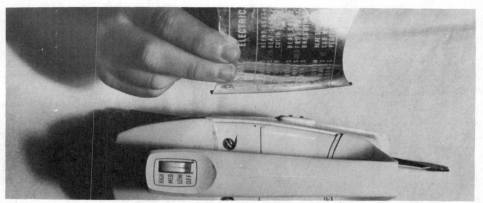

Figure 12. Many times the most difficult part of appliance repair is getting the appliance open. Disassembly screws may be hidden, as they are here beneath the nameplate.

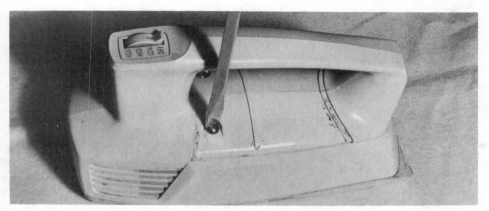

Figure 13. Once you have found the disassembly screws, remove them and carefully open the case. One of the most common reasons to open the case is the presence of a faulty on-off switch. A tip-off is if the switch suddenly becomes "sloppy" as it is manipulated.

hardware store.

Notice that one end of each brush is curved so it will fit, more or less, the configuration of the commutator on which it rides. When new brushes are installed, they may spark for several minutes until they shape themselves exactly to the commutator. This is nothing to be concerned about.

However, if sparking continues for more than 10 minutes or so, make sure that brushes are not loose in their holders. Check springs for tension. If they are weak, replace them. Also see to it that brush caps are tight.

4. **By this time,** the food mixer

should be running again, but if not, you may have one with a faulty on-off switch. Sometimes this suspicion is confirmed by a switch that suddenly becomes "sloppy" as it is manipulated.

To check the switch, open the case (Figures 12 and 13). (At this point, you can also check out the line cord as explained before unless you have a cord that can be detached from the mixer externally and has already been tested.)

Disconnect the wires from the switch—if possible without breaking a solder joint—and remove the part from the case. Inspect the contacts for pit marks and burned spots. You can often clean dirty contacts, if they aren't too badly eroded. Use a fine-cut file or fine sandpaper. An excellent tool to use for this is an ignition-point file which you can purchase at an automobile supply store. After filing or sanding contacts, wipe them off using a clean cloth or paper towel which is moistened with alcohol.

Now, test the switch for continuity. Lay the switch on your workbench and connect the continuity tester across the switch's terminals. Plug the tester into a wall socket (make sure the switch has been flicked "on".) The tester's light should go on. If it doesn't, replace the switch.

In many units, switch leads are soldered to the switch. Conduct continuity tests with the switch in place (Figure 14). If the switch is bad, break the soldered joints, remove the switch, and solder the wires back into place.

5. **Examine the mixer** closely to see if it is equipped with a centrifugal switch. If so, the cause of your appliance failing to run may be that the switch's contacts are stuck in the open position. After locating the switch, test the contacts by moving them carefully with your finger. They should move together and apart easily.

Examine the contacts for dirt and pit marks, which may be preventing good contact. Clean them with fine sandpaper and an alcohol wiping. Add one or two drops of lightweight household oil to the pivot point and move the arm back and forth so oil works in.

Centrifugal switches seldom go completely bad. The treatment mentioned here usually is all that is needed to repair one.

6. **If your mixer does not start** at this point, you can conclude that the motor is defective. Either the field coil is open or an armature is open or shorted out. However, motor failure is not common. In any case, it does not pay to replace the motor. A new food mixer costs very little more.

Important: If the motor does not start, but it does hum, the cause of the trouble is probably not a defective motor, so don't throw the appliance away. As explained below under "motor runs, but beaters don't turn," the cause of the trouble is probably a frozen bearing or defective gear.

Figure 14. Here we are testing the continuity of the wire running between the line-cord contact connections and the switch. On small appliances you don't need a wiring diagram.

Figure 15. Brushes of portable electric food mixers are usually inside the unit. To get at them in this model, it is necessary to first remove the brush-holder retaining plate. If the brushes are old and spark excessively, new brushes may be needed.

when the motor has no pep

IF THE MIXER runs too slowly and lacks power, the operator may be doing one of two things wrong. Make sure that the variable-speed control switch is positioned at the right speed for the preparation that is being mixed. Also determine if the appliance is being called upon to mix something it is not capable of mixing. Perhaps the mixture is too stiff.

Worn brushes are the main reason for lack of speed and power. Other causes include a centrifugal switch that is stuck in the closed position.

Handle this just as you would a centrifugal switch stuck in the open position, as discussed previously.

If switch and brushes check out okay, test to see if the field coil is grounded. Connect one end of your continuity tester to the housing. Connect the other end to a known ground, such as a pipe. If the lamp lights, the field coil is grounded, and you should consider replacing the appliance.

Remember: The appliance must be disconnected from the wall plug during continuity tests.

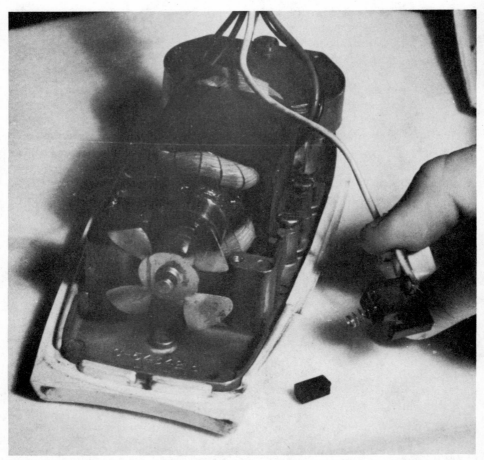

Figure 16. The brush holder is removed gently from its seat, and brush and brush spring are released for inspection. Also check the brush-spring tension.

if the motor sparks

AS YOU HAVE DISCOVERED, this is a normal condition when new brushes are installed. Sparking continues for a few minutes until the brushes wear down sufficiently to fit the contour of the commutator. However, if new brushes have not been installed and the unit sparks excessively, it indicates that old brushes may be wearing out, so inspect them (Figures 15 and 16). Also check brush spring tension.

Another reason that AC-DC universal motors spark is because of a dirty commutator. The commutator may be cleaned by polishing its surface lightly with a piece of fine sandpaper (Figure 17). Do *not* use emery cloth.

The most unlikely cause of sparking is a shorted or open armature. An indication of this is burn marks near the edges of the commutator. If all other reasons for the condition have been ruled out, it may be time to replace the appliance.

motor operates, beaters don't

VERY OFTEN THIS TROUBLE is

preceded and/or accompanied by unusual noise coming from the appliance as it operates. The reasons for it are worn beater shafts, chipped or broken gear teeth, and a bad bearing.

Examine the beaters first. See if the shafts are worn or are so badly beat up that they don't lock securely. If beaters are damaged, replace them.

Open the gear case. Examine the gears closely for chipped and broken teeth (Figure 18). See if the lubricant has dissipated, leaving gears to run dry and noisily. Replace damaged

gears and lubricate them with gear lubricant for appliances. Your dealer can help you select the correct lubricant.

when the motor overheats

IF THE APPLIANCE SEEMS TO GET UNUSUALLY HOT when it runs, turn it off at once and disconnect the line cord from the wall plug. Examine the case to see where ducts are located. Mixers possess small fans at one end of their motor shafts to provide cooling, but if the ducts are

Figure 17. The pointer is pointing to the commutator. If it is dirty or slightly pitted, gently polish it with a piece of fine-grit sandpaper. It is not advisable to use emery cloth to polish a commutator.

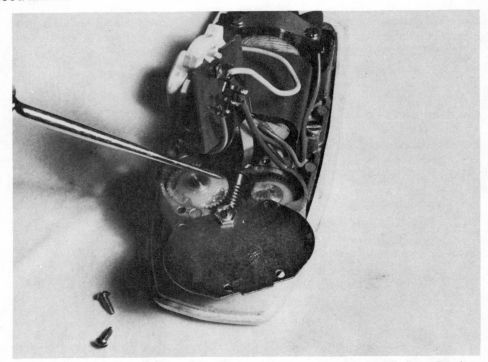

Figure 18. The gear arrangement in a food mixer consists of a worm gear (being pointed to) on the end of the armature shaft which rotates two pinion gears. Gears seldom fail. However, lack of lubricant or chipped and broken gear teeth may cause trouble.

Figure 19. This small fan on the end of the motor shaft cools the inside of the food mixer. If there's a problem of overheating, it's not often the fault of the fan.

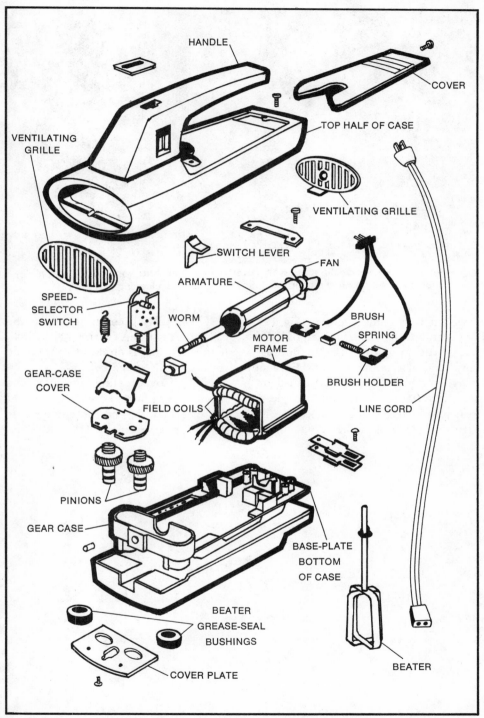

HANDLE

COVER

TOP HALF OF CASE

VENTILATING GRILLE

VENTILATING GRILLE

SWITCH LEVER

FAN

ARMATURE

SPEED-SELECTOR SWITCH

WORM

BRUSH

SPRING

MOTOR FRAME

BRUSH HOLDER

GEAR-CASE COVER

FIELD COILS

LINE CORD

PINIONS

GEAR CASE

BASE-PLATE BOTTOM OF CASE

BEATER GREASE-SEAL BUSHINGS

COVER PLATE

BEATER

This drawing shows the breakdown of a typical food mixer. It may be helpful to you in locating and removing parts, and understanding functioning.

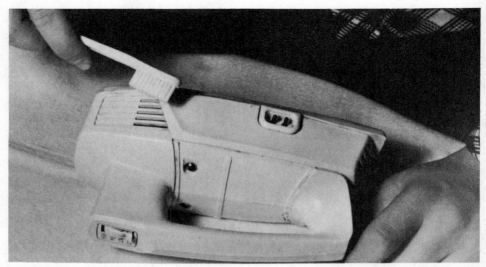

Figure 20. The free passage of air prevents overheating. Clean dirt from the ducts, using an old toothbrush and if possible a hand vacuum. Do not use any cleaning solvent.

blocked, air cannot enter (Fig. 19).

Clean out the ducts with an old, dry toothbrush (Figure 20). Do not use any kind of cleaning solvent. Solvent may contain chemicals that can damage internal components. To do a really effective job, suck debris from ducts with a hand vacuum.

If overheating continues, open the case to see if the centrifugal switch, if there is one, is shut closed. Handle this as we discussed before.

Now, if overheating continues, the problem is a shorted or grounded field coil or armature, and the appliance is ready for replacement.

Chapter 3

Food blenders

You may never experience a problem with this reliable appliance, because it is operated for only brief periods. But it's reassuring to know that if failure occurs, repair usually is simple

IF YOU CAN REPAIR an electric food mixer, you can repair an electric food blender. The two appliances have practically the same components (Figure 1).

The heart of an electric food blender is an AC-DC universal motor, which is the same kind of motor used in food mixers as explained in Chapter 2. Generally, blenders employ more powerful motors than mixers since they have to do heavier work, such as chopping and shredding food.

A major difference between food blenders and mixers is in placement of the motor. In a food mixer, the motor is above the mixing bowl and is horizontal. In a food blender, the motor is below the mixing bowl and is vertical. Blenders have cutting knives as the working element, while mixers have beaters.

Another major difference between the two is the way in which the working elements are driven. In a food blender, the motor shaft is coupled directly to the cutters (Figure 2). There are no gears. In food mixers, the motor turns gears which turn the beaters.

Blenders have as many or more speeds than food mixers. Some

Figure 1. This blender is about 15 years old and still going strong. See illustrations in Chapter 2 for tips on taking it apart.

Figure 2. The cutter is the part that does all the work. Attached to the shaft, it is rotated directly by the motor.

blenders have as many as 15 different speeds. Most have between eight and ten, but old models may have as few as three.

One way in which variable speed may be attained in a blender is by the tapped field-coil method. As described in Chapter 2, each switch taps one coil of the circuit, shortening or lengthening the coil to produce a different speed. If a tap is engaged so the coil is lengthened, a higher speed results.

Not all blenders use the tapped field-coil method of attaining variable speed. Some food blenders use a line

of different resistors in series with the motor. Each resistor (they are called "dropping resistors") has a different resistance to electricity. As each button of the blender is pushed, engaging the resistor, a different speed is obtained.

what can go wrong?

THESE ARE THE PROBLEMS you may encounter in the order of likelihood:

• Motor runs slowly or erratically
• Motor doesn't run at all
• Motor runs okay at some speeds, but doesn't run at other speeds
• The bowl leaks

Let's examine each condition to see how it should be handled.

slow or uneven operation

IMPROPER USE OF THE BLENDER —such as overloading—or dirt is usually the cause of this problem. A simple way of determining if the difficulty is internal or operator-caused is to operate the appliance with the bowl in position but empty. If the motor runs normally, then the trouble is not inside the unit, but is with the operator.

Figure 3. To open up this blender, it is necessary to remove the cap screws in the feet. Notice the ventilation holes for cooling.

Too much food in the bowl, or food not recommended for blending, puts an unusual strain on the unit. This can lead to major damage. Overloading should be avoided. Consult the operating instructions that came with the appliance to determine what can and what cannot be blended, and how much food can safely be placed in the bowl.

The cause of erratic operation may also be a knife assembly that is hampered by encrusted food. This can be determined easily by operating the blender without the bowl. If the unit whirrs at a good rate of speed, there is nothing wrong with the appliance. The knives just need cleaning.

Mix up a solution of hot water and detergent, and immerse the knife assembly. Let it soak.

if there's motor trouble

IF THE MOTOR DOESN'T RUN AT ALL, the first things to check are (1) the wall plug (test the plug with a lamp you know is working), and (2) the line cord.

If the line cord is the type that can be detached from the blender, test it by attaching it to another appliance you know is working. If that appliance won't operate with the cord, then you know the cord is bad. Get a new one.

If the line cord is the type that cannot be detached from the blender, then test it for continuity (see Chapter 2). Remember, though, an indication of a lack of continuity is not conclusive. The switch may be bad—not the line cord. You will have to open up the unit to make sure.

The reason the blender fails to operate may be found inside the unit itself. Worn motor brushes are the usual cause. Unfortunately, with a blender, you usually have to open up the case to get at brushes. There are no caps which can be removed to get brushes out of the unit, as in a mixer.

See if there is a large nut on top of the blender's base. Unscrew it with a pair of pliers or a wrench. Inspect the bottom of the base. If there are screws, remove them. Sometimes screws are screwed directly into the feet and may be hidden, so look for them (Figures 3 and 4).

When the baseplate is removed, exposing the motor, you may find the motor covered by a heavy paper-like fabric that protects the unit from

Figure 4. A cap-screw remover similar to this tool may be purchased. But a small screwdriver should do as well.

dust. Remove this very carefully, and be sure to return it to place later when you button up the unit.

Brush retainers will be visible. Remove brushes and measure them. If they are ¼-inch or less in length, replace them.

If brushes are in good shape and the motor doesn't work at all in any switch position, then you can conclude that the motor itself has burned out. Replace the appliance.

a switching problem? . . .

A SWITCHING PROBLEM is apparent when the unit runs at some speeds, but not at others. If this happens with a tapped-coil switching setup, the problem could be a defective switch or an open field winding.

Perform continuity tests to determine if the switches are bad. Connect the continuity tester to the switch terminals. If the tester does not indicate "life," replace the switch.

If the switches test out well, then the reason for the switching problem is probably an open field winding. You can continue using the appliance at whatever speeds are working, but

it won't be long before everything goes bad. At that point, scrap the blender.

Where dropped resistors are used to control speed, the cause of the unit failing to operate at one or more speeds could be a defective switch or a defective resistor. Continuity testing of switches will lead you to the faulty component. If switches prove okay, then you should replace the resistor of that speed which is not working.

Resistors are normally soldered in place. You have to break the connection and solder a new resistor into position.

Important: Be sure that the new resistor has the same value as the old resistor. Values are usually marked on these parts.

when the bowl leaks

IF FOOD JUICES start running from the bowl and the cutter assembly is screwed on tightly, the bowl seal is shot. Repair it by disassembling the cutter assembly and replacing the seal with a new one.

Chapter 4

Vacuum cleaners and electric brooms

It may seem somewhat odd for vacuum cleaners and electric brooms to follow a discussion of electric food mixers and blenders, but it's logical. These cleaning tools use an AC-DC universal motor, just like mixers and blenders

VACUUM CLEANERS come in all shapes and sizes. Electric brooms come in one general shape and size. An electric broom is merely an underpowered vacuum cleaner that has enough power to clean a floor, but should not be used extensively for cleaning carpeting.

A vacuum cleaner can be a small, hand-held unit that is slung over the shoulder for cleaning drapes and cushions, but has limited value for floors; a self-contained upright unit that is pushed and pulled across carpeting or floors (an electric broom falls into this category); or a tank or canister model, having separate hoses and accessories (Figures 1, 2, 3 and 4).

We can dismiss the hand-held unit with a shrug. It is classified as a vacuum, because it has a universal motor which revolves a small fan to create suction and pull dirt into a disposable bag. The same general repair information which applies to the bigger models applies to hand-held models.

Essentially, vacuum cleaners can be divided into two main groups: upright, and tank and canister. There are some major differences between the two, other than the fact that one is pushed and pulled, and the other is dragged. These differences have a bearing on repair.

upright versus the drags

IF YOU HAVE AN UPRIGHT unit around, get it out and turn it upside down. Notice that it has a brush in its base (you may have to remove a cover plate to see all of it) (Figure 5).

This brush rotates when the vacuum is operated, and beats against the carpeting. The brushing action stirs up dirt and foreign objects so they can be easily sucked up into the nozzle and into the bag. The brush is driven by a belt which is coupled to the motor.

Let's make this point right now, because it can save you a lot of headaches and maybe even the cost of a new vacuum cleaner: The most common complaint against an upright vacuum cleaner is that it "doesn't run as good as it did." In other words, it isn't picking up dirt.

Right off, turn the vacuum over and inspect the drive belt. If it is worn or broken, the brush won't revolve, and vacuuming will be reduced to practically nothing. Replace the belt with one for your model (Figures 6 and 7).

33

vacuum cleaners and electric brooms

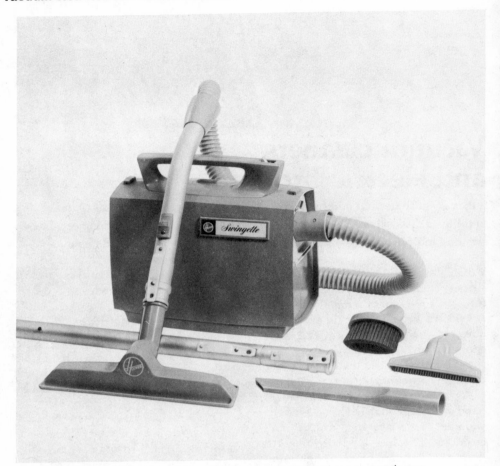

Figure 1. Small, hand-held vacuum cleaners (above) are ideal to vacuum drapes.
Figure 2. Upright vacuum cleaners (right) have long been mainstay for cleaning carpeting.
Figure 3. Canister or tank models (below) can reach way under beds and into crannies.
Figure 4. An electric broom (far right) should be used primarily for cleaning floors.

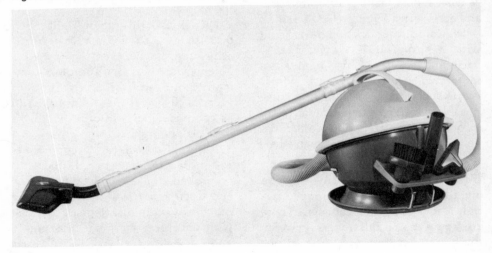

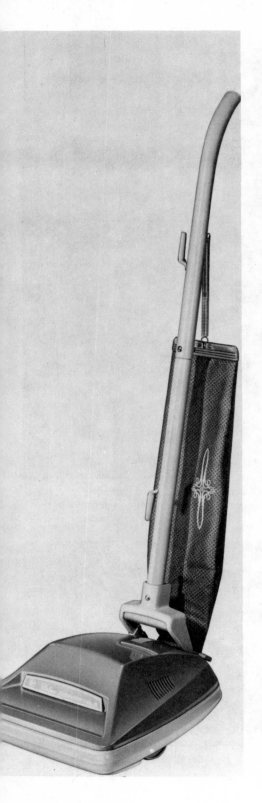

Figure 5. The part of an upright vacuum cleaner which does the actual gathering of dirt is this roller; bristles on it scoop up the dirt. The roller is driven by a belt, which in turn is driven by the shaft of the motor. The belt should be inspected frequently for wear.

Figure 6. In this model, the roller is held in place by clips on each side (see clip at tip of screwdriver) and the roller is removed by pulling the roller from the clips. The clips are not pried, pulled, pushed or otherwise disturbed, which would cause damage.

Also inspect the brush closely. With use, the brush eventually wears away because of constant rubbing. In time, bristles no longer reach the carpeting. Goodby effectiveness.

To compensate for wear, most vacuum-cleaner manufacturers make the rotating brush adjustable. It can usually be moved closer to the floor. However, if the brush is completely worn out, remove and replace it with a new one.

Tank and canister vacuum cleaners do not have rotating brushes. (Neither do electric brooms.) To compensate for a lack of brushing action, manufacturers of tank and canister models usually equip their units with more powerful motors.

Motors used in tank and canister models are as powerful as ¾ horsepower. Those used in upright models can be as small as ¼ horsepower.

Whatever the model, the principle of operation is the same.

how vacuum cleaners work

THE AC-DC ELECTRIC MOTOR is the heart of the system. The purpose of the motor is simply to rotate a fan and, as we have seen in the case of upright units, to drive a rotating brush. The fan is basically an exhaust fan—that is, it pulls air through and out the vacuum at a very high rate of speed (Figure 8).

The rate of speed at which a vacuum-cleaner motor operates can be as high as 10,000 revolutions per minute. It creates the suction to pull dirt into the unit. Air passes through a bag. The bag is porous, but is of such fine mesh that particles cannot pass through. Thus, dirt is trapped in the bag, but air is permitted to flow out.

The path that air follows is somewhat different for an upright and electric broom than it is for canister and tank models. In an upright vacuum, air and dirt are sucked into the nozzle as it rolls across the surface. The air flows around the motor, into the bag (where dirt is deposited), and out of the bag.

In the case of an electric broom, there is no bag, as such, where dirt is deposited. There is a bag through which air and dirt flow. But dirt is deposited in a plastic cup, which can be removed and cleaned out.

Dirt that is deposited on an upright

Figure 7. When a belt is replaced, the roller is pulled from its seat and the belt is simply slid off. Examine the roller whenever you check the belt just in case bristles have worn away. If bristles are worn, cleaning will be less than adequate. Replace the roller.

bag's linings can be cleaned away by pushing the bag up and down to dislodge dirt.

In canister and tank models, the bag is positioned at the air intake. Dust-ladened air enters the bag first. Dirt is deposited, and cleaned air proceeds through the bag, past the motor and out the rear of the machine.

Remarkably, vacuum cleaners and electric brooms remain reliable for many years despite the fact that they are subjected to more dirt and foreign matter than any other household appliance (Figures 9 and 10). They are also abused. Line cords are tugged and run over, hoses are pulled, and motors are run for long periods.

In time, of course, a vacuum cleaner breaks down. Problems can be divided into two groups: those occurring in the air-intake system; and electrically oriented problems. Determining where the trouble lies is usually very easy.

If the motor fails to run, the problem is electrically oriented. If the motor operates smoothly, but the vacuum lacks suction and fails to pick up dirt, the problem is concentrated in the air-intake system. The only time you will have difficulty deciding where trouble exists is when the motor runs sluggishly. It could be the fault of the motor (electrical) or it could be caused by a blockage in the air system that is putting a strain on the motor.

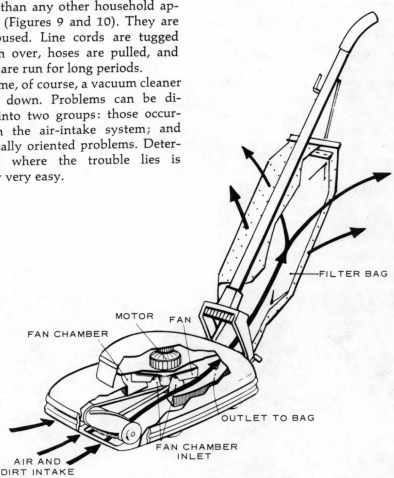

FILTER BAG

MOTOR   FAN

FAN CHAMBER

OUTLET TO BAG

FAN CHAMBER INLET

AIR AND DIRT INTAKE

Cutaway shows how a vacuum cleaner works. Whatever kind you own, the principles are the same.

Figure 10. We reached inside the "empty" bag and got this dirt. The unit worked like new after the bag was brushed out inside.

For example, lint wrapped around the rotary dust pickup brush of an upright vacuum may be impeding motor operation. However, whenever you have to make a decision between an electrical or an air-intake system approach, opt for the air-intake system. The procedure is simpler.

air-intake repair

THE SUREST WAY of knowing whether the air-intake system needs servicing is to test it the professional way. Scatter some sawdust on the floor and attempt to vacuum it up. If some remains, there is a malfunction that needs correction.

Observe whether dust is being blown from around connections and hose. This indicates a leak. Leaks in canister and tank models occur where

Figure 9. Most people think all you have to do to clean an electric broom is to empty the cup, as here. But see Figure 10.

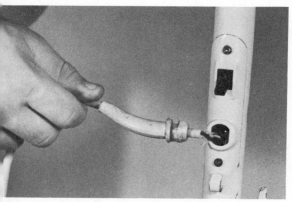

Figure 11. This is what can happen to a line cord if you're not careful. The cord had to be spliced to restore operation.

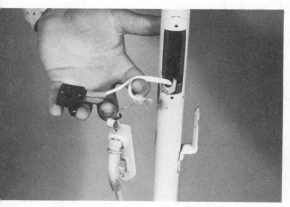

Figure 12. To replace a switch or repair line cord is usually simple. We removed the cover plate to allow access for this purpose.

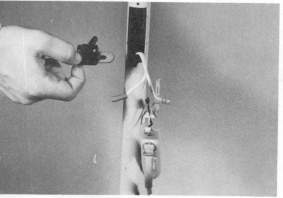

Figure 13. This switch lead simply pulled from the switch terminal. Then the lead was just pushed onto the new terminal.

the hose connects to the vacuum and through the hose itself. Leaks in upright models occur where the bag attaches to the unit.

Make sure that connections are tight. If a leak persists, see if a gasket is used at the connection point. It may be damaged and should be replaced. The final solution is to replace the hose or bag.

If dust is leaking through cracks or holes in a hose, you may be able to repair the hose with electrician's tape. If not, replace the hose.

As pointed out before, if an upright unit fails to pick up, inspect the rotary brush for wear. Follow this by making sure that the dust bag is not full. If there is one thing that most often cuts the efficiency of all types of vacuum cleaners and electric brooms, it is a filled dust bag or cup.

In an upright, the dust bag's bag (that is, the porous bag in which the disposable dust bag fits) may be clogged. After many years, it is possible for the bag's pores to close. This will hinder the free passage of air.

To check the efficiency of this fabric or plastic bag, detach it from the unit and turn the machine on. Place your hand over the connection on which the bag fits. You should feel strong suction. If you do, replace the porous bag.

Caution: When operating a vacuum cleaner or electric broom minus its dust bag or dust cup, place it in a position where it cannot pick up. Do not operate the unit in its cleaning position. Dust that is drawn in can damage the motor.

Tank and canister models fail to dr. w in dirt primarily because of a filled dust bag or a wad of dirt crammed into the flexible hose. After checking on the bag, use a long-handled brush to clean out the hose.

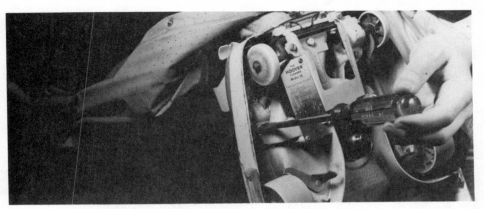

Figure 14. Look and you will find. Let's say you want to save the cost of a new vacuum by replacing worn brushes. Getting at the brushes may be the hardest part of the job. Investigation reveals that a few screws have to be removed to remove the cover over motor housing.

Figure 15. With the screws out, we are able to remove the cover. The rest is easy. We now find the brush holders. One holder is at the tip of the white arrow. The other holder is located on the opposite side of the motor.

Figure 16. Unscrew the brush holder, and the brush spring can then be pulled from the brush housing. You can see the brush spring (arrow). Discard the worn brush for a new one, but re-use the spring if it hasn't lost its resiliency.

electrical problems

THE MOST COMMON electrical failure is a damaged line cord. People who operate vacuum cleaners abuse the cord. A common practice, for example, is to disconnect the cord from a wall plug halfway across a room by pulling on the cord.

Examine the cord over its length for damage. Pay particular attention to where the cord connects to the machine, which is the weakest point. If the cord is frayed at this point, failure is a likelihood (Figure 11).

Open the case. Disconnect the cord's leads from the switch. Wrap the ends of the cord together, and test the cord for continuity. Replace a bad line cord.

Another common area of failure is the on-off switch, especially of canister and tank models that have foot-operated switches. In time, they can fail because of heavy footwork. With the case open, test the switch for continuity by removing it from the case and connecting your continuity tester across the terminals. Flick the switch on. If it shows lack of continuity, replace it (Figures 12 and 13).

The third common reason for electrical failure is worn brushes. Information provided about brushes in the previous chapters applies as well to brushes of vacuum cleaner motors (Figures 14, 15 and 16).

Seldom does a vacuum cleaner or electric-broom motor fail. However, if the motor does not operate after the line cord, switch and brushes have been checked, the motor is probably burned out. Purchase of a new vacuum cleaner should be considered.

Chapter 5

Floor polishers

**Floor polishers are serviced in much the same way as are electric
food mixers and blenders because they, too, have AC-DC universal motors**

SURPRISINGLY, floor polishers are
most similar—not to vacuum cleaners
as you would imagine—but to food
mixers. Although vacuum cleaners
and floor polishers both employ AC-
DC motors of comparable drive
power, floor polishers are equipped
with gears. Vacuum cleaners are not
(Figure 1).

In a floor polisher, the revolving
AC-DC universal motor causes two
main gears to rotate. The gears are
positioned so they turn opposite to
one another—that is, one turns to the
left and one turns to the right (Figure
2).

The gears turn drive shafts to
which brushes are attached. The opposing rotary motion is thus transferred to the brushes, which polish
the floor.

Let's not belabor the point. If a
floor polisher fails to operate, it is because of one of the following reasons,
which are presented in the order of
likelihood:

1. Faulty line cord
2. Faulty on-off switch
3. Worn motor brushes
4. Damaged gears
5. Burned-out motor

Check the chapter on food mixers,
and go through precisely the same
procedures to repair a malfunction in
a floor polisher (Figures 3 and 4).

Figure 1. This is a typical floor polisher.

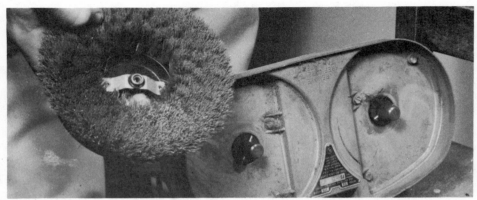

Figure 2. Here is what the bottom of a typical floor polisher looks like. There are two chucks, each holding a scrubbing-polishing brush. The brushes rotate in opposite directions.

Figure 3. Dirt is the chief enemy of cleaning appliances. A dirt buildup like this reduces the effectiveness of a floor polisher and also causes the motor to run at a higher temperature. Over a period of time, this excessive heat could result in serious damage.

Figure 4. The motorized parts of a floor polisher that you should be familiar with are the: 1. Gear case; 2. Motor (notice the commutator); 3. Gear case. To get at the motor and brushes of this particular unit, it's necessary to remove the cover over the motor.

Chapter 6

Electric knives

**This very reliable and useful kitchen utensil has a motor similar
to that of an AC-DC universal motor, but with a few differences. In addition,
other interesting innovations are packed inside its relatively small body**

WHEN YOU EXAMINE an electric knife that needs repair, picture it as three assemblies: the *motor* which provides the driving force; the *gear train*, which is a unique assembly that converts rotary power into reciprocating motion; and the *blade assembly* (Figure 1).

The three work together as one. The *motor*, which is a direct current (DC) motor, drives a shaft that has a geared end. This, in turn, drives a so-called *pinion gear* which is arranged to convert the rotating motion of the shaft into reciprocating, or al-ternate back-and-forth, motion (Figure 2). The *blade assembly* is connected to the gear train. It consists of two serrated knife blades that are in contact with each other (Figure 3). The blades move in opposite directions a fraction of an inch at a time. It is this reciprocating action that enables you to carve a turkey, roast, or whatever neatly and effortlessly.

an interesting motor

THE DIRECT-CURRENT MOTOR in an electric knife is similar to the universal AC-DC motor discussed

Figure 1. This electric knife receives its current from a wall outlet via a line cord. Others are battery-powered, while still others can run either on battery or household current. The cutting knife is always an assembly of two individual blades.

earlier in that it possesses an armature and brushes. However, there are several significant differences between the two.

An AC-DC universal motor can operate on either alternating or direct current. A DC motor uses much less current than an AC-DC motor, and it has a permanent magnet rather than a wire-wound field. Thus, the magnetic field needed to rotate the armature is created by a magnet rather than by a coil.

At this point, you may note that some electric knives you've seen run when plugged into a conventional 115-volt *AC* wall plug. Yet, from what has been said, an electric knife operates only on *DC*. What's the story?

This is what makes the DC motor in an electric knife so interesting. The typical electric knife contains a rectifier, which converts alternating current to direct current, and a transformer which "drops" the voltage to a level that is low and safe. An electric knife operates on 5 to 6 volts of direct current.

In considering an electric knife that you have to repair, you should determine the kind of DC motor it has. A DC motor is a DC motor, but there are variations—in fact, there are three:

1. Some knives have DC motors which operate only when plugged into an AC wall outlet (Figure 4). Generally, these are older models, with motors consisting essentially of an armature, brushes, permanent magnet, transformer and rectifier.

2. Some knives—so-called "cordless" models—operate only on batteries that are rechargeable. They are usually nickel-cadmium cells and come as a "pack."

A battery pack consists of four or five batteries connected in series. If

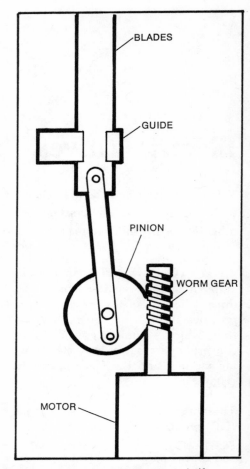

Figure 2. In gear train of electric knife, pinion converts rotary to back-forth motion.

one goes bad, all have to be replaced. Each battery (cell) provides 1.5 volts of direct current. Totally, then, a battery pack of an electric knife emits 6 to 7.5 volts, but when the knife is operating, voltage drops to 5–5.5 volts.

The battery pack of a cordless electric knife can be charged by means of a battery charger that comes with the knife at the time of purchase. Battery chargers contain diodes, which permit the batteries to receive just the right amount of the right kind of current. When the battery charger is plugged into a wall outlet, the diodes convert

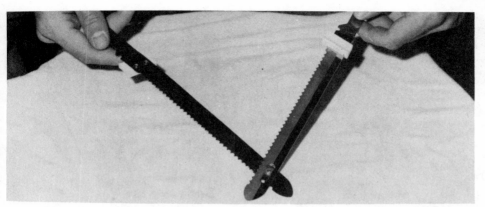

Figure 3. Electric knife blades are interconnected by means of a male fitting which is part of one blade that fits into slot in other blade. Do not use damaged blades.

Figure 4. The major power assemblies of an electric knife are the (1) gear train and (2) motor. This particular knife is an older model that can use only household current.

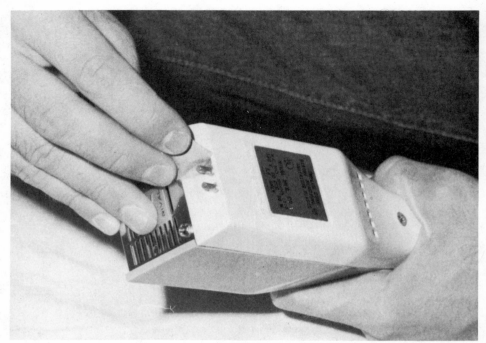

Figure 5. Carefully burnish contacts if they appear oxidized, using a pencil-type ink eraser or very fine sandpaper. This may reestablish contact between the knife and electric source.

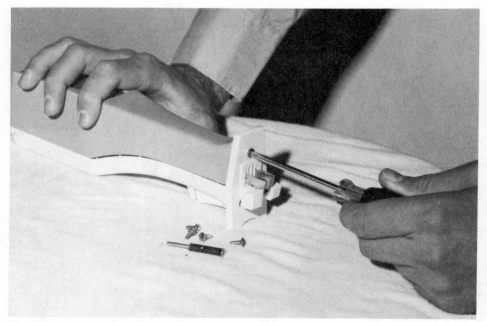

Figure 6. Never force open the case of an electric knife or any other appliance. Find and remove all screws. Forcing will crack the case.

AC to DC. When the batteries are charged, the diodes switch the current off so the batteries will not over-charge. Every cordless appliance utilizes a similar battery charger.

3. The third type of motor used in electric knives is one that can operate both when plugged into an AC wall outlet and on battery. These are generally referred to as convertible knives. They combine components of the other two types of motors.

It is very important to keep in mind that the motor of a convertible electric knife always operates on current supplied by the batteries although the appliance may be plugged into a wall outlet. In other words, alternating current is converted into direct current, which passes through the batteries to the motor. One problem that sometimes hampers convertible knives is refusal of the motor to run when it is being operated on battery, although it functions when plugged into an AC outlet. This is almost always a sign that the batteries are depleted and won't hold a charge. Replace the battery pack.

On some models of convertible electric knives, the batteries may be charged continuously when the knife is being stored. This is made possible by internal charging diodes. Other convertible knife models, however, require that the knife be connected to an external battery charger.

checking a motor problem

MOTOR PROBLEMS make themselves known in one of two ways: the knife refuses to operate at all, or it operates very slowly. The latter deficiency may be caused by a malfunction in the gear train. Keep this in mind should an investigation of the motor turn up nothing.

If the knife refuses to function and it is a standard or convertible unit, make sure that the wall outlet is "live" and that the line cord isn't damaged. The line cord probably attaches to two small contacts projecting from the rear or side of the knife. Make sure that these contacts are clean. If they aren't, polish them off with a small piece of fine sandpaper (Figure 5). Also make certain that the plug of the line cord is firmly set on the contacts.

If it is necessary to open the case, remove all the screws that you can find (Figure 6). The top of the appliance has to be removed to observe the interior.

Caution: It is very easy to overlook some screws, especially if they are hidden beneath a nameplate that has to be removed by prying. If the top of the case does not come apart when you have removed all the screws that you think are there, do not apply force. You may break the case. Carefully examine it for additional screws.

Once you have opened the case of an electric knife which doesn't operate at all, first examine the on-off switch. Connect your continuity tester across the switch, plug the tester in, and see if there is continuity. If the test light doesn't light, showing lack of continuity, replace the switch.

If you are handling a standard model, and all tests and examinations reveal no problem to this point, you can pretty well conclude that the reason it doesn't operate at all is because of a motor malfunction. The reason for this may be worn motor brushes, a worn commutator, or a bad transformer. You may be able to inspect the brushes and replace them if they are worn as described in other chapters discussing brush replacement of universal motors. Other than this repair, however, it is not financially

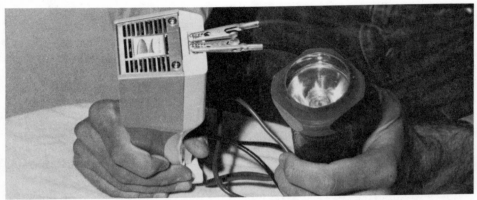

Figure 7. Here we are checking an electric knife for continuity. We connect the continuity tester across the two line-cord contacts. No continuity indicates motor trouble.

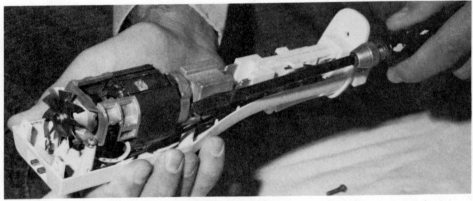

Figure 8. To get inside the gear case of this knife, it is necessary to remove the entire motor-gear assembly from the case. This becomes rather tricky and should be handled with caution. Make notes as you go along so you can easily reassemble the unit.

feasible to repair an electric knife motor—assuming that you can find the trouble. Uncovering the cause of the problem would require a multitest meter you probably don't have. And even then, parts may cost as much as a new knife.

To satisfy your curiosity, though, and learn whether the problem is indeed inside the motor, connect your continuity tester across the motor terminals—that is, across the two contacts to which the line cord attaches. If there is no continuity, the knife has motor trouble (Figure 7).

With convertible and cordless mod-

els, failure of the knife to operate may be caused by a mator problem, but it's more likely that the power pack has failed. Keep the appliance turned off and connect a voltmeter across the power pack. You should get a reading of 6.0 to 7.5 volts, depending upon whether the power pack consists of four or five batteries, respectively.

Now, turn the appliance on. The battery voltage as recorded by the voltmeter should drop to between 5 and 6 volts. If the battery voltage does not respond in the manner described, the reason for the malfunction is a dead battery. Replace the

a unique gear train

WHEN THE MOTOR of an electric knife operates, it turns. This rotary motion causes the armature shaft to turn. How come, then, that the knife blades move in back-and-forth reciprocating fashion?

The secret lies with the appliance's gear train, which consists essentially of a worm gear and pinion gear. The knife blades are attached to the pinion (or reduction) gear. The worm gear is cut into the end of the armature shaft.

What happens is this: The worm gear drives the pinion gear. There is an eccentric on each side of the pinion gear. Eccentrics are in the form of either small gears or wheels which are set off-center to the worm gear. As the worm gear rotates, eccentrics turn with an oscillating motion. Levers positioned on the eccentrics change the oscillating motion to reciprocating motion, so that the pinion gear moves back and forth instead of revolving. This, in turn, forces the knife blades to work in reciprocating fashion.

Problems that can afflict an electric knife because of a malfunction in the gear train include blades that don't move when the motor operates, and failure of the blades to move fast enough. If your electric knife has the former problem, examine the pinion gear. Most are made of plastic or a fibrous material that eventually will wear (Figure 8). If the pinion-gear teeth look worn, replace this gear. It is unlikely that the worm gear will wear since it is usually made of hardened steel.

If the knife operates sluggishly and the trouble is not with the motor brushes, the cause may be a gear train that needs lubrication (Figure 9). Be aware, too, that the gear train is equipped with tiny bearings, such as the one at the front end of the worm-

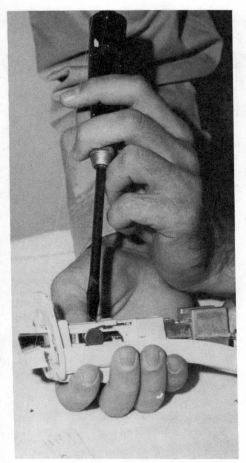

Figure 9. The roller pointed to is a part of the gear train. Dirt trapped behind it can cause the blades to move sluggishly.

battery pack. If the batteries do respond, probably the trouble is inside the motor.

Important: It is seldom that the motor of an electric knife fails, so make sure that you have tested all other possibilities correctly before concluding that the motor is bad.

A knife that functions but with reduced power may be afflicted by worn brushes, dry bearings that are part of the gear set, or gears that require lubrication. Check the brushes for wear, and if all is well, turn your attention to gears.

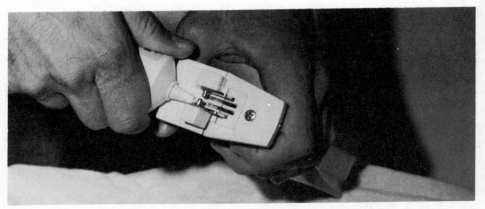

Figure 10. Repair cracks when they are small, if possible. This prevents them from getting larger and more difficult to handle. Use a good-quality plastic cement.

gear shaft. This may require oiling.

There is a special cream lubricant for gears that is sold by appliance dealers. Follow directions and lubricate the gears.

If the bearings run dry, which is rare because they are prelubricated at the factory for lifetime service, apply one drop of lightweight household machine oil to each bearing you find. Once bearings lose their factory lubricant, it usually becomes necessary to oil them annually.

physical damage

AN ELECTRIC KNIFE may sustain physical damage. This is usually in the form of bent knife blades or a cracked case. If the knife blades bend, do not attempt to straighten them. You won't be able to. Buy a replacement set. A cracked or broken case can be cemented together again with a good-quality plastic cement available in a hardware store (Figure 10).

Chapter 7

Electric toothbrushes

This chapter is brief, because you cannot repair an electric toothbrush—well, hardly. However, it is now a common appliance, and deserves to be understood so you can take proper care of it

INSIDE THEIR CASES, cordless electric knives and cordless electric toothbrushes are virtually the same. Like an electric knife, a cordless electric toothbrush contains a small DC motor that operates on rechargeable batteries (Figure 1). The motor drives a small gear set that converts the rotary motion imparted by the motor into reciprocating motion which allows the brush to make rapid up-and-down movements.

Unlike a cordless electric knife, a cordless electric toothbrush is a completely sealed unit. This is done to prevent moisture from damaging internal parts. Should anything go wrong inside the case, such as a dead battery cell or failure of a motor component, the problem cannot be repared by the homeowner. The appliance should be returned to the manufacturer's factory service center.

Important: Many manufacturers of electric toothbrushes have a liberal exchange policy. They will sell you a new unit at a substantially reduced price plus trade-in of the old appliance.

The batteries of a typical cordless electric toothbrush are kept charged by placing the appliance in a battery

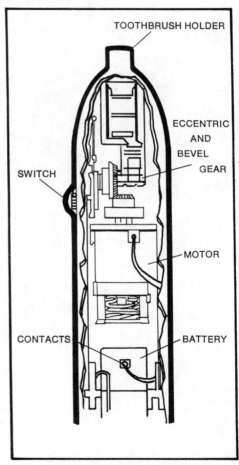

Figure 1. The cordless electric toothbrush is completely sealed. No repairs can be made, not even changing a dead battery.

Figure 2. Electric toothbrushes with cords are also sealed units. The only repair possible is repair of external line cord.

failure of the toothbrush may be caused by a malfunction within the charger, so keep this in mind.

Examine the charger's power cord and switch. You can connect a continuity tester across the power-cord prongs, plug in the tester and turn on the charger's switch. Lack of continuity indicates a defective power cord or a bad switch. Usually these can be replaced by the home appliance repairman. Also, clean contacts with a piece of fine-grit sandpaper.

To check on the internal condition of the charger, you should connect a voltmeter across the charger's output terminals. These are the terminals on which the toothbrush sets. Plug the charger's power cord into a live wall outlet and turn on the switch. Lack of voltage indicates a malfunction of the internal mechanism of the charger —possibly, the transformer has burned out. Replace the charger using the exchange privilege provided by the manufacturer. Repairing a charger is not economically feasible.

Electric toothbrushes aren't always cordless, of course (Figure 2). Some operate only when plugged into a wall outlet. As with other appliances having DC motors, this type of electric toothbrush contains a transformer to reduce voltage to the level required.

Even so, an electric toothbrush with a cord is a sealed unit just like its cordless counterpart. No repair should be attempted.

charger that is plugged into a wall outlet. The charger develops approximately 1.25 volts of direct current to charge the batteries. It is possible that

Chapter 8

Electric shavers

It is smaller than most other appliances, but that doesn't mean it's easier to repair. In fact, the electric shaver heads the list of appliances we urge you to approach with caution

THE ELECTRIC SHAVER is one of the most complicated appliances in the home, and it is not advisable for someone without experience to attempt repairs. Part of the complexity stems from the different variations employed by manufacturers in making the instrument.

Some shavers, for example, use vibrating mechanisms that move back and forth at a rate of about 7200 strokes per minute to move tiny cutters fast enough to cut whiskers. Other shavers employ a small pinion-gear setup, similar to that of an electric knife, that moves a series of razors reciprocatingly. Still other shavers employ cutting heads that revolve.

Another reason for the complex nature of shavers is the variety of means that are employed to power them. Some have small universal motors which are not unlike those used in electric food mixers. Other shavers are cordless models similar to cordless electric toothbrushes (Figure 1). They contain a small direct-current motor that is operated by nickel-cadmium cells which are recharged either by inserting the shaver into an external battery charger or by connecting it

to a transformer which is plugged into a wall outlet (Figures 2, 3, 4 and 5).

However, the main reason electric shavers are so complicated to repair is that, generally speaking, manufacturers don't want you to repair them. A shaver may be as delicate as a watch and require special instruments for making adjustments and repairs.

Manufacturers literally hide disassembly screws, making them so difficult to find that you would swear they don't exist (Figures 6 and 7). Replacement parts are not usually available either, even if you can take your shaver apart and find the cause of its problem. Generally, manufacturers want you to return an inoperative shaver to the factory.

It is very difficult, therefore, to go into any detail regarding electric-shaver repair. If you have an old shaver you wouldn't mind ruining, then you may want to experiment. The troubleshooting chart below may help. Otherwise, we suggest that you don't do anything to your electric shaver except to follow the brief manufacturer's instructions that came with it. These instructions will help you keep the shaver clean.

More electric shavers fail more of-

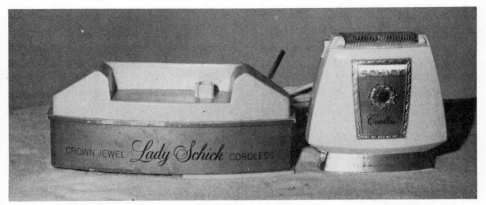

Figure 1. One of the many different types of electric shavers is the cordless model shown here. As with a cordless electric toothbrush, this unit has a small direct-current motor that is operated by nickel-cadmium cells which are periodically recharged.

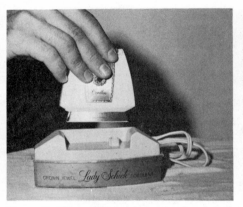

Figure 2. This cordless shaver is charged by positioning the shaver in a battery charger which is plugged into a wall outlet.

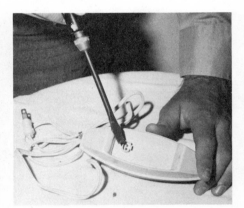

Figure 3. Contact points in the base of the battery charger connect with a transformer inside which produces low-voltage current.

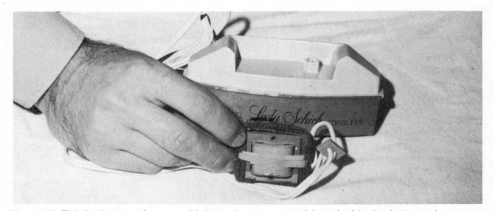

Figure 4. This is the transformer, which has been removed from inside the battery charger. The use of a two-step method makes shaver more convenient.

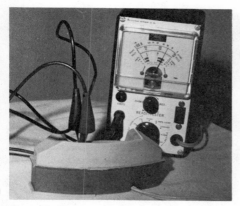

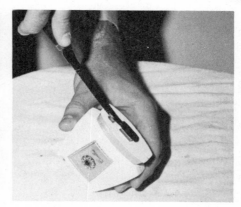

Figure 5. Here we test the battery charger with a multitester to see if it is putting out the proper amount of voltage.

Figure 6. Removing this clip and one hidden in the razor's head allows separation of this razor's two shells, for disassembly.

Figure 7. Once inside, there is little you can do to repair an electric shaver, because generally speaking manufacturers do not make repair parts available. However, maybe a good cleaning and tightening of connections will revive a dead unit.

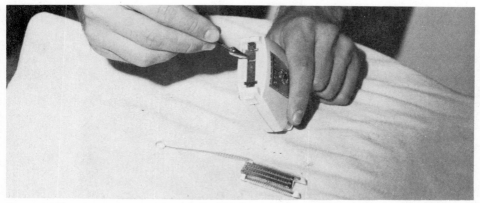

Figure 8. Keeping your razor clean is the chief way to assure good performance of the unit. Electric shavers fail more often because of dirt than for any other reason.

ten because of dirt than for any other reason (Figure 8).

some troubleshooting

THE FOLLOWING CAUSES of electric shaver problems apply primarily to shavers employing point-contact mechanisms. In this type of shaver, the motor causes spring-activated contact points to open and close approximately 8000 times per minute to allow cutters to oscillate.

Problem	Causes	Repairs
Shaver does not run	• Defective power cord • Capacitor is shorted • Loose or broken wire • Defective motor coil	• Replace cord • Replace capacitor • Resolder wire • Replace motor
Shaver doesn't give a close-enough shave	• Dull cutting edges • Cutting-head springs are weak • Worn oscillator • Motor runs too slowly	• Replace cutting head • Replace springs or cutting head • Replace oscillator • See below
Motor runs too slowly	• Cutting head is clogged • Incorrect point-gap adjustment • Contact points are worn or burned	• Clean • Adjust point gap to factory specification • Replace motor
Shaver is noisy	• Worn oscillator • Cutting-head springs are weak	• Replace oscillator • Replace springs or cutting head

Chapter 9

Electric can openers

This is the first of the appliances we shall discuss that uses a shaded-pole motor, which is a simple device that can't fail—unless someone makes it fail

THE SHADED-POLE MOTOR is much different from the high-speed, brush-equipped AC-DC universal motor that we spoke about in reference to electric food mixers, food blenders, and vacuum cleaners. For one thing, the shaded-pole motor turns at a relatively slow rate of speed. For another, it doesn't have brushes.

A shaded-pole motor is made up of a single field coil that lies at the base of a motor consisting of a rotor (the revolving part) and two other coils that are wrapped (shaded) with copper. Current enters the field coil and is transferred to the shaded coils, creating a magnetic force that causes the rotor lying between the shaded coils to revolve.

The speed of a shaded-pole motor cannot be varied. It is constant. Neither can direction be reversed. A shaded-pole motor revolves in one direction only.

Shaded-pole motors are used in appliances that do not require great speed or driving force. The electric can opener is representative. All that has to be turned is a serrated drive wheel (or sprocket). The sprocket, which is turned by the action of the rotor, turns the can. The lid of the can

Figure 1. The purpose of the shaded-pole motor in an electric can opener is to turn the serrated wheel which turns the can.

Figure 2. Many electric can openers also can sharpen knives. The shaded-pole motor drives shaft that rotates a grinding wheel.

Figure 3. Pressing a button allows the cutting assembly of this can opener to be detached and slid off for cleaning.

is pressed against a sharp cutting blade on a pivoting wheel. The lid is sheared off smoothly by the cutter (Figures 1 and 2).

To do this, more torque is needed than is provided by the rotor of the shaded-pole motor alone. Sufficient torque is obtained by incorporating reduction gears into the appliance. Reduction gears cut back the speed at which the rotor turns the sprocket. When speed is reduced, torque (power) is increased.

A shaded-pole motor cannot be damaged except deliberately. However, electric can openers can fail to operate properly.

dirt is enemy number one

THE MOST COMMON problem afflicting electric can openers is skipping. The cutting knife skips over and fails to cut a section of the can lid. The condition is caused by a dirty cutting mechanism.

Getting dirt on the cutting knife cannot be avoided. When cans are opened, some of the contents stick onto the cutting wheel, and splash onto the magnet and driving-wheel sprocket. When enough dirt gets on these parts, the cutting operation is hampered.

With some can openers, you can easily disengage the cutting wheel and magnet, as an assembly, from the can opener simply by pressing a button and pulling the assembly from the unit (Figure 3). If this is possible, remove the mechanism often and allow it to soak in household detergent solution and hot water. Use a small brush to remove stubborn dirt. This little bit of maintenance will prevent problems with the cutter.

If the cutting mechanism cannot be disengaged easily from the can opener, try brushing hardened food from the cutting blade and magnet. If this doesn't do much good, scrape the cutter with a very thin screwdriver or the point of a dull knife to loosen dirt. Then, brush.

Caution: Before fooling with the cutter, pull the line cord from the wall socket—to avoid any possibility of electric shock.

The final solution for cleaning a cutting blade that is not easily removed is to unscrew it from the can opener. Notice the shoulder location on the wheel, so you will be able to reassemble the unit properly.

Incidentally, if the cutting wheel has dulled, you can probably get a replacement through the dealer from whom you purchased the appliance or by writing the company that manufactured it.

Before reassembling the cutter, it is a good idea to clean out the teeth of the serrated sprocket. Use a small brush or a dull tool (Figure 4). If the sprocket gets badly clogged with dirt, cans will not hold and will fall from the can opener.

Before putting the cutting wheel back in place, place a drop of lightweight household oil or powdered graphite on its small shaft. The cutting wheel has to turn a bit as it punctures the can. If this shaft gets dry, the wheel may bind, making a mess of can lids. Also lubricate the assembly shaft to allow easier disengagement (Figure 5).

other problems

OTHER TROUBLES that can strike an electric can opener are failure of the unit to run at all, and a motor that hums but a sprocket that doesn't turn.

Reasons for an inoperative can opener (motor does not run or hum—it's lifeless) are a damaged line cord or faulty on-off switch. Obviously, a

Figure 4. Use an old toothbrush to clean the serrated drive wheel. Do this often; it is the most important maintenance measure.

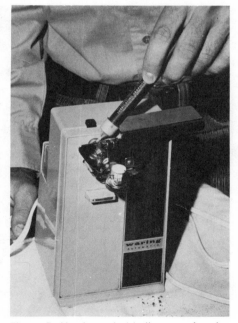

Figure 5. Use household oil or powdered graphite to lubricate the assembly shaft and the cutting-wheel shaft.

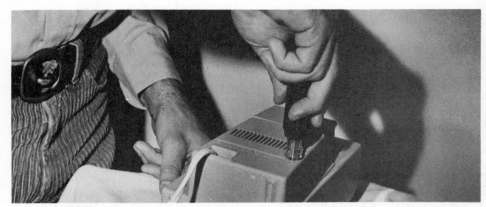

Figure 6. As with other appliances, assembly screws are often difficult to reach unless you have the proper-size tools. Here the case is being opened up.

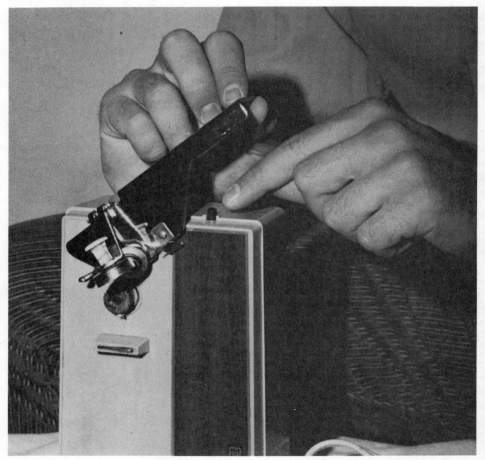

Figure 7. The switch, being pointed to, and the line cord are the two troublesome areas in an electric can opener. However, remember that a dirty cutting assembly, although easier to remedy, is a more frequent cause of problems.

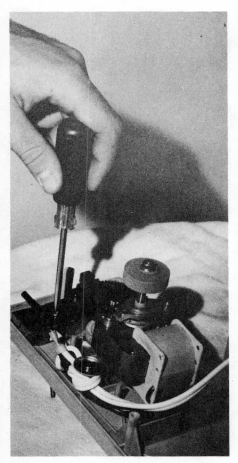

Figure 8. To get at the switch in this can opener, you must split the case and remove the cover over the switch housing.

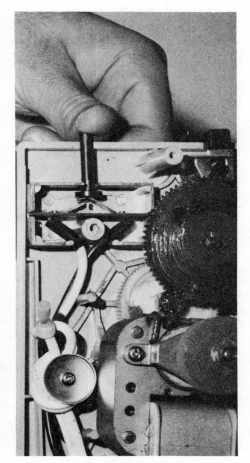

Figure 9. The switch consists of two contacts which, when pressed together, allow current to flow to the motor.

burned-out motor would also cause the condition, but this is extremely rare.

Line cords of electric can openers fail for the same reason as line cords of other appliances: misuse. Advise the user never to pull on the cord when disconnecting it from a wall socket. Pull only on the thick plug.

To determine definitely whether the line cord is causing trouble, or the fault lies with the on-off switch, you must open up the appliance's case (Figure 6). Disconnect the line cord

from the switch, wrap the exposed leads together, connect the continuity tester, and check the line cord for continuity.

Caution: The line cord must be disconnected from the wall outlet to prevent serious injury.

Next, check the on-off switch for continuity by attaching the continuity tester across the switch terminals (Figures 7, 8 and 9). Replace a bad line cord or a bad switch (Figure 10).

If tests reveal that the motor is burned out (if line cord and on-off

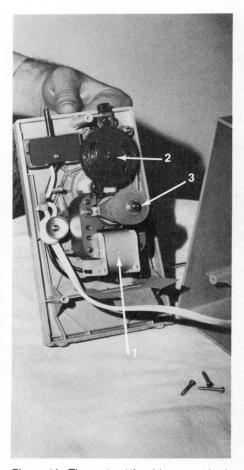

Figure 10. To remove the line cord here, pull off connector (pointed to) and disentangle the wires.

Figure 11. The motor (1) seldom goes bad. If a gear (2) breaks it can be replaced. Grinding wheel (3) sharpens knives.

switch show continuity, the cause of the trouble could only be the motor), it usually does not pay to replace the motor. A new can opener can be purchased for practically the same cost.

If the motor hums, but cans do not turn, one of the gears inside the can opener is damaged. New parts usually can be obtained from an appliance dealer or from the manufacturer of the can opener (Figure 11).

Open the case and find the bad gear. Normally, gears go bad when teeth break. Remove the bad gear and get an exact replacement.

Chapter 10

Hair dryers and hot combs

**Like hair-dos, hair dryers come in different sizes and shapes. Combs
and brushes may be attached to some hand-held models. Others of larger size
have long nozzles and head bonnets. Whatever the design, all hair dryers are
basically the same, and problems that occur in one model can occur in others**

INSIDE WHERE IT COUNTS, all
hair dryers possess the same parts
(Figure 1). First is the **motor** (usually
a shaded-pole type, so see the introduction to this section and the chapter
on electric can openers). The motor
drives a small **fan** or impeller made of
metal or plastic which circulates air.
The third necessary component possessed by all hair dryers is a **heating
element**—more than one, actually, so
that different variations of heat are
offered.

Hair dryers and room heaters are,
strangely enough, basically the same
appliances. That is why I suggest you
read simultaneously with this chapter
that portion of the introduction to this
section and that portion of the chapter
on room heaters dealing with heating
elements.

Up front at the "working" end, different types of hair dryers hardly
resemble each other. Some are simple
blower units that you hold in your
hand. All they do is dry hair.

Other models, also hand-held, are
more sophisticated, allowing you to

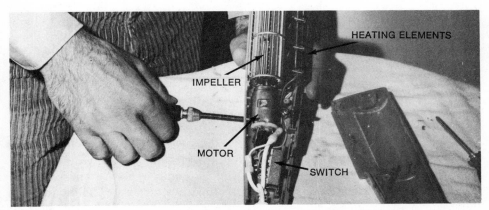

Figure 1. When you get inside a hair dryer, its main parts become readily apparent. They
are the heating elements, the impeller or fan and the motor which drives it.

Figure 2. Over the years, hair dryers have become more sophisticated. This model can take several different kinds of attachments, such as a comb and brush.

connect attachments. You can comb or brush your hair as you dry it (Figures 2, 3 and 4).

Still other models, larger in size, resemble hair dryers found in beauty shops. They may have a long hose, which is attached to the mechanical section of the dryer. The other end of the hose has a bonnet which is placed over the head.

Whatever model you have in your home, except for some physical damage to up-front parts (a split hose, for example, or missing teeth in a comb), all hair dryers are basically the same, and their repair is handled in the same way.

how hair dryers work

LET'S START WITH THE MOTOR, which probably is a shaded-pole type that operates only on alternating current. The shaded-pole motor, as pointed out in the introduction to this section and the chapter on electric can openers, has a low starting torque and low power. Since it drives a small fan that moves air, and since air offers little resistance, practically no load is imposed on the motor. For this reason, the motor of a hair dryer seldom causes trouble.

Most hair dryers allow the user to select various degrees of heat. Degrees of heat are normally stipulated on a selector switch as "low," "medium" and "high." The three heat positions are made possible by the inclusion in a dryer of two heating elements, which in most cases are rated at 100 and 200 watts.

When both heating elements are operating at the same time, maximum heat is applied. When the 100-watt heating element is working alone, low heat is applied. When the 200-watt element is working alone, medium heat is applied.

Typically, the heating elements are wired together in series with the motor. This means that the elements cannot function unless the motor is operating. A heat-selector switch permits the user to select any degree of heat by making contact (or not making contact) with various terminals (Figure 5).

The reason that the motor and heating elements are wired together in the same circuit is to prevent heat from being generated without being circulated. This is a very important safety feature because, if heat were allowed to build up and concentrate

Figure 3. The attachment is detached by pressing the spring-loaded detaching button (at point of arrow).

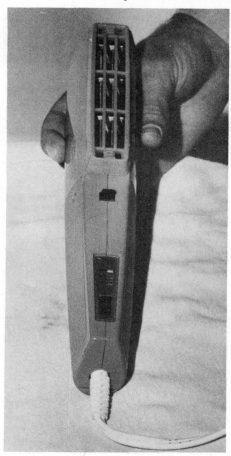

Figure 4. Devoid of the attachment, the appliance becomes an ordinary hair dryer. Notice the three-phase selector switch.

itself inside a hair dryer, it could cause irreparable damage and create a fire hazard.

Suppose, though, that for one reason or another the motor suddenly fails to function, making it possible for the heating elements to operate without the motor running. This would raise the dangerous situation just referred to, but fortunately it cannot happen because practically every hair dryer includes a safety thermostat which is wired in series with the power cord. If the internal temperature reaches a dangerous

level, the thermostat opens and voltage to the unit is shut off.

Although the switch that operates the motor and the one that allows selection of the various heat positions perform two separate functions, they are normally combined into one rotary-type switch so both functions occur simultaneously. In most dryers, it is possible to operate the fan so only unheated air is supplied. Thus, a dryer may have five switch positions, as follows:

1. Motor and heating elements are off.

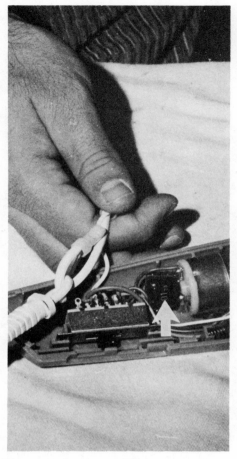

Figure 5. This is the heat-selector switch. Notice tapped terminals. The arrow points to the safety thermostat.

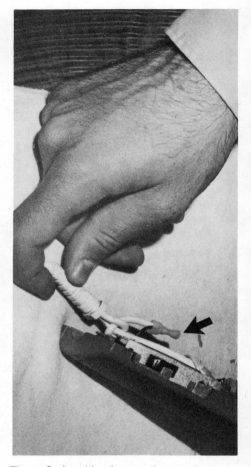

Figure 6. As with other appliances, the chief cause of trouble in a hair dryer is a damaged power cord. Check connections.

2. Motor is on and heating elements are off, providing cool air.

3. Motor is on and the low heating element is on, providing low heat.

4. Motor is on and the high heating element is on, providing medium heat.

5. Motor is on and both heating elements are on, providing high heat.

what can happen?

WHEN A HAIR DRYER GOES HAYWIRE, it can:

• Cease to function at all.

• Function in one way or another, but not in all ways. For example, the

motor may run, but the heating elements may not heat.

When a hair dryer refuses to function, there is a loss of voltage before voltage reaches the motor and heating elements. True—a hair dryer wouldn't function at all if the heating elements and motor failed at the same time, but this is extremely rare.

Other than a dead wall outlet, voltage can be cut off from the unit for one of three reasons: (1) power-cord trouble; (2) a safety thermostat that has failed; (3) a bad switch. Finding the problem area is easy enough.

It would be redundant to go into

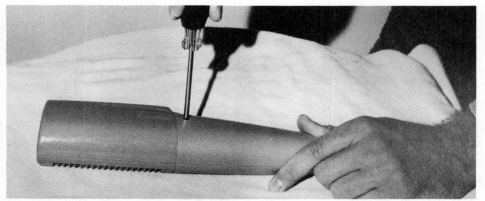

Figure 7. The hardest part in repairing a hair dryer may be in opening the unit. This photo and Figures 8 and 9 show how this is done in this model. One screw holds the case.

detail concerning the examination and testing of power cords (Figure 6). Continuity testing and how to inspect for broken wires and bad insulation have been discussed in several other chapters (see Index).

To check the safety thermostat, open up the unit and find the part (Figures 7, 8 and 9). In most dryers, it is positioned in line with the power cord, between the power cord's plug and the appliance's switch. Test the thermostat for continuity.

Caution: The dryer must be disconnected.

If there is no continuity, the reason for the failure is a bad thermostat. Replace with an identical part.

To determine whether a bad switch is preventing operation, attach a jumper lead across the switch leads. Plug the power cord into the wall outlet. If the hair dryer now works, replace the switch.

The switch of a hair dryer that provides various heat choices has several different wires attached to it. In many cases, these wires are color-coded. Carefully note where on the switch each wire attaches. If the wires are not color-coded, label them in some way for easy identification. Wires must be attached to their respective correct terminals when you install a new switch.

when one function fails

IF THE HEATING ELEMENTS work but there is no air circulation (assuming the safety thermostat hasn't activated), or if there is air circulation but no heat, obviously there is a problem in the motor circuit or in the heating-element circuit.

In the motor circuit, a malfunction in the motor itself, the fan or impeller, or in the switch can result in lack of motor function. The likelihood is that one contact of the switch has gone bad, so test this first by connecting a voltmeter to the output (motor) side of the switch. Plug the appliance into a wall outlet and turn the switch on.

If there is no voltage, replace the switch. If voltage is getting through to the motor, check the fan or impeller for freedom of movement. Spin it by hand. It should turn freely. If it doesn't, look for a foreign object, such as a hairpin, that might have become entwined and is preventing the fan or impeller from moving.

A fan or impeller may also be stuck because of a frozen bearing. Usually

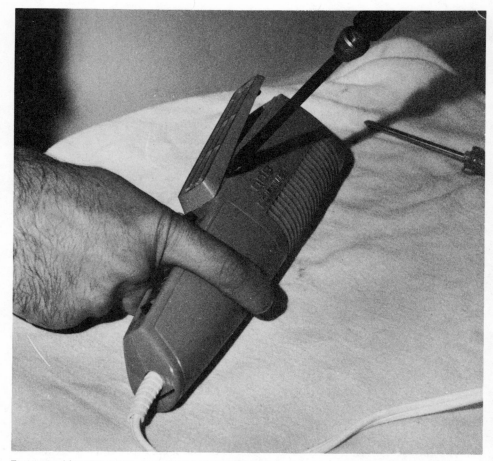

Figure 8. After the screw or screws holding the case are removed, the head at the dryer's blower end is taken off so the unit can be split into its two halves.

this can be repaired, but the motor will have to be taken apart. Keep a careful record of the order in which parts are removed, so reassembly will be easier. When you reach the bearing, clean the area thoroughly with solvent, such as mineral spirits, let the part dry, and oil the bearing with lightweight machine oil.

As mentioned before, there is little likelihood of motor failure, but that is exactly your problem if at this point you haven't uncovered the cause of lack of air circulation. You may be able to buy a replacement motor from a dealer who sells the particular make

of hair dryer, but compare its price with the price of a new, comparable dryer. The latter purchase may prove to be more sensible.

A problem in the heating-element circuit may be caused by a faulty switch or by an element that has failed. Probably the switch is to blame if there is no heat in the "high" heat position, or in both of the other positions, since it is hardly likely that both heaters will fail at the same time. Check the switch by connecting a jumper across its terminals and trying to operate the appliance in each of the various heat positions. If the unit

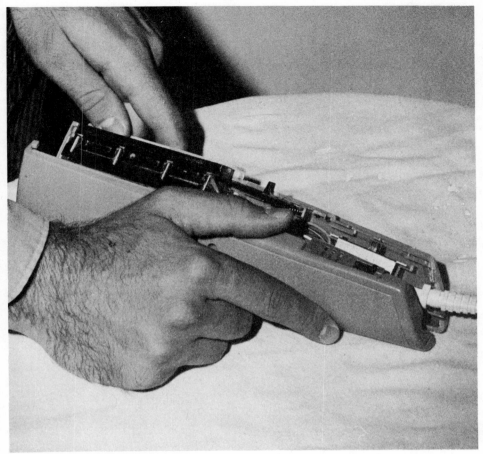

Figure 9. The unit may then be pried open, with a screwdriver or thin-bladed tool. The halves of the dryer are held together by a cam-slot arrangement. One slip can crack the case.

works, replace the switch.

If one heater doesn't work, but the other does, clean off the switch contacts with mineral spirits. Dirt may be preventing a good connection (Figure 10). If the heater still fails to work, it has burned out. Again, you may be able to get a replacement, but check its price against the price of a new hair dryer.

repairing physical damage

MOST HAIR DRYERS ARE PLASTIC, and plastic may crack if accidentally dropped or knocked against a hard surface. Often, however, a cracked or broken case can be repaired with one of the strong adhesives sold in hardware stores. Clear household cement or plastic mending adhesive usually will do the job.

To seal a crack, carefully pry the cracked edges apart with a small wedging tool, such as a thin knife. At the same time, apply adhesive into the crack. To avoid a possible mess, apply the adhesive to a wood or plastic applicator first, and use this to line the cracked edges. The wood or plastic dowel used as part of a cotton swab will do nicely as an applicator, but don't apply adhesive with cotton.

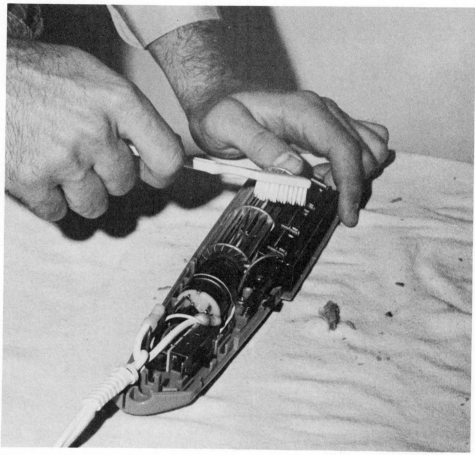

Figure 10. This dryer had been suffering from a case of poor heat output. We found dirt over the impeller and heater system; it was impeding heat flow. A good cleaning was the cure.

Close the crack and press the edges firmly together, clamping them in place until the cement sets.

Hair dryers that employ flexible hoses can be damaged if the hoses are manhandled. If a hose tears and a replacement cannot be found, buy a roll of pressure-sensitive vinyl adhesive tape at a hardware store and seal the crack with tape.

Chapter 11

Small electric fans

Simply built and usually reliable, small electric fans used in the home come in two varieties: cooling fans and exhaust fans. They are really the same machine, so you can use the same repair techniques

COOLING AND EXHAUST FANS consist basically of an on-off switch, motor and blades. By itself, a fan is a useful appliance. But in addition as you will see in other chapters, fans are necessary components of other appliances. For example, room heaters and hair dryers have small electric fans built into them.

Small cooling and exhaust fans have motors of less than ¼-horsepower. They are either shaded-pole or split-phase types. Both shaded-pole

and split-phase motors have low starting torque since air doesn't offer much resistance.

The functioning and upkeep of a *shaded-pole motor* are described in the introduction to this section and in the chapter on electric can openers, which also employ shaded-pole motors.

Since the *split-phase motor* is widely used in small electric fans as well as in other appliances, you should understand the way it works.

Figure 1. This is a low-horsepower split-phase motor which drives the electric fan seen in the rest of the pictures in this chapter. Some fans have shaded-pole motors.

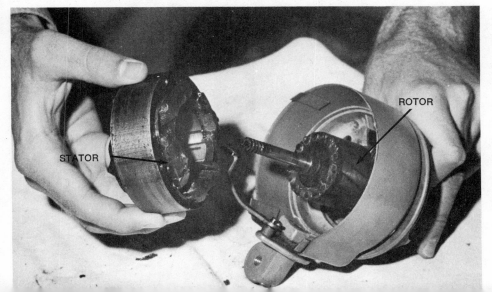

STATOR

ROTOR

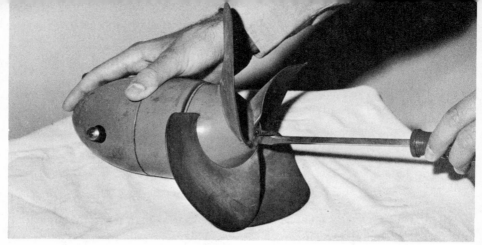

Figure 2. It is not likely that the rubber blades of this fan will ever have to be replaced. But if they did fail, they could be removed by unscrewing the large retaining screw.

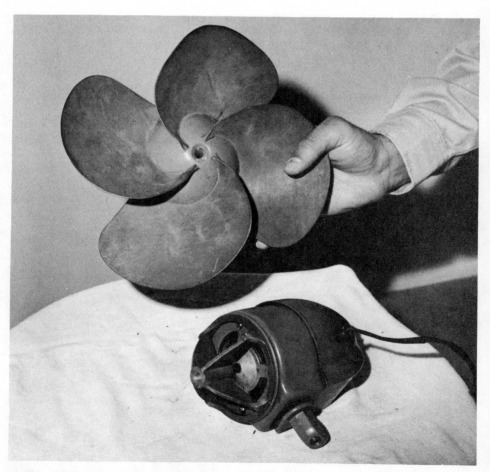

Figure 3. With the screw out, the blade assembly is taken from position. The retaining screw must also be removed if you wish entrance inside the fan housing.

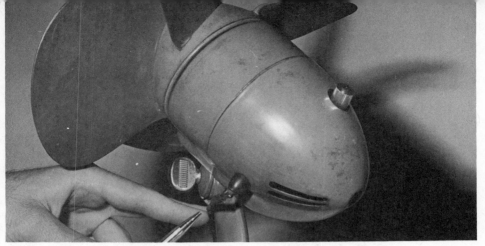

Figure 4. A power cord that looks like this should be suspected if there is a failure. To prevent failure, the cord should be taped with electrician's tape.

However, electric fans also employ smaller, less powerful split-phase motors. More powerful split-phase motors are installed in clothes washers, clothes dryers and dishwashers.

split-phase motor facts

SPLIT-PHASE MOTORS are made in several different horsepowers, including ¼, ⅓ and ½. The horsepower rating of the motor is significant in regard to its starting torque (power).

More powerful split-phase motors have a greater starting torque, because they must turn heavier loads. A washing machine, for example, has to turn a loaded tub from scratch. Conversely, the less powerful motor of a small exhaust fan only has to start revolving a lightweight blade.

Whatever its power rating, a split-phase motor consists essentially of a stator (stationary member) and rotor (rotating member) (Figure 1). The stator is made up of a coil of wires which is generally called the field coil. It is connected to the motor's frame and develops a magnetic field with the rotor as the rotor revolves.

The rotor is positioned inside the stator. A shaft that is part of the rotor is supported on bearings which

are mounted on the motor frame. This keeps the rotor suspended, but permits it to turn freely.

A stator and rotor by themselves produce power once the rotor starts to turn. However, a necessary member has to be added: a unit that will start the stator and rotor. This is called the starting coil.

The starting coil injects the electricity to start the rotor turning so it can interact with the current that is sent through the stator to create a magnetic field. Once the rotor and stator coil are able to operate independently, the starter coil is turned off by a centrifugal switch. This is done so no extra strain, which may cause premature failure of the starter coil, is exerted on that coil.

Incidentally, the centrifugal switch is a spring-type device. Spring pressure is overcome when the rotor attains a certain speed.

The split-phase motor is one of the most reliable motors used in appliances. It seldom fails, so if a malfunction within an appliance should occur, the cause of it should be sought carefully in other areas before the decision is made that the split-phase motor has malfunctioned.

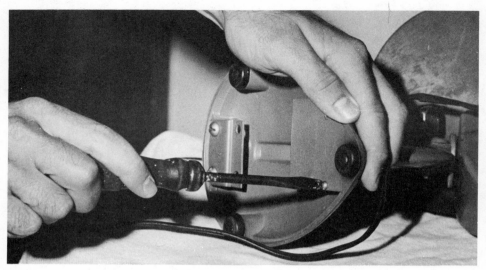

Figure 5. To replace a switch in this fan, we start by removing the switch-housing cover. The fan housing itself need not be dismantled.

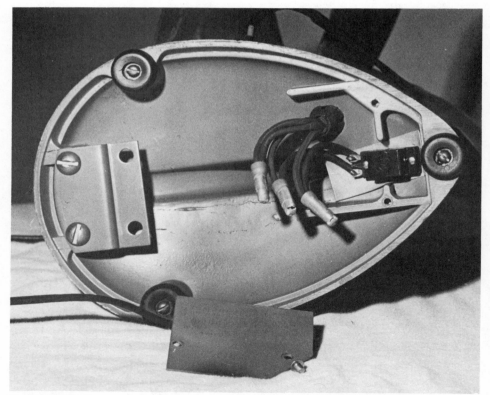

Figure 6. With the cover removed, wire-connecting nuts are exposed. These connect the switch and power cord. Notice that the switch is soldered to the wire. Without soldering equipment, replacing the switch is not possible.

some common troubles

ONE PROBLEM THAT IS COMMON to all small electric cooling fans is damage caused by accidentally dropping or knocking the fan over. This can throw the blade out of balance, allowing it to rub against the grille and create noise. The blade assembly may also vibrate when one blade is bent. Another cause of noise brought about by accidentally knocking a fan over is a bent grille portion, which the fan blades hit as they revolve.

One way to determine what is causing the noise or vibration is to rotate the blades slowly by hand. If the blades are scraping against the grille because the grille is bent, carefully bend it back into shape.

Caution: Just to be on the safe side, pull the power cord from the wall outlet before testing the blade-grille relationship.

If only one blade is bent and is hitting against the grille, carefully bend the blade back. Sometimes you can't straighten a blade back to its original

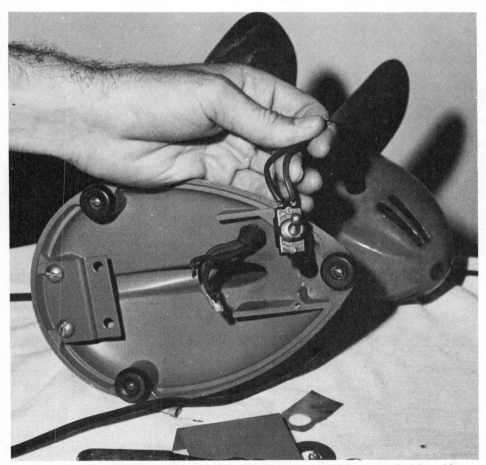

Figure 7. With wires disconnected and soldering connections broken, the switch bezel is unscrewed and the switch is removed. For the small price of a new switch, plus a fair amount of your time, you've saved the price of a new fan.

shape, but you can usually do a good enough job to reduce the amount of noise to an acceptable level.

To determine if the blade assembly is out of balance, creating a vibration problem, hold a sharp pencil steadily against one of the bars of the grille so the pencil point just barely touches one of the fan blades. Rotate the assembly slowly by hand. The pencil point should touch each blade leaf at the same spot as it touched the first leaf.

If an entire blade assembly is so badly damaged that the blades cannot be straightened or restored to balance, or if one of the blades is broken off, you may be able to get a replacement assembly (Figures 2 and 3). See if the damaged assembly can be removed from the shaft by unscrewing a fastener. This fastener is often in the form of a retaining nut.

Incidentally, if the blades are out of balance it is possible that this retaining nut has vibrated loose. Make sure it is tight.

Another operational problem resulting from bent blades may be sluggish action on the part of the fan. Usually, however, this is caused by a lack of oil.

Examine the fan carefully for oil ports and apply several drops of 20-weight household machine oil. Start the fan, allowing it to run for a minute or so. Turn it off. Apply more oil, and keep following this procedure until the blades spin at a proper rate of speed.

Reminder: Many fans require periodic lubrication, which is often called for annually. Let's hope you still have the owner's instructions you got when you purchased the fan. They'll tell you exactly where to lubricate.

Another condition that may cause fan blades to operate sluggishly is

dirt which accumulates around the fan motor shaft and blades. Disconnect the unit and wipe off all dirt. If necessary, wash this portion of the fan with a solution of household detergent and water, but don't let any water enter the motor housing. It can damage windings.

You will notice that a fan-motor housing has slots in it. These are necessary for air to enter the housing and cool the motor. Slots should be kept open. If they are clogged, clean the dirt out with a small putty knife or wooden scraper.

when a fan won't operate

IF A FAN MOTOR REFUSES to run, the problem can lie in only one of four places: the **wall outlet, power cord, switch,** or **motor.** It is easy enough to pinpoint the trouble area.

Is the wall outlet "live?" If you aren't sure, plug in a lamp you know is good.

Is the power cord in good condition? You could dismantle the fan to conduct a continuity test of the cord, but first examine it closely for cuts and breaks (Figure 4). On the chance that the wire is split internally, insert the plug into a wall outlet, switch on the fan, and bend the line cord back and forth over its entire length. If the cord has broken strands that do not allow electricity to get to the motor, the strands are likely to come together during a "bend" and will let the fan operate momentarily.

Flick the on-off switch. Often, a switch that has failed feels "sloppy" (Figures 5, 6, and 7).

At this point you have a choice to make. You can take the time to dismantle the fan and verify the cause of the problem, or you can simply assume that the **motor** is burned out and replace the fan. If you decide to be "mechanical," here is how to pro-

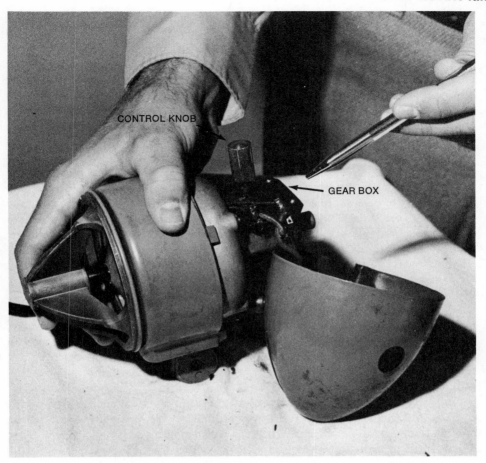

Figure 8. Many small desk fans, as well as larger fans, are designed to spread their breeze from side to side. Here are two main components of the oscillating mechanism: the gear box and the control knob, which are located at the rear of the motor.

ceed once the fan is dismantled.

Check the line cord for continuity as we've discussed many times before. Check the switch by connecting the continuity tester across the switch terminals. If the test light flares, the switch is good. Another way to test a switch is to connect a jumper lead across the terminals and plug the power cord into a wall outlet. If the fan runs, the switch is bad.

If testing indicates a burned-out motor, discard the appliance for a new one. It is not economically feasible to repair the fan.

when a fan won't oscillate

MANY SMALL DESK FANS oscillate. This motion is made possible by a small gear box attached to the rear of the motor (Figure 8). The gear setup includes a clutch that connects a pinion gear to an eccentric arm (Figure 9). The clutch is controlled by a knob on top of the gear box. When you turn the knob in one direction, the fan oscillates. When you turn the knob in the other direction, the pinion slips on its shaft, stopping the oscillation.

79

When a problem occurs with the oscillation mechanism, the fan will either oscillate sluggishly or fail to oscillate at all. Sluggish oscillation is usually caused by dirt and/or lack of lubricant on the eccentric arm. Repairing the problem may involve disassembly of the oscillating mechanism for a thorough cleaning and oiling with lightweight household machine oil.

If the fan fails to oscillate, the trouble probably is a stripped or worn part in the gear train. The entire gear box should be replaced, or you can choose to operate the fan without oscillation.

all about exhaust fans

MANY HOMES have exhaust fans mounted in the ceiling or wall of a kitchen and/or bathroom (Figure 10). Usually the fan is controlled by a regular on-off switch mounted on a wall. The switch connects to an electric outlet into which the fan power cord is plugged. The fan itself is mounted on several metal arms which are attached to wall studs. Most have rubber bushings (mountings) between the metal arms and wall studs to reduce vibration and noise.

Power-cord problems are virtually non-existent with exhaust fans because the line cord is seldom disconnected.

The exhaust fan also has a decorative grille that covers the hole in the ceiling, making it less conspicuous. The grille permits air and odors to pass through. Above the fan there is a movable cover that stays closed when the fan is shut off to keep out cold air and weather. When the blast of air from the fan hits it, the cover swings open to allow exhaust to escape.

One problem that may in time strike an exhaust fan is the drying up of its lubricant. The motor of practically every exhaust fan is lubricated in manufacture so that homeowner lubrication isn't required for many years. However, the large oil-soaked wick placed in many fans can dry out eventually. An indication that this may have happened is a very slow-turning fan. Also, if a fan motor is allowed to dry out too much, the fan can begin making a scraping noise.

To see if an exhaust fan needs re-lubrication, shut off the power and remove the grille. Spin the fan blades by hand. The fan assembly should spin easily and coast to a stop. If the assembly halts abruptly or displays resistance, lubrication is needed.

Some manufacturers install oil ports in their exhaust fans, so look the housing over carefully. If you see oil ports, squirt in several drops of lightweight household machine oil. Then, turn on the fan and allow it to run for about a minute. Turn it off and apply several more drops. Keep following this procedure until the fan runs smoothly.

If the motor housing has no oil ports, detach the fan from its mounting in the ceiling or wall. Pull the power cord from the plug. Now, place the fan on a workbench and remove the end cap. You should find a cloth oil wick. Saturate this with lightweight household machine oil, reassemble the unit, wipe off excess oil, and reinstall it in its mounting. Start the fan and allow it to run for several minutes.

The only other problem that can affect an exhaust fan is total failure—no movement at all. The first thing to do is to check for continuity by pulling the line cord and connecting a continuity tester across the plug's prongs. If there is continuity, failure of the fan to operate when you flip the wall switch probably is due to a

Figure 9. The third major component of an oscillating fan includes the pinion gear and eccentric arm. When the knob is tightened, it engages a clutch connecting gear and arm.

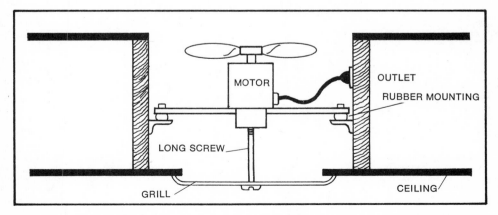

Figure 10. An exhaust fan is nothing more than an ordinary electric fan. The only difference is that it's mounted in a wall or ceiling, and blows out.

faulty switch. If there is no continuity, the cause of the trouble can be a burned-out motor, which should be replaced.

needed: occasional maintenance

AN EXHAUST FAN can get so badly clogged with grease and dirt that it will refuse to run, but this is unusual. What is more likely to occur is a slowing down of fan action.

To avert this problem, occasionally wipe off all grease and dirt with paper towels. Non-electric parts, such as the grille, end cap, and blades may be washed with detergent and water solution, but make sure that no water works its way into the fan motor.

Chapter 12

Home workshop motors

Believe it or not, the general-purpose motor in your home workshop is very similar to the starter motor in your car; the small universal AC-DC motors in food mixers and blenders; and even the 500–1500-volt motors that drive electric railway cars

DON'T LET ITS SIZE fool you or dismay you. The home workshop motor is nothing more than an oversize universal AC-DC motor of the kind we have discussed in several chapters in this section on small motorized electric appliances. Basically, it is a machine which produces rotary action. It converts electrical energy to mechanical action.

Stripped of its outside case, a typical home workshop motor is seen to contain coils of wire wound around a cylindrical rotor called the armature. Coils are wound so their sides are parallel to the armature shaft.

The armature is free to move; that is, although it is supported, it is not held firmly. One end of the armature shaft is the end that turns a pulley to operate a home-workshop tool, such as a grinder. Interestingly, most home-workshop tools, including drill presses and table saws, work on this kind of motor.

Among the elements required to get the armature (motor) shaft rotating are the field coils. The field coils are wound wires which are attached to the frame and are in series with a coil wound around the armature. This is one of the reasons a home workshop

motor often is referred to as a series motor. An electromagnetic force is created between the field coils and the armature coils; this force causes the armature to revolve.

There is, however, another element which is required. There must be a connection between the armature coil and the field coil. As you know from our discussion in previous chapters, this connection is accomplished by means of carbon elements called brushes which are held by springs in contact with the end of the armature called the commutator.

The commutator is an assembly of copper bars which are mounted compactly around one end of the armature shaft. Each of the individual bars of the commutator is connected to the endings of the coils of wire which comprise the armature coil.

Brushes and commutator work as a team. One brush is positive, and the other brush is negative. They are spaced directly opposite each other and are held in firm contact with the commutator by springs.

Brushes are connected directly to the field coils. This entire setup establishes an electromagnetic force. In other words, the brushes are spaced around the commutator so that when the south pole wires on the armature come under a north pole of the field coils, the bars of the commutator to which they're connected are given a definitive physical direction because of strong opposing (magnetic) force. When the same wires rotate under the south pole, the commutator bars connected to the wires are between brushes with an opposite attraction, and the rotary motion is maintained.

The result, then, is very rapid rotary movement of the entire free-moving armature, which culminates in mechanical energy at the output end of the armature shaft.

little cause for concern

THE HOME WORKSHOP MOTOR probably is the most reliable machine in the home. This truism applies to appliances in general which are equipped with the armature-brush-field-coil setup. Home workshop motors seldom fail to the point of needing major overhaul or discarding. Even when they do break down, the reason for the occurrence is usually of such minor consequence that it's easily eliminated.

Let's run down a list of the more common home-workshop-motor failures and discuss what you should do when one strikes:

1. **A loose pulley.** The pulley at the output end of the machine may in time become loose. This can cause vibration and a loss of power. To tighten the pulley, tighten the set screw that holds the pulley to the shaft (Figure 1). In many cases, this is an Allen-type set screw, and you will need an Allen wrench which fits exactly. Allen wrenches are available in hardware stores.

2. **A loose wire.** If the motor sparks, refuses to start one time but starts another, or refuses to start at all, a wire

Figure 1. Keep the pulley tight. A loose one causes vibration, loss of power and damage to the parts of the motor involved.

connection may be loose. Typically, motors possess end covers that can be removed easily to expose connections (Figure 2). Remove the two or three screws holding the cover.

With the cover plate off (make absolutely certain that the workshop motor's line cord is disconnected from the electric source), use a small wrench to tighten all connections (Figure 3).

3. **Bad brushes.** One of the most common repairs which is made to a home workshop motor is brush replacement. Brushes wear as they rub against the commutator. Depending upon the extensiveness of use to

which you put the motor, brushes may wear away in a matter of months or may last many years.

When brushes are worn and should be replaced, the motor will start sluggishly and may spark.

Brushes of some home workshop motors can be reached externally by removing slotted caps from the outside of the machine. Remove caps carefully so the spring-loaded brushes won't fly out, and take care not to damage the brush springs. If the springs are resilient, they can be reused.

When the brushes have been removed, replace them with new ones. You can buy brushes of the type needed by your home workshop motor from a hardware store or an establishment that specializes in home power tools.

In other motors, the case has to be disassembled to get at brushes. In most instances, the pulley has to be removed from the output shaft before the case can be taken apart. Then, the long screws that project horizontally through the motor can be loosened. These are usually held by nuts (Figure 4).

If housing components "stick" and won't budge apart, don't force anything. Rather, take a block of wood and lay it on each component of the casing. Tap the wood gently with a hammer until the component loosens.

With both ends of the motor housing off, you will spot the brush holders at the commutator end of the armature shaft (Figure 5). The brush holders may be held in place by small screws or clips. Take these off carefully, pick the holder off the motor, locate the brush and brush spring, and replace the brush.

4. **Frozen bearings.** This is not a common failure, but it may happen, especially if your motor is designed to be lubricated and you fail to do this. The tip-off that bearings are going bad is that the motor suddenly runs noisily. If the condition becomes very serious, the motor may hum when you turn it on, but it won't revolve.

Bearing replacement is a job for a professional power-tool mechanic who possesses the necessary pullers for removing bearings from the end cap. You can ruin a perfectly sound

Figure 2. To ascertain the existence of a loose wire, remove the end cover. This is usually an easy job accomplished simply by removing two or three screws.

Figure 3. With the cover removed, you are able to reach inside with a small wrench and tighten wire connections.

Figure 4. Getting inside the motor to make repairs and replace worn parts entails removing the pulley and disassembly bolts.

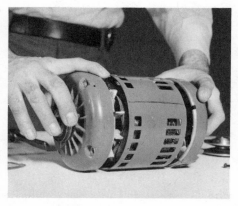

Figure 5. With the bolts out, the end covers can be removed, exposing the brushes and other parts. Proceed carefully.

motor by using home-grown methods, such as knocking bearings from the end cap with a hammer. We advise that you not take the chance.

a word about maintenance

A HOME WORKSHOP MOTOR requires very little care. The most important procedure, though, is to keep the unit clean. Since it is used for home workshop projects, it will get dusty and dirty.

Your motor may or may not be designed for lubrication. If the motor possesses oil cups, apply a drop or two of machine oil to the motor periodically.

How often? That depends on the recommendations of the manufacturer, but if you have lost the maintenance instructions, apply a few drops of oil every few months, but more often if the motor is used frequently.

If there are no oil cups, the motor was pre-lubricated at the factory during manufacture. There is nothing you can do.

Section 2
Small Appliances
Without Motors

Chapter 13

Introduction

With one exception, the appliances discussed in this section either keep you warm (Chapters 12–16) or cook food (Chapters 18–24). The exception is the electric iron, which is discussed in chapter 17.

THERE IS ONE APPLIANCE in this section which cannot truly be called an appliance without a motor, and that is the room heater. It has a small motor which drives a fan.

However, we have placed room heaters in this section—in fact, we have made it the first chapter of the section following this introduction—because its non-motorized characteristics predominate. These characteristics are the same or similar to those possessed by most of the other appliances which follow it in this section.

As mentioned above, the section divides itself at chapter 17 between small non-motorized appliances which are used for cooking and those that perform other functions. Whatever the appliance, though—cooking or non-cooking—each one discussed in this section has a feature in common with all other appliances discussed in this section: it produces heat.

Every appliance we discuss in Section II possesses some sort of heating element and thermostat. The way in which elements and thermostats work, as well as the functioning of other dominant features possessed by each appliance, are discussed in detail throughout the section. Naturally, the most emphasis is placed on troubleshooting and repairing each of the appliances.

These are the chapters included in this section:

Chapter 14. Room heaters
Chapter 15. Electric blankets
Chapter 16. Heating pads
Chapter 17. Electric irons
Chapter 18. Waffle irons
Chapter 19. Electric coffee percolators
Chapter 20. Electric pop-up toasters
Chapter 21. Toaster-ovens
Chapter 22. Electric roasters
Chapter 23. Electric skillets, sauce pans and fry pans
Chapter 24. Hot plates and hot trays

Room heaters

Also called a space heater, this appliance saves the day when a home heating system doesn't warm a room properly. Although fairly reliable, it may fail because of the heavy amount of electricity it draws.

ROOM HEATERS are available in a variety of shapes and sizes. However, they all work on the same simple, basic principle, and the problems that afflict them are common. So are repairs.

Basically, a room heater consists of two circuits: a heating circuit and an air-driving (motor) circuit (Figure 1). Neither is particularly complex in makeup or function, but at the outset we must caution you about one pitfall—

Caution: Room heaters draw a great deal of electricity. Unless you are 100 percent sure of yourself, when a heater fails you should leave repair to a professional technician. There are two dangers involved.

First, there is the danger of personal injury. If you are not careful, you can receive a severe shock when making repairs. Furthermore, anyone using the heater can receive a serious shock after repairs are made if the work wasn't done properly. Also, there is the danger that an improper repair will cause fire.

In this chapter, we examine the problems that can affect a room heater and, in general, how to tackle them with all the necessary precautions.

However, if you decide to proceed with repair, but for some reason or other you get hung up, do not take chances. Abandon the project and consult a serviceman.

how you make "heat"

THE HEATING CIRCUIT of a room heater consists of one or more heating elements, a thermostat, probably

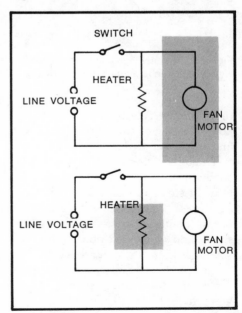

Figure 1. Every space heater has a fan-motor circuit (top) and a heating circuit.

Figure 2. Screwdriver points to shaded-pole motor which drives the fan. The back cover of this room heater had to be unscrewed to reach the motor and remove reflector pan.

Figure 3. The man has just spun the plastic fan impeller. This is a good way of checking whether the fan is binding and restricting the flow of warm air.

one or more selector switches to enable selection of a desirable heat level, and a tip-over switch.

The air-driving circuit consists of a shaded-pole motor which drives a relatively small fan blade. The fan circulates the heated air through the room (Figures 2 and 3). This is the same kind of shaded-pole motor that small desk fans use, and which was discussed in the chapter on fans. If the fan motor gives you any problem, review chapter 11.

Now take a look at the way in which a simple room heater works. It consists of a single heating element,

thermostat, tip-over switch and air-driving motor (Figure 4). When its line cord is plugged into a wall socket, voltage is applied through the tip-over switch and thermostat across both the heating element and motor. Simultaneously, then, the heating element gets hot, and the fan moves the hot air.

How does the heating element get hot? The element is made of a special alloy wire (usually a nickel-chromium alloy called nichrome) that is both heat-resistant and has resistance. Both characteristics are necessary for an electric heater to do its job.

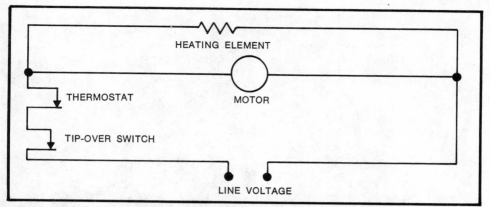

Figure 4. This schematic depicts the layout of a one-element electric room heater. This type of heater has only one setting.

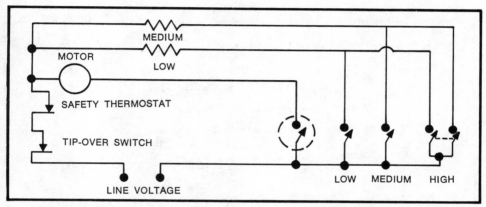

Figure 5. In a two-element heater, the Low element has less resistance than the Medium and produces less intense heat. A High setting activates both Low and Medium heating elements.

The special-alloy wire has a high melting point that enables it to withstand the great amount of heat the wire itself produces. The amount of heat created depends on the amount of wattage the element produces. Depending on the element, this could be as little as 500 watts or as much as 5,000 watts. In other words, elements differ from room heater to room heater. Some have a higher wattage capacity than other. Elements having higher ratings draw more electricity and create more heat. Those with lower capacities draw less electricity and produce less heat (Figure 5). This

is true not only of room heaters, but as you will see throughout this section, it is also true of other heat-producing appliances.

a little theory (sorry)

LET'S GET a little theoretical, so you can better appreciate the tremendous job that a heating element must do.

When we say that a heating element has *resistance,* we mean that it allows only a certain amount of electricity to flow through it at a time. Resistance depends upon such factors as the type of wire, the gauge of wire, and the number of coils into which

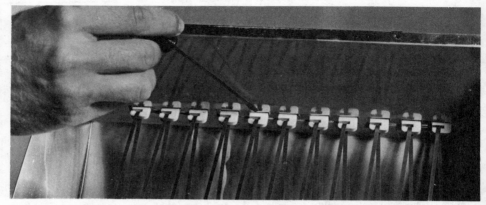

Figure 6. Insulators hold the bands of heating element wire. The characteristics of the wire and number and size of insulators produce electrical resistance which creates heat.

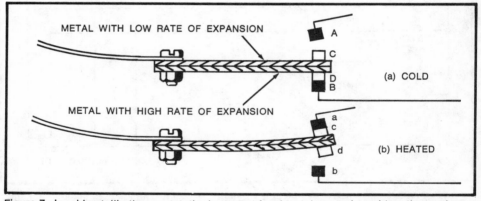

Figure 7. In a bimetallic thermostat, the bottom strip of metal expands and lengthens when heated, causing the strip to curl up and away from electric contact point, breaking circuit.

the wire is fashioned. It also depends on the type and size of the ceramic or porcelain insulators to which the element is attached, because insulators, too, have resistance (Figure 6).

To determine how many watts (and, hence, how much heat) a room heater can give, you always start with a constant figure. This is the amount of available voltage (or electric pressure). The voltage coming from the wall outlet is a known factor. In most U.S. homes, for example, it is 115 volts, give or take a few volts.

The speed at which voltage flows through a circuit depends on the size and makeup of the wire (that is, on the wire's resistance). Some wires—copper and silver, for example—offer little or no resistance. This kind of wire is called conductive wire.

Other wire—nichrome is one—impedes the flow of voltage. It slows electricity down and is referred to as resistance wire.

The rate of speed of electricity through a circuit is measured in amperes. Opposition to amperage is measured in ohms.

As electricity flows through an element which has resistance, the element "strains" under the load and

Figure 8. Many people are not aware that when they set the "heat" of an electric room heater, they are manipulating the thermostat to "make" and "break" earlier or later.

gets hot. This heat (power) output is wattage. The number of watts you get from an element depends on voltage (electric pressure) and amperage (electrical speed). In other words—

Watts = volts × amperes

This, however, can be somewhat misleading because, as noted above, voltage usually is a constant 115 volts. Amperage, then, is the critical factor. The greater the ampere flow through an element, the greater will be the wattage (heat output).

Suppose the heating element in your heater allows a 10-ampere flow through it. The output of the heater will be 1150 watts—115 volts × 10 amperes = 1150 watts.

On the other hand, suppose your heater has an element that permits a 25-ampere flow. The output of this heater will be 2875 watts—115 volts × 25 amperes = 2875 watts.

heating elements, thermostats

A ROOM HEATER CIRCUIT, as mentioned earlier in this chapter, consists of a heating element that creates a certain amount of heat, depending upon the element's resistance to electricity. When the room that the heater is supposed to heat gets warm

enough, the heating element automatically turns itself off, thanks to the thermostat. On the other hand, when the area cools down below a certain temperature, the thermostat permits the heating element to turn itself on again.

The purpose of a room heater's thermostat is to maintain a certain comfort level. A thermostat is simply a heat-sensitive switch that is composed of two different types of metals which are securely fastened to each other (Figure 7). For this reason, most thermostats are called "bimetallic thermostats."

One of the metals of this bimetal assembly has a very high rate of thermal expansion, while the other has a very low rate of thermal expansion. The former metallic strip expands rapidly when subjected to heat. This causes the metal to increase in length. Since the other metallic strip—the one resisting heat—remains more or less the same size, the bimetallic strip bends out of shape, which snaps the strip away from an electric contact point. This "breaks" the circuit, shutting off electricity to the heating element.

When electricity is shut off, the heating element starts to cool down.

Figure 9. This is the tip-over switch. When heater falls over, the heavy counterweight pulls the thermostat apart, breaking the circuit and cutting off electricity.

Figure 10. Although electric room heaters vary in style, this breakdown of a typical heater and the photos in this chapter will help you troubleshoot and repair any unit.

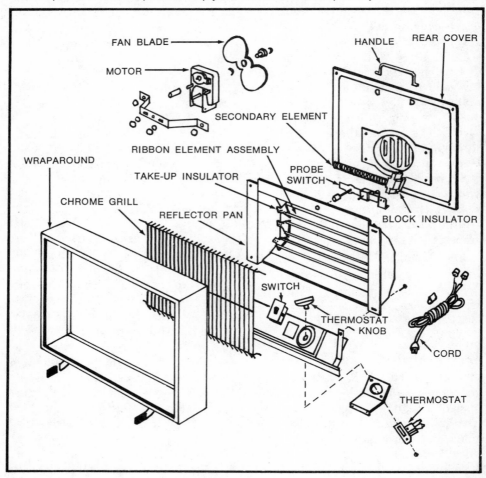

The bimetallic strip also cools down and starts contracting, eventually assuming its original shape, which places it once more in contact with the electric contact point. The circuit is "made"—that is, electricity is once again permitted to flow through the heating element.

Most thermostats are adjustable. They can be set to make and break a circuit at different temperatures. You do this by setting a temperature-control knob, but in effect what you are doing is adjusting the distance between the bimetallic strip (thermostat) and electric-contact point (Figure 8). This permits the room heater to cycle off and on more or less frequently, giving more or less heat. It's as simple as that.

One of the most important parts of a room heater is the tip-over switch. It is a safety device to prevent fire.

The tip-over switch is a spring-loaded switch that must be pressed in for contact to be maintained and for the heater to operate. It closes the circuit.

The tip-over switch is allowed to be pressed in only when the heater is in its normal, upright operating position. If the heater is accidentally tipped over, the spring pulls the switch off its electric contact, breaking the circuit (Figure 9).

troubles are little ones

SINCE A TYPICAL room heater contains only a limited number of parts, troubleshooting a defective one is fairly simple (Figure 10). The cause of the problem may be a dead wall plug, a bad line cord, a faulty thermostat, a sticking tip-over switch, a loose connection, or a bad heating element.

Experience suggests that the parts least likely to fail are the tip-over switch, thermostat, and shaded-pole motor. Parts most likely to go bad are the line cord, connections and heating element.

An electric room heater can fail in one of two ways: Either it will not work at all, which is the most common way in which the unit goes bad, or it will ground itself. Grounding is serious business, because someone touching the unit may receive a severe shock. In cases of grounding, which is another term for short-circuiting, the house fuse or circuit breaker on the line in which the heater is plugged will often blow or trip.

If the unit does not turn on when it is plugged into a wall outlet, it's possible that the wall plug is dead. This is easy enough to determine. Plug a lamp that you know works into the wall outlet and turn it on. If it doesn't glow, something is wrong with the house current.

If the lamp does turn on, examine the room heater's line cord. Spread the prongs slightly and plug them back into the wall outlet (Figure 11). Perhaps the prongs weren't making good contact. If the unit still doesn't work, check the line cord for damage. At this point, you should take off the grillework and/or cover so you can get inside the unit.

Caution: Make certain that the line cord is pulled from the wall plug before you start taking the room heater apart (Figure 12). The shock you get from a heavy-drawing unit such as a room heater is enough to knock you into the middle of next week.

Once inside the unit, here is what to look for:

- Check all insulators for cracks and breakage. Replace damaged insulators (Figure 13). Parts for room heaters are available from electric-parts supply stores.
- Inspect open-wire heating elements

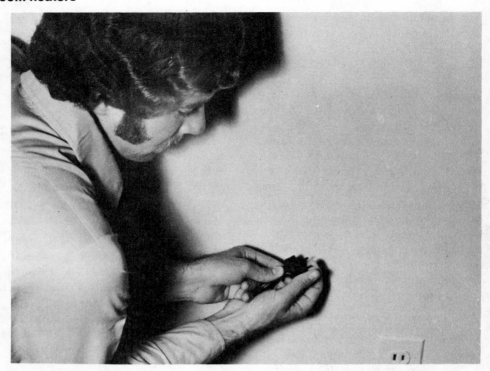

Figure 11. Often, the simple repair will be the one that works. Here, it's just a matter of slightly spreading the prongs of the heater's line cord so they make contact in outlet.

to see that they are taut. Open-wire elements should not sag, since a sagging element could touch the metal case, causing a dangerous grounding condition. Heating elements of many room heaters are insulated. Make sure that insulation is not burned away in any one spot.

- Inspect heating elements closely to see if there is a break in the wiring. Breaks interrupt the circuit, causing the heater to cease functioning.

- Find the thermostat and tip-over switch (Figures 14 and 15). With your finger, carefully pull each off its electric contact and inspect if the thermostat is accessible. If the metal element sticks, or contacts are pitted or badly oxidized, replace the part with one of exactly the same rating.

- Inspect all electric connections.

They should be clean and, above all, they should be tight. In fact, those connections held by screws and nuts should be given a tightening in the event that one or more have come loose (Figure 16).

If you have failed to find the cause of the trouble by this time, the various parts of the heater should be tested for continuity using a continuity tester or a multitester. Multitesters come with complete instructions. Follow them.

If you use the continuity tester, make sure that the device is connected between the points you are testing before plugging it in.

One additional point should be made about repair: Before replacing a heating element, you should obtain the cost of the element and compare it to the cost of a new room heater.

Figure 12. Here's good advice when repairing *any* appliance. Be safe and pull the plug from the wall before you start working. Handling a "live" appliance could be deadly.

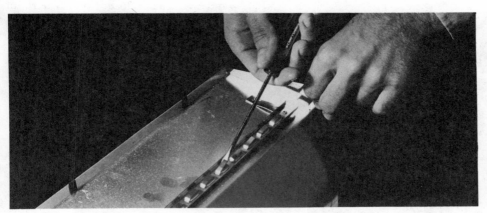

Figure 13. Damaged insulators (see Figure 6) can usually be replaced. Here, reflector pan had to be removed because prongs on top of pan hold the insulators.

Figure 14. The thermostat switch in this heater is easily replaced, because wire connections are held by a cap rather than being soldered. The cap is removed.

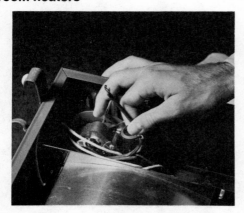

Figure 15. The wires are then separated; switch is removed and replaced.

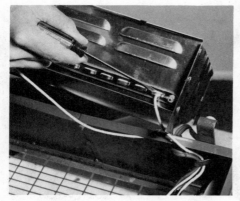

Figure 16. Tightening a loose wire connection may restore service.

You may find that the cost of repair is not justified.

the most important step

ASSUMING YOU HAVE MADE a repair and the room heater has been reassembled, there is a very important safety check to make *before* you plug the heater into a wall outlet and touch it to turn it on. If you have accidentally short-circuited (grounded) the heater, touching it may cause serious injury.

The check is made with a test lamp consisting of an insulated socket that is equipped with a low-wattage bulb and two leads. Do *not* plug the room heater into the wall outlet. First, connect one of the test leads to a clean, bare (unpainted) metal part of the room heater. Connect the other lead to a good clean ground. A water pipe is ideal.

Turn the room heater on. Now, plug it into the wall socket.

The test lamp should *not* glow. If it does, the heater is grounded and is dangerous (Figure 17).

If the lamp does not glow, pull the plug from the wall outlet, reverse it, and plug it back into the outlet. Now, if the bulb does *not* glow, you can conclude that the room heater is safe.

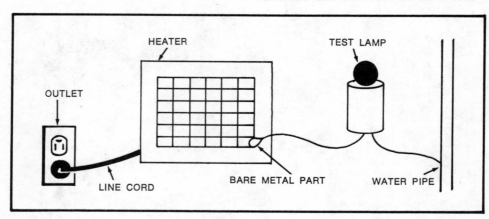

Figure 17. This diagram shows you how to make the ground test following repair.

Chapter 15

Electric blankets

The electric blanket on my bed has given warm service for over ten years. When it finally does fail, I may try to fix it—and then, again, I may not. It all depends on where the failure occurs.

AN ELECTRIC BLANKET is a relatively simple appliance, consisting essentially of flexible heating elements that are sewn between two sections of material. The material is lightweight enough to allow warmth from the elements to pass through.

Electric blankets generally have two heating elements. One element heats each half of the blanket, and these two elements have a common element between them (Figure 1). Thus, it is conceivable that half of an electric blanket can fail while the other half gives heat.

The operational controls of an electric blanket consist of (a) a two-wire line cord that connects into a (b) control box and a (c) three-wire line that runs from the control box to a (d) connector at the foot of the blanket that attaches the line to the heating elements. In practically every blanket (perhaps all) the control box and lines can be disconnected from the blanket itself, so the blanket may be dry-cleaned and/or folded for storage during warm weather.

An electric blanket for a twin bed normally has a single control box. The two heating elements sewn inside the blanket are controlled simultaneously by the one control, which contains a

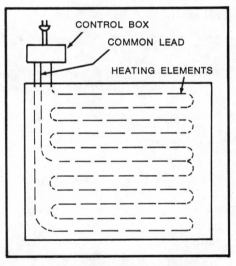

Figure 1. There are two heating elements in an electric blanket, with a common lead.

thermostat. The thermostat permits variations of temperature from very cool to very hot.

Electric blankets for double beds have virtually the same setup, except that there are two control boxes so each partner can set warmth to his or her desire in his or her half of the blanket (Figures 2 and 3). Almost every one of the control boxes of these doube-bed blankets contains its own thermostat.

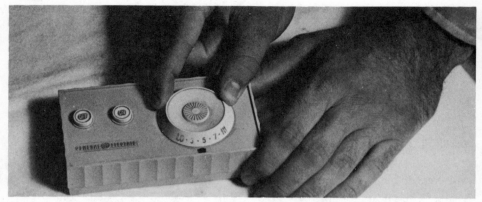

Figure 2. The degree of warmth is adjusted by a dial which simply applies more or less tension to the thermostat. The thermostat controls the amount of heat produced.

all about the thermostat

THE THERMOSTAT of most electric blankets is what is called the "magnetic contact" type (Figure 4). If you use an electric blanket, you have heard the clicking sounds coming from the control box. These are the thermostat contact points coming together with sufficient force to make them click.

The typical thermostat contains a lower contact point which lies on the end of a stationary control arm in the base of the control box. The contact point is attached to an iron washer.

The other part of the thermostat is an upper contact point which is positioned on the end of a flexible bimetal control arm. This control arm moves in accordance with temperature. The contact point itself lies in the center of a cup-shaped magnet.

Suppose the temperature in your bedroom falls below the particular setting at which you have the temperature control knob set. As you know, the outside of the control box has a movable indicator of some sort (knob or whatever) and a series of numbers, ranging, say, from one to eight, with one being the coolest setting and eight the hottest.

When you set the indicator dial, you are in reality manipulating the flexible (movable) thermostat arm. Setting the indicator at the lower settings places less tension on the arm, which in turn allows the contact points to open more readily. Conversely, placing the indicator at the upper settings places more tension on the arm, which keeps the contact points closed longer.

As long as the contact points remain closed, electricity flows through the elements sewn in the blanket, and the elements give off heat.

When the temperature in the room falls below the established "heat" setting, the thermostat's bimetal arm starts to straighten out (coolness causes it to contract), and the magnet draws closer and closer to the iron washer on the end of the stationary (bottom) arm, eventually coming close enough so magnetic attraction draws the two contact points firmly together . . . click.

Unlike most other appliances, the electric blanket uses this magnetic set of points. Why? To assure that contact points make *firm* contact. Without the magnetic feature, points would bounce, and the electric current would "make" and "break" in-

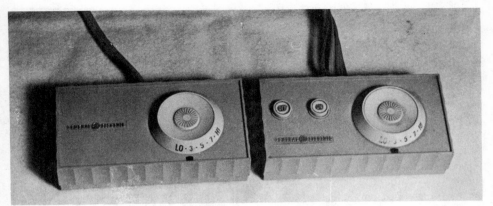

Figure 3. These controls serve an electric blanket for a double bed. This older unit, unlike newer models, does not have "on-off" switches on both control boxes.

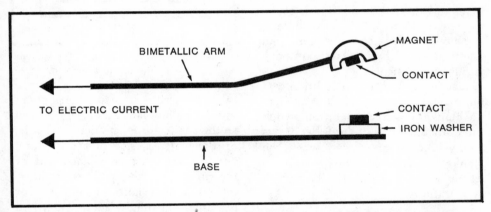

BIMETALLIC ARM

MAGNET

CONTACT

TO ELECTRIC CURRENT

CONTACT

IRON WASHER

BASE

Figure 4. This illustrates the magnetic-contact bimetal thermostat which allows for rapid cycling and maintenance of desired temperature within close tolerance.

discriminately, leading to erratic heating.

Now, when the two contact points meet, of course, the electric circuit is completed, and electricity flows through the blanket's heating elements. But now, let's say, the temperature reaches the desired level. If the contact points remained together, heat would continue increasing, and someone would get very hot indeed. However, such is not the case.

As the temperature increases, heat acts on the bimetallic arm of the upper thermostat section. Heat causes the arm to "expand"—that is, to bend

back. A point is reached at which the force of the thermostat arm bending back is sufficient to overcome the magnetic force between the magnet and iron washer. The two are pulled apart, causing the two contact points to separate. The rest is obvious. The electric circuit is interrupted, no more electricity gets to the heating elements, and the heat simmers down.

I should point out here that most blankets have thermostats sewn into the blanket, too, in series with the heating elements (Figure 5). This is not the same kind of thermostat as the one in the control box. It is a thermostat which acts as a protective device.

The points of this thermostat are designed to stay closed until a very high (dangerous) temperature is reached. Thus, if there is a malfunction and the heating element starts to get hotter and hotter to a point, let's say, where it can cause a fire, the thermostat sewn in the blanket would "open"—in fact, it would open much before a critical temperature is reached, interrupting the electric flow.

You can determine if your blanket has a protective thermostat sewn in it by running your fingers over the blanket. Where the smoothness of the element is interrupted by a "bump" or "bumps" (there could be more than one protective thermostat), you have verified its existence.

Just for the record, in addition to a thermostat, the control box of an electric blanket possesses an on-off switch and a small neon pilot light that draws a tiny amount of current when the blanket is turned on. The light glows, letting you know that the blanket is in operation.

when your blanket fails

LET'S PUT THINGS into perspective. There are only three problems that can affect an electric blanket:

1. The blanket fails to heat at all.
2. The blanket gets too hot.
3. The blanket gives some heat, but not enough.

The most common problem of all, believe it or not, however, is the person using the blanket. There is, for example, a right way and a wrong way to place an electric blanket on a bed, and many people for some reason always manage to do it the wrong way.

"Right" and "wrong" can be determined by the connector at the foot of the blanket into which the line cord plug connects. In practically every

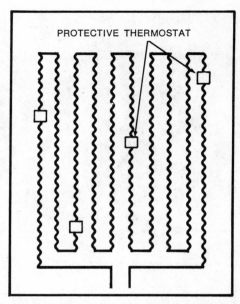

Figure 5. Electric blankets have protective circuit-breaking thermostats sewn in.

case (if there is an exception I don't know it), the blanket must be placed so the connector is "hidden"—that is, on the mattress side of the bed and not in view. Incorrect placement of the connector creates an erratic heating situation (Figures 6 and 7). For example, you might get warm when you want to be cooler, and your partner may get cool when she (or he) wants to be warmer.

Caution: To avoid operational problems with an electric blanket, read and follow manufacturer's instructions on how to connect a blanket. In many cases, these instructions are printed on a label that is sewn to the blanket as well as in an instruction book accompanying the appliance.

Another mistake frequently made by people is abusing the blanket. They place heavy objects on the unit; they crumble it up; they sit on it; they stick pins into it; and who knows what else.

Please remember that the heating-

Figure 6. If the connector is placed wrong side up, the blanket will not work right.

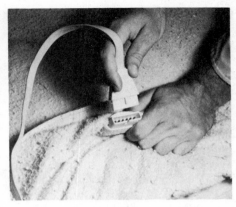

Figure 7. Firmly set the plug connecting the blanket to the control.

element wires in these electric blankets are not the strongest in the world. Once a wire breaks, you can kiss the blanket good-bye

Let me stress this point. *You* cannot repair an open heating element wire. The task requires opening the stitching, taking the materials apart, and finding and fixing the broken wire.

Most professional appliance repairmen won't do the job either. It is just not worth the effort, and they would charge you more than the blanket is worth. It's wiser to exercise some care. If you do, that blanket will serve you for many years to come.

damage outside the blanket

IT COULD HAPPEN, and when it does, the most common reason is a break in a line cord, which often can be fixed. The second most common cause is an ornery control box, but even this may be repaired.

Let's consider the most prevalent external trouble. Let's say the blanket doesn't heat up at all. Here's what to do:

1. At the wall receptacle, make sure the line-cord plug prongs are pushed in firmly. Spread them slightly

so they make firm contact when inserted.

2. At the blanket connector, make sure the line-cord plug is firmly connected—and also, as we said above, that the blanket is positioned properly.

3. Is the wall plug "live?" Pull out the electric blanket's line-cord plug and connect a lamp. Switch it on. If it doesn't light, there is nothing wrong with the blanket. Your problem is with the circuit breaker or fuse, or maybe the receptacle is "dead."

4. The line cord may be the trouble. Remember, though, that there are actually two line cords serving an electric blanket. The two-wire cord extends from the control box to the wall plug. Then there is the three-wire line cord extending from the control box to the connector at the foot of the blanket. The break in a line cord can be anywhere.

But practically speaking, these wires are covered with heavy insulation and won't usually get damaged unless they were subjected to all kinds of ill treatment.

However, on the chance that there is a break, connect the line-cord plug to the wall receptacle and to the connector at the foot of the blanket. Turn the blanket on. Now, flex all segments of the line cord. Flexing will connect a broken strand of wire, completing the circuit, and causing the blanket to turn on. The neon signal light will glow.

You can usually fix a break in the line cord of an electric blanket. Here's how:

(a) *Caution:* First thing, unplug that line cord from the wall outlet.

(b) With a sharp knife, carefully strip the insulation away on both sides of where you determined the break to be. Keep removing layer after layer until the broken wire is revealed.

(c) Buy a strip of the same gauge wire (consult the appliance dealer—he can tell you what gauge your blanket employs). To do the most effective job, solder the piece of wire to the two ends of the break. Then, with insulating electrician's tape, neatly cover the wire.

(d) If you don't care to use a soldering iron, take the piece of repair wire and twist it between the two ends of the break. Just make sure the twist is really twisted, so the wires won't come apart. With the splice made, cover the wires with electrician's tape.

5. Still no heat? Then, my friend, you have to open up the control box (Figure 8). You will have to feel your way, because each box differs to some extent from others and my suggestions have to be general.

In some boxes, for instance, the indicator knob can just be pulled off. In others, the knob is held in place by a set screw that has to be loosened.

6. With the control knob off, turn the box upside down and see if there are attaching screws. Remove them and open the box.

Caution: By this time, I shouldn't

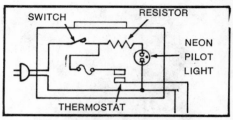

Figure 8. Electric blanket control box.

have to remind you to make sure that the line cord is pulled from the wall receptacle.

7. Make a visual inspection of the "guts" in the box. Look closely for loose connections or broken wires. Make necessary repairs.

8. Turn your attention to the thermostat. Although it isn't too likely, dirt may have gotten on the contact points, which may be keeping them from closing. Take a strip of clean paper (a business card is ideal) and pass it through the points.

9. Gently push the movable bimetal thermostat arm down to see if the magnet on its end and the iron washer on the stationary thermostat arm click together. Magnets can lose their attractive force. If this is what's happened, see if the magnet is replaceable by checking with a dealer who sells the make of blanket. If the company doesn't make replacement magnet sets, see if the thermostat comes as a replacement part. If not, you will have to replace the entire control box.

10. Has nothing worked so far? Then there is a break in the heating element or in the protective thermostat wired into the heating element. Buy a new blanket.

If a blanket provides too little or too much heat, placement of the control box may be at fault. Keep it away from heat-duct or window drafts.

Some control boxes have a temperature calibration screw you can adjust. It is on the bimetal removable thermostat arm. Turn it only slightly.

Chapter 16

Heating pads

Great for sore muscles, a heating pad will continue to relieve pain for many years unless it is misused or abused. When the pad does fail, it can often be fixed.

A HEATING PAD is just a bit more complicated than an electric blanket, which was discussed in the previous chapter.

A heating pad consists essentially of a two-wire heating element (Figure 1). Each heating element is composed of a different-gauge wire to provide differing wattages. More about this in a minute.

The heating elements are sewn inside a flexible cover. A control box with various temperature settings and line cords complete the typical unit (Figure 2). However, many heating pads have safety thermostats sewn into them which are in series with the heating elements. These are protective devices which "open" if a safe heat limit is surpassed. When the thermostat does open, the electrical flow to the heating elements ceases—so does heat output.

A heating pad, obviously enough, applies more intense heat in a concentrated area than an electric blanket. The cover surrounding the heating elements is normally made of a rubberized material which allows unimpeded passage of heat and also permits flexibility so the pad can be shaped to conform to the contour of

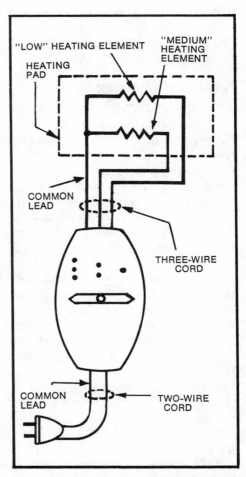

Figure 1. Schematic illustrates elements of a typical heating pad.

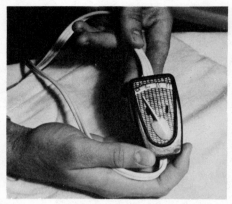

Figure 2. The control box is the heart of the unit. Typically, it allows you to set but three heat settings.

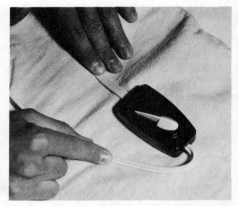

Figure 3. Two wires enter the box and three exit. One lead is a common lead. Either heating element or both may be activated.

that part of the body being heated.

The rubberized heating pad is usually enclosed in a cloth cover that can be slipped off for washing.

consider the heating elements

AS MENTIONED, there are normally two heating elements sewn into a heating pad. Each element is rated differently.

In a typical pad, one heating element may be rated at 20 watts, while the other may be rated at 40 watts. The deviations in wattages permit, in a typical pad, the selection of three heating temperatures: Low, Medium, and High.

The two heating elements are wired together in parallel. They are joined by a third wire, which is a common lead. All three emanate from a control box, which also possesses an ordinary two-wire line cord and plug. However, one of the wires of the line cord passes right through the control box into the heating pad to become the "common" lead (Figure 3).

Another important part of a heating pad is a "flick" switch that can be rotated among the various temperature settings (Low, Medium, and High), and also Off. This rotary

switch possesses a metal bar. When the bar comes into contact with one of the electric heating elements (assuming, of course, that the appliance is plugged into a wall outlet), the circuit is completed, and current flows through the particular heating element. Ah, feel the heat relieve that soreness!

Let's take a closer look at the rotary switch and its relation to the heating elements (Figure 4). With the rotary switch in the Off position, the metal bar is "nowhere," so to speak. No current flows. No heat is produced.

Now, move the rotary switch to Low heat position. The metal bar comes into contact with the wire leading to the 20-watt (Low) heating element. The circuit is closed, and current flows to provide 20 watts of heat, which is enough to offer relief for minor muscular aches.

However, suppose you overdid it beyond the minor stage, and muscle soreness gets no relief from Low heat. Rotate the switch to Medium. The bar comes into contact with the wire leading to the 40-watt (Medium) heating element. The circuit is closed, and you get 40 watts of heat.

If you are in really "bad" shape,

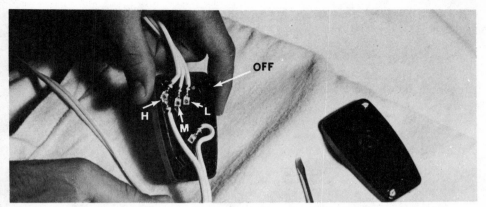

Figure 4. The operation of the switch is illustrated. This is a so-called tapped switch. Notice that wires are soldered to the taps.

you can move the rotary switch to the High setting on the control box. The metal bar comes into contact with wires leading to both Low (20 watt) and Medium (40 watt) heating elements. You get a maximum of 60 watts of heat concentrated on that sore spot, and if that doesn't help, it might be wise to call your doctor.

what can happen to a pad?

NOT TOO MUCH if you don't heap abuse on the poor thing. A heating pad if damaged, however, may fail to heat at all, or it may provide only partial heating.

If the heating pad doesn't heat up at all in any temperature position, you can be pretty sure that the trouble is not in the heating elements. It would be something short of a miracle for *both* heating elements to fail at the same time.

So check the obvious, and that means you begin with the line cords, because when complete failure to heat occurs, this is where the cause usually lies. All information concerning checking and repairing line cords that we gave in the chapter dealing with electric blankets applies to electric heating pads, so there is no sense repeating it here. Just flip back a few pages.

But if line cords are okay, open the control box. Make sure that the rotary switch hasn't fouled. The switch should rotate freely and the metal bar should make firm contact with wire terminals.

Look that bar over pretty carefully. Although it doesn't often get dirty or rusty, it just might be. If so, clean the dirt from the bar with a clean business card. If the bar is rusty, try rubbing it lightly with very fine sandpaper to remove rust. If this doesn't help, see if you can get a replacement switch.

Caution: Need I remind you that while making checks and repairs, the line cord must be detached from the wall outlet?

Examine the inside of the control box carefully, looking for disconnected or loose wires. A break in a wire may stop electrical flow and heat. It is probably necessary to solder the wire into position.

Notice that I haven't made mention of a thermostat inside the control box. There is none, because with a heating pad, heat is not variable, except by switching the rotary switch from one temperature setting to another. At any one setting, heat output will remain constant.

However, as I mentioned above, there may be a thermostat sewn into the pad in series with the heating elements to serve as a protective device. Run your hand over the pad. Where the "smoothness" of wiring is interrupted by a "bump," you have found a protective thermostat.

If a protective thermostat fails in the closed position—that is, if it sticks and won't open up—the heat output will be maintained. But watch it. You may be tempted to use the pad, but it is possible for the wire to overheat. If heat seems to be more intense in any one position than before, it would be wisest to discard the heating pad.

If a protective thermostat opens, electrical flow will cease, and there will be no heat. Discard the pad.

It is very, very rare for a protective thermostat to fail in the closed position. It usually opens up.

no heat from just one setting?

THEN ONE of the heating elements has opened up because of damage or because it has burned out. If there is no heat in Low position, the Low (20 watt) heating element is shot. If there is no heat in Medium (40 watt) position, the Medium element has burned out. In either event, you will not get maximum (60 watt) output.

If a heating element goes bad, you are stymied, because elements are sewn into the pad and taking that pad apart is really rough. However, retain the unit. You can still use it at the setting at which it works.

Chapter 17

Electric irons

**It's not very difficult to understand how this appliance works,
whether it's a dry iron or a steam iron. But when it comes to repair—
well, that's another matter. Sometimes it doesn't pay.**

THE TWO BASIC TYPES of electric irons found in homes today are the dry iron and the steam iron. Electrically speaking, the two are the same, consisting of a line cord, heating element, and thermostat. In fact, the only real difference between them is that the steam iron has a water chamber built into it; the dry iron, of course, doesn't (Figure 1).

The way in which an iron works can be summed up in one sentence: you plug it in, turn it on and the heating element heats the sole plate—that's the part that does the pressing.

Yet, with all its apparent simplicity, an electric iron can be difficult to repair. There are several reason for this.

First of all, over the years manufacturers have built more and more refinements into electric irons. More parts added to an appliance means more parts that may have to be removed when making repairs (Figure 2).

Another reason that an electric iron may be difficult to repair is that there are variations in basic components— irons which are alike basically may not be alike in construction. For example, there are three different kinds of heating elements and two different types of thermostats.

Still another reason for difficulty when making repairs is the apparent intention by manufacurers to *make* repairing difficult. Assembly screws, for example, are hidden in the damndest places.

In this chapter we will discuss the differences in basic components among electric irons and explain what may go wrong with an iron. However, it is not possible to cover all makes and models. If you decide to make repairs (there is no reason you shouldn't at least try) go slow and make detailed notes of what you removed, where. Then reassembly won't be too much of a problem.

how electric irons differ

TO BEGIN WITH, there are three different types of heating elements although every iron uses a nichrome wire element (for a discussion of nichrome, see the chapter on room heaters). The types differ in the manner in which the nichrome is fashioned and also in where it is positioned.

The nichrome element may be in the form of a ribbon wound on a sheet of mica, which is an insulator. Usually this type of element can be replaced when it fails, because it is

111

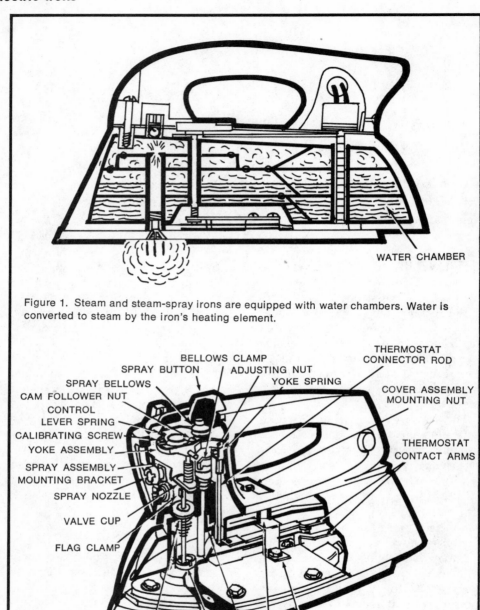

WATER CHAMBER

Figure 1. Steam and steam-spray irons are equipped with water chambers. Water is converted to steam by the iron's heating element.

BELLOWS CLAMP
SPRAY BUTTON
ADJUSTING NUT
YOKE SPRING
THERMOSTAT CONNECTOR ROD
SPRAY BELLOWS
CAM FOLLOWER NUT
CONTROL
LEVER SPRING
CALIBRATING SCREW
YOKE ASSEMBLY
SPRAY ASSEMBLY
MOUNTING BRACKET
SPRAY NOZZLE
VALVE CUP
FLAG CLAMP
COVER ASSEMBLY MOUNTING NUT
THERMOSTAT CONTACT ARMS
VALVE STEM ASSEMBLY
GASKET
VALVE BODY
COVER MOUNTING BRACKET
COVER MOUNTING SPACER

Figure 2. Steam created inside a steam iron is sprayed over clothes through holes in the soleplate. Make sure that the holes are kept open.

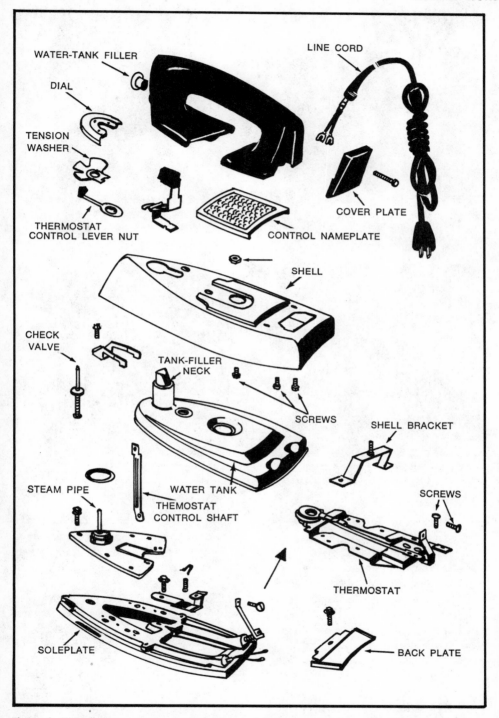

Figure 3. This diagram of a steam iron shows a base-expansion thermostat (arrow). The thermostat in most irons is part of the soleplate.

Figure 4. Very often manufacturers hide disassembly nuts beneath the nameplate. This was the case here, and the nameplate is being pried off to get at the nut.

Figure 5. You need a properly fitting tool to remove the nut. Once the nut has been removed, the iron should come apart easily.

not integrated into the sole plate. However, not many models use a ribbon-type element any longer.

The other types of heating elements are cast into the sole plate. When they fail, it is virtually impossible to replace them; replacing the sole plate and element would be too expensive. It is wiser financially to replace the iron.

One type of cast-in element is nichrome wire that is fashioned into a coil. The other type, which is usually used in a steam iron where water may come into contact with the element, is a band of nichrome that is covered

with a metal insulator. A trade name for one kind of element of this sort is Calrod, and it is basically the same as the element used in dishwashers and electric ranges.

Thermostats in electric irons also differ. Basically there are two varieties: bimetal and base-expansion.

The bimetal thermostat is the same as the one we have discussed in previous chapters (see the chapter dealing with room heaters, for example). It is simply a strip consisting of two different metals, each having its own thermal characteristics.

As the temperature in the iron

Figure 6. If your iron needs a new part, find the unit's model number and order the part for your model. There is no general parts standardization among models.

Figure 7. The soleplate can be kept in good shape by washing and buffing. Buff with fine steel wool and then polish with a soft, dry cloth.

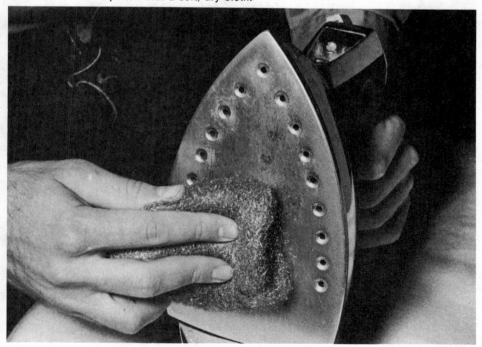

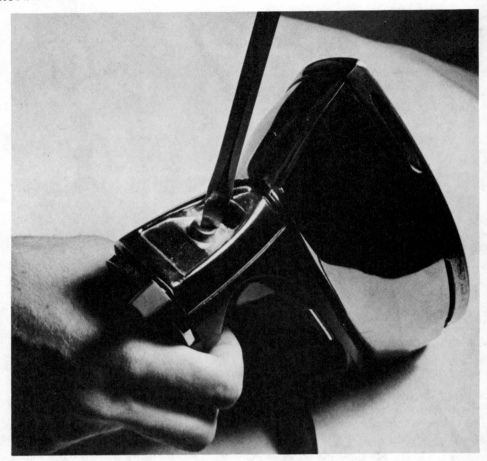

Figure 8. If the spray function fails, remove the notched spray nozzle. This can usually be done easily by using a screwdriver.

changes, one strip expands or contracts more than the other, causing the strip to bend or straighten out in relation to an electric terminal. Contact is either made or broken, and current either flows or it doesn't flow to make heat.

The base-expansion thermostat is similar, but it is a homogeneous metal strip that is welded to the base. As the base contracts or expands in respect to heat, the thermostat rises or falls, making or breaking contact with electric terminals (Figure 3). Heat in the base (at the sole plate) is maintained at a specific pressing temperature.

In the case of both types of thermostats, you control "making and breaking" by selecting a pressing temperature. This puts more or less spring tension on the thermostat so the desired temperature is maintained by having the thermostat cycle on or off.

There is a difference between steam and dry irons—naturally—but there is also a difference in the types of steam irons which are available. Some have a tank that serves as a boiler to convert water into steam. Other models allow water to drip into a steam chamber in the hot sole plate where it vaporizes.

Problem	Causes	Procedure
Iron won't heat	1. Blown fuse or tripped circuit breaker	1. Replace or untrip. If the trouble recurs, check the iron for shorts.
	2. Defective line cord	2. Test continuity. If the cord is defective, replace it with one of the same rating.
	3. Defective thermostat	3. Bypass the thermostat with a jumper lead. Turn the iron on. If it now gets hot, replace the thermostat.
	4. Loose connection	4. Make sure all connections are tight
	5. Defective heating element	5. At this point, nothing else remains. If the element can't be replaced, discard the iron.
Iron doesn't get hot enough	1. Low line voltage	1. Possible, but not likely. If in doubt, consult your electric company.
	2. Defective thermostat	2. See above under "iron won't heat".
Iron produces too much heat	1. Defective thermostat	1. Replace.
Sole plate sticks to clothes	1. Dirty sole plate	1. Wipe the sole plate down with a damp cloth. Buff it with fine steel wool, and then polish it with a soft, dry cloth (Figure 7).
	2. Temperature setting is too high for fabric	2. Consult the manufacturer's instructions and lower the temperature.
	3. Excessive starch	3. Reduce the amount of starch being used.
Sole plate stains clothes	1. Starch is caked on the sole plate	1. Clean the sole plate as described above under "sole plate sticks to clothes".
	2. Excessive minerals in water (steam iron)	2. Follow the manufacturer's instructions regarding water quality.
	3. Sediment in steam tank (steam iron)	3. Clean the tank by filling the tank with vinegar and turning the iron on.
Sole plate tears or snags clothes	1. Damaged sole plate	1. Try to remove the damage by polishing the sole plate as described above under "sole plate sticks to clothes." If this doesn't work, discard the iron.

Problem	Causes	Procedure
Steam iron leaks water	1. Tank is being over-filled 2. Parted seam or weld 3. Damaged tank gasket	1. Do not fill the tank to the top, because water expands when heated. 2. If a seam or weld of the tank has separated, replace the tank if possible. If not, replace the iron. 3. Examine all gaskets. If damaged, replace them.
Steam iron doesn't produce steam	1. Tank is empty 2. Setting is wrong (valve is off) 3. Clogged steam ports 4. Thermostat is out of calibration	1. Fill the tank. 2. Check setting just to be certain. 3. Fill the iron with vinegar and turn it on to clean minerals from ports. In the future, use low-mineral, soft, or distilled water. 4. Replace the thermostat. You need a special tool to recalibrate.
Steam iron spits	1. Thermostat is set at wrong setting 2. Tank is being over-filled 3. Mineral deposits	1. Set the thermostat higher, because spitting usually is caused by the control being set too low. 2. Don't fill the tank to the top. 3. Clean out the iron with vinegar as described above under "steam iron doesn't produce steam."
Steam spray doesn't function	1. Defective control	1. Disassemble the plunger and spray assembly. Clean and replace damaged parts, if possible, or the entire assembly (Figures 8, 9, and 10).
Iron produces shocks	1. Defective line cord 2. Heating element is grounded 3. Thermostat insulator is broken	1. Check cord for bare wires and frayed areas. Replace the cord if it is damaged. 2. Test for grounds as explained in the text. If the element is grounded, discard the iron. 3. Examine the thermostat for a broken insulator. Replace if necessary.

Caution: The iron must be disconnected when making continuity checks. If replacement parts are needed, be sure to use only those parts made for the iron by the manufacturer.

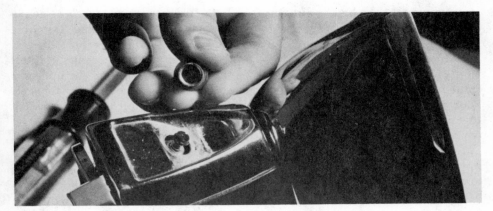

Figure 9. After removing the notched spray nozzle, look inside. The tiny spray holes may be clogged, and a simple cleaning can restore the spray function of the iron.

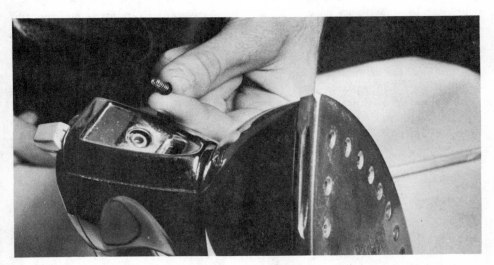

Figure 10. Remove and check the plunger assembly behind the spray nozzle. Clean out any dirt and determine whether the spring has sufficient tension.

Important: The kind of water used affects the longevity of the sole plate in particular. Holes may clog. Use the water specified by the iron's manufacturer. Chances are he recommends distilled water or tap water that is pre-filtered. However, there are models that can use water drawn straight from the tap.

some repair tips

HERE ARE SEVERAL HINTS that might make disassembly and repair-ing of an electric iron easier for you:

1. Never force an iron apart. You can ruin it. If it was put together, it can be taken apart without force. The trick is to find the key. The one nut you may have to discover in order to disassemble an iron, for instance, may be hidden beneath the name-plate, which may be pried off with a screwdriver (Figures 4 and 5).

2. In some models, you first may have to pry the temperature scale for-ward and off to get at a nut that al-

lows you to take the handle off. Once the handle is off, you can get inside the base.

3. In other models, you may have to pry off an indicator arrow in the front handle and remove the control knob and adjustment screw. Beneath that you will find a square hole in which there is a Phillipshead screw. This is the main assembly screw.

4. On some steam irons, you have to pull the filler tube forward and out before you can lift the handle off, which allows entry into the base.

5. The line cord and its connectors are the chief cause of electric-iron problems. It's easy to see why. During pressing, the line cord constantly is being flexed, bent, and otherwise manhandled. In most irons, the cord is attached to terminals with two spade lugs. To replace the cord, loosen the two terminal screws (you don't have to remove them) and pull the spade lugs off.

6. Another major cause of electric-iron damage is dropping the iron. Broken parts have to be replaced.

7. When making repairs, protect the sole plate by laying the iron on a soft cloth. If the sole plate gets scratched, the iron loses its pressing qualities.

troubleshooting electric irons

ONCE AN IRON has been taken apart, it is relatively simple to locate the cause of a problem and fix it, if it can be repaired (Figure 6). The troubleshooting charts on these pages will help to guide you.

After repairs are made and the iron is reassembled, you must safety-test the iron for grounding. This is something that should be done for every appliance that uses heating elements. A grounded appliance can cause serious shock. The ground safety test is explained in the chapter on room heaters.

Chapter 18

Waffle irons

It used to be that "sticking" batter was the main and usually only problem you'd encounter in using a waffle iron. But now with the development of non-stick coatings for the grids, even that annoyance has vanished.

A WAFFLE IRON consists of a line cord, switch, thermostat, two heating elements, and in some units a pilot light which indicates when the waffle iron is hot enough to use. There is nothing esoteric about this appliance.

The two heating elements, which are coiled lengths of nichrome wire, are separated. There is one in each half of the waffle iron; that is, one heating element heats the bottom grids, while the other element heats the top grids. Each heating element is supported by porcelain insulators.

The two heating elements are wired together in parallel so they turn on and off at the same time. This is done by connecting the two together by means of wires which in most waffle irons pass through a spring near one of the hinges. This spring is normally a coil spring which can take extraordinary abuse. It has to. The door of a waffle iron is opened and closed countless times.

In a typical waffle iron, the line cord is connected directly to the heating element in the lower half of the unit (Figure 1). This passes voltage to the upper heating element through the wires which are protected by the coil spring. It's as simple as that.

Figure 1. The line cord of a typical waffle iron is separate from it, and plugs into connectors in the base of the unit.

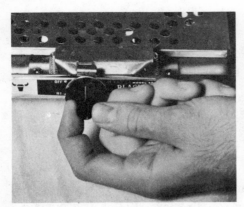

Figure 2. If the unit fails to operate, the switch might be bad. If so, it may reveal itself by a "sloppy" feel when activated.

Figure 3. Waffle irons are among the easiest small appliances to repair. Fasteners that hold parts are usually exposed.

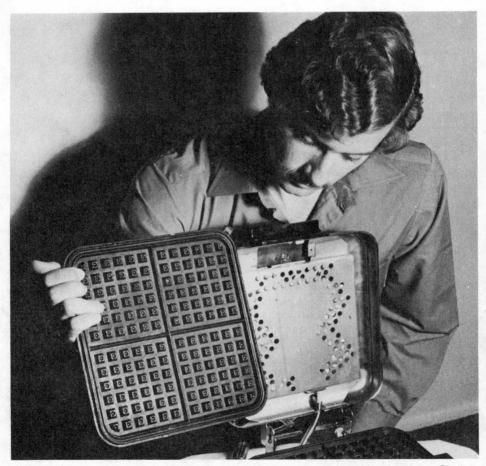

Figure 4. Suppose you are looking for an open heating element or broken insulator. Start by removing the grid. This will reveal a protective cover.

Figure 5. In this unit, the cover is held by two small metal tangs, which are straightened so the cover can be removed.

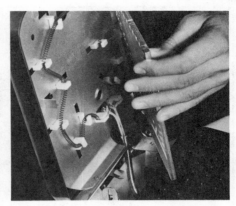

Figure 6. Once the cover is removed, the element and insulators are exposed. One look may reveal the problem.

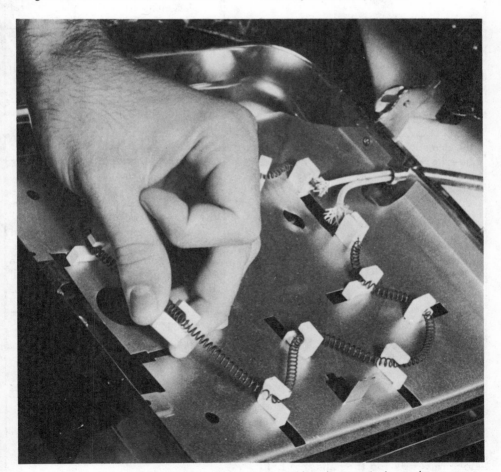

Figure 7. If element is broken, it can be removed from this unit, except where wire comes in from below. At this point, quick disconnects are used or wires are silver-soldered.

waffle irons

Problem	Cause	Procedure
Waffle iron doesn't get hot at all	1. Dead wall outlet	1. Bring it back to life.
	2. Defective line cord	2. Check out the line cord as we have explained in previous chapters. If it is defective, get a new one of the same rating.
	3. Loose connection	3. Check all connections for tightness and integrity.
	4. Defective (open) thermostat	4. Check the thermostat for continuity. If it fails the test, replace it.
	5. Defective switch	5. Ditto (Figures 2 and 3)
	6. Open element or broken insulator	6. Look for broken wires and cracked insulators (Figures 4, 5, 6, 7, 8). Elements may be replaced if replacement parts are available for the waffle iron from a dealer.
Waffle iron doesn't get hot enough	Thermostat opens too soon	This may be caused by a temporary low-voltage condition in the area (brownout). But if voltage is normal, undoubtedly the thermostat is at fault. Replace it.
Waffle iron gets too hot	Thermostat is not opening	Replace it.
One element gets hot—the other stays cold	The "cold" element has opened, or the wires encased in the coil spring have failed	Check the non-heating element for continuity. Replace it if it's bad. If the top heating element is the cold one, it's possible that the wires passing through the coil spring have become damaged. There are two wires going through that coil spring. Replace them both, even if only one is in bad condition (Figures 9, 10, 11, 12). If one has broken, the other probably will break soon. Allow about five inches of slack in the new wires.
User gets a shock	The waffle iron is grounded	Locate the short and fix it.

In addition to an electrical problem, a waffle iron may suffer actual physical damage; specifically, a broken handle or broken legs. These can be replaced if you can find the parts. To remove a broken component, probably you will have to remove the grids and the pans that hold the elements. Note the position of the elements, so they can be replaced properly.

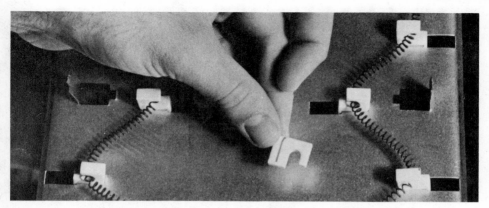

Figure 8. Insulators in this unit are easily removed for inspection by sliding them from their seats in the housing. Replace damaged insulators.

Figure 9. Let's take a closer look at the connection between lower and upper heating elements. Two wires inside protective coil spring connect the elements in parallel.

Figure 10. The wires connect to the elements. In checking for failure, first see if connections are tight, and if not, tighten them.

Figure 11. The arrangement for the lower unit is identical, with the connecting wires attached to the lower heating element.

what can happen to a waffle iron

WAFFLE IRONS SELDOM GO BAD, but I'm not telling you anything you don't know. How long has it been since you have *had* to buy a new waffle iron?

However, when a waffle iron does fail, it can do so in one of the following ways:

1. It won't heat up at all.
2. It doesn't get hot enough.
3. It gets too hot.
4. One side gets hot—the other stays cold.
5. You get a shock when you use the unit.

Factors that cause each of these problems have been discussed in previous chapters in connection with other appliances. But in the following chart, we sum up the causes and cures of waffle-iron problems—in case you really want to cure an ailing iron. Perhaps the unit is so outdated that you'd rather buy a new one.

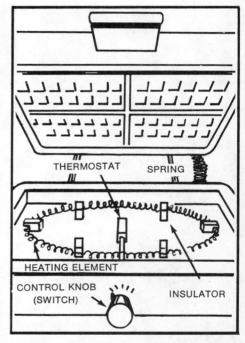

Figure 12. This drawing shows what you'll see when you remove the protective cover from the lower part of a waffle iron.

Chapter 19

Coffee makers

There are variations in circuitry between different makes, but whether your electric coffee percolator is a nine-cup or 30-cup unit, the principles of operation are the same (Figures 1 and 2). So is the method of repair—and it's easy!

THE BASIC CIRCUITRY of an electric coffee percolator is not much different from that of a room heater, waffle iron or any other electric appliance in which heat is created to do work. That circuitry always includes a heating element, which is made of resistant-type wire, and a line cord.

When you plug the line cord into a wall outlet, electricity attempting to flow through the heating element meets resistance, causing the element to get hot. This causes the water to boil (or waffles to bake, or air to heat). Water spurts up and falls back onto a bed of ground coffee. The result is hot coffee.

Of course, you don't really believe that the electric percolator is as simple as this. Obviously, there are refinements which are necessary both for safety reasons and to permit the making of a *good* pot of coffee. Still, even with refinements the electric coffee percolator hardly is a complicated appliance.

Figure 1. This is a nine-cup electric coffee percolator. Its line cord is detachable.

Figure 2. A 30-cup urn like this possesses the same basic parts as the smaller unit.

And it has another virtue. The electric coffee percolator is a most reliable machine. I have owned a 30-cup unit for 15 years, and it is still going strong.

two types: automatic and not

LET'S TALK FIRST about non-automatic units. They are a bit old-fashioned, but many are still in use.

A non-automatic electric coffee percolator does not shut itself off when the coffee is brewed. You have to judge when brewing is completed and pull the line cord plug from the wall outlet.

The basket and overflow tube are then removed from the pot, and the line-cord plug is inserted back into the wall outlet. This keeps the coffee warm without perking it further.

The electric circuit of a non-automatic electric coffee percolator consists only of a line cord, heating element and a fuse.

The fuse protects the percolator from carelessness. If the coffee maker is accidentally left plugged into the wall outlet after all coffee has been poured from the pot, causing the element to overheat, the fuse blows and trips the circuit. The current is prevented from reaching the heating element, which cools. If this did not happen, the heating element would burn itself out.

The actual brewing process that takes place in a non-automatic electric coffee percolator is the same as that occurring in an automatic percolator. One very key component is the innocuous-looking flared bottom of the overflow tube. This acts to meter out exact amounts of boiling water, which spurt up the overflow tube.

Although the way in which this part acts varies somewhat from coffee maker to coffee maker, because the part itself varies in makeup, the acutal function is pretty much the same. Let's take a typical example.

Notice that the bottom of the overflow tube sits in a depression (well) in the base of the percolator (Figures 3 and 4). It is at this point that the greatest amount of heat is applied.

Also notice that there is a series of tiny holes around the top-side of the bottom of the overflow tube. Look at the underside of the tube (Figures 5 and 6). There you will see what appears to be a washer. Basically, that's what it is, but it is a movable part that fluctuates up and down—to create a small pump.

When the pump drops, the holes in the base of the overflow tube open up to let water flow into the well. When the well fills, water gets hot (boils) and pressure forces the pump up. This pushes hot water up the tube.

The hot water spews from the top of the tube, hits the lid of the percolator, and spreads itself over the basket cover. The cover is perforated, so water seeps through it to the ground coffee in the basket. The bottom of the basket is also perforated, and the liquid hot coffee drops down into the pot.

non-automatic troubles

NOT MUCH ELECTRICALLY can go wrong with a non-automatic percolator. At this time we won't speak about other possible failures that are mechanical in origin. They are reviewed later, because they are common to automatic percolators as well.

When an electrical failure takes place, the percolator will not heat. The trouble can be in only one of three places:

1. Line cord.
2. Fuse.

Figure 3. The base of this nine-cup electric coffee percolator has a deep well fashioned into it. The greatest amount of heat is concentrated here.

Figure 4. The base of this 30-cup coffee urn also has a deep well. However, notice the large retaining nut, which has to be removed to remove the main heating element.

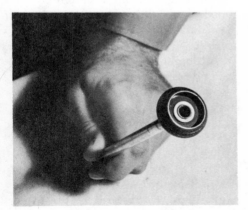

Figure 5. Base of overflow tube contains a movable washer that acts as a pump. The base must be set firmly in the well.

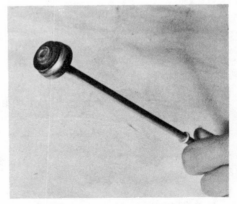

Figure 6. Overflow tube of 30-cup coffee maker looks different but works the same. If washer is damaged, get a new tube.

Figure 7. The bottom of a coffee maker can be removed by unscrewing the fastener.

3. Heating element.

The electrical components are housed in a plastic case, beneath the coffee maker, which can be opened by removing the screw or screws (Figures 7, 8, 9, 10). Check the line cord, fuse and heating element for continuity. Replacement parts usually can be obtained from a dealer who sells percolators of this make. You should get parts which have the same rating as the original parts.

servicing the automatics

AUTOMATIC ELECTRIC COFFEE PERCOLATORS also contain a heating element, or elements, and line cord. However, they do not have a fuse. Instead they have a thermostat which allows the automatic feature—the percolator shuts itself off when brewing is completed, and then keeps heat applied so the coffee stays hot.

Circuits differ somewhat from coffee maker to coffee maker. For example, some have signal lights that turn on when the coffee is finished percolating. Others allow you to make an adjustment for weak or strong coffee, with degrees in between.

How your automatic works: Many automatic coffee percolators possess two heating elements—one for brewing (a main element) and an element that keeps coffee hot when brewing is completed. Let's say you set up a fresh pot filled with cold water and ground coffee, and plug it in. The thermostat is closed (cold makes it so) and full-line voltage is applied across the main element, which lies beneath the depression in the base of the pot and the "pump" we spoke about earlier.

This causes the water to boil, and percolating begins. But boiling is confined only to this one area. Water on the "outskirts" remains relatively cool at first.

As boiling water permeates the ground coffee and hot liquid drips into the pot, more and more cold water enters the pump for boiling and percolating. The coffee gets stronger and hotter. When brewing is done, the object is to keep the coffee hot.

This is easy enough, because the main element, warming element, and signal light, if there is one, are wired in series. When the coffee reaches a particular temperature, heat causes the thermostat to open, shutting off

Figure 8. The cover is lifted off, exposing electric components. If unit was submersible in water, it no longer is because opening it breaks the seal.

full-line voltage to the main heating element.

Most of the voltage is transferred to the warming element, which is made of a "weaker" wire than the main element, and thus doesn't generate as much heat. Only a slight amount of current goes to the main element—certainly, not enough to permit percolation. In other words, the heat put out by the warming and main elements is enough to keep the coffee hot, but is not enough to cause it to boil.

Some models have a control to adjust the strength of the coffee. All this does is to control the opening and closing of the thermostat so the temperature at which the thermostat opens (or the length of time it remains closed) can be set. The functioning is similar to the thermostat we discussed in the chapter on waffle irons.

troubleshooting an automatic

THIS IS NO BIG DEAL if the fault is electric. Suppose your automatic percolator won't perk. The trouble lies in the line cord, main heating element, or thermostat. Find out where by making continuity tests.

The thermostat has to fail in the open position for it to prevent percolating. But if the trouble is a bad thermostat only, water gets warm, but it won't perk, because current still gets through to the main and warming elements.

If the thermostat fails in the closed position, percolation takes place, but it does not stop.

What happens if the warming element is the only one to fail? Well, brewing does occur. At the completion of percolation, the brewing process ceases, and you get a hot cup of coffee. But you'd better get it quickly, because the coffee will not stay hot.

The same failure occurs if the signal light goes bad. The signal light acts as a fuse. If its element opens, the current is interrupted.

When you have completed an electrical repair on an automatic or non-automatic coffee maker, be sure to perform a ground test afterward. Connect a test light from the metal pot to a ground, such as a pipe. Plug the percolator into a wall outlet. If the test light lights, the percolator is grounded and is not safe to use until the short is located and repaired.

As for non-electrical problems that

coffee makers

Figure 9. Parts of the electrical circuit include: (a) main heating element; (b) low heating element; (c) thermostat.

hamper a coffee maker, the chief one is a damaged pump. The washer in the base of the overflow breaks or is otherwise damaged. You can conclude that this is what has happened if the coffee maker works, but coffee does not brew. Usually this part can be replaced without replacing the entire overflow tube.

A coffee maker can also sustain physical damage because of an accident or misuse. Most parts that do break, such as the plastic housing for electrical components and handle, can be replaced. Consult a dealer who sells your make of percolator.

Many electric coffee percolators can be submerged in water for washing. This means that they have to be well sealed. If you have to open up a coffee maker, make absolutely certain that you get the necessary gaskets and/or sealers to assure proper resealing.

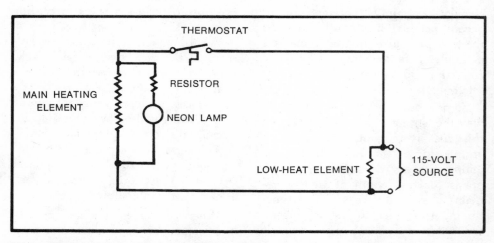

Figure 10. This is a simplified wiring diagram of a typical electric coffee percolator for your use in troubleshooting and making repairs.

Chapter 20

Electric pop-up toasters

The electric pop-up toaster is one of the most intricately designed small appliances in the home. But it is also one of the most reliable.

THE ELECTRIC POP-UP TOASTER is not an appliance that is easily repaired if it suffers a major parts failure. How it operates is not difficult to comprehend, but in practice the various mechanisms, levers, elements and switches make this one of the most difficult appliances in the home to salvage if a major breakdown occurs (Figure 1).

Fortunately, there are several redeeming factors. First of all, the electric pop-up toaster is probably the most reliable small appliance you own. It probably will last a score of years or more. An automatic pop-up toaster I own, for example, was purchased in 1952 and is still going strong.

When a toaster finally does succumb to old age, the homemaker usually is satisfied and looks forward to purchasing a newer, fancier model. This is okay because by present standards, a new toaster cannot be called an expensive appliance. In fact, prices are quite reasonable.

There is still another encouraging factor about an electric pop-up toaster which more than compensates for its complex nature. If it does develop a malfunction within a relatively short period of time, the cause more often than not is a *minor* one that is easy to fix. The pitfall in this case is that the home repairman may fall into the trap of looking for skeletons in the closet, because he becomes awed by the complexity of the appliance.

Keep things in perspective. Do not probe for complex answers to simple problems. (This is good advice for anyone attempting appliance repair, no matter what the appliance.)

The information in this chapter is arranged in order from the simple things to look for when a problem occurs to the more complex. This is the way you should tackle any problem.

Naturally, the pop-up toaster is not the only kind of toaster in use, although it probably is the most common. Another popular type is the toaster-oven, which is dealt with in the next chapter.

how electric pop-ups work

AN ELECTRIC POP-UP TOASTER must perform several distinct functions in order to give you your morning toast. It must latch the cradle (carriage) holding bread firmly in

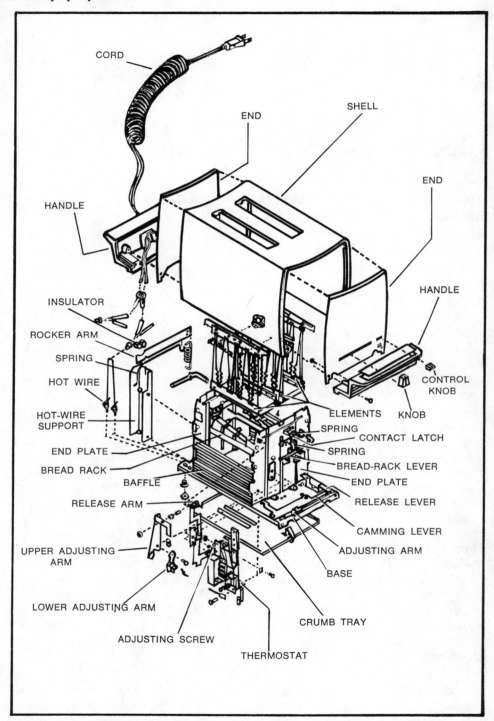

Figure 1. This drawing of a typical electric pop-up toaster shows what you face when you attempt to repair one. With all of its mechanisms, it is one of the most intricate small appliances, and one of those most difficult to repair.

place when the lever controlling the cradle is pushed down. It must then turn on electricity so the heating elements that do the actual toasting can begin glowing.

As with room heaters (see Chapter 14), the heating elements in a toaster are commonly made of a nickel-chromium alloy, called nichrome. Elements are connected in parallel in most toasters, so they are controlled by a common conductor.

Smaller toasters have three elements so two slices of bread may be toasted simultaneously. Larger toasters have more than three elements so that four or more slices of bread can be handled at a time.

Caution: A toaster's heating elements are not insulated. Touching

one, even if the toaster is not turned on, may result in serious injury since one side of the heater circuit is always "live"—it is in constant touch with the wall outlet. When working on a toaster, make certain that it is disconnected from the wall plug except when taking voltage readings. In this case, keep the toaster disconnected until the voltmeter is connected—then plug it into the outlet, but keep your hands away from "live" elements.

Another function that an automatic toaster must perform is to shut off the current to the elements when the toast is done. At the same time it must trigger a latch that allows the cradle to surface. However, the spring-loaded cradle must have a brake on it to prevent it from snapping up too

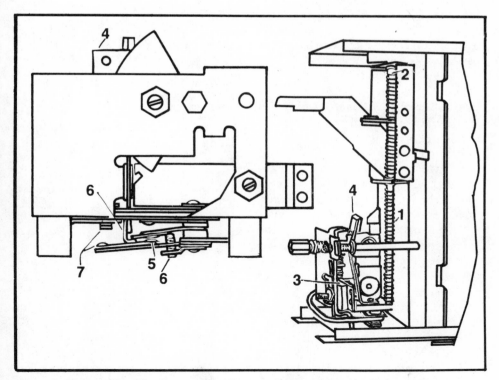

Figure 2. Major parts of the thermostatically controlled cradle mechanism are: (1) rack-return spring; (2) guide rod; (3) latch mechanism; (4) metal blade; (5) contact points; (6) hooking mechanism; (7) contact points; (8) adjustment mechanism.

forcefully, which could cause the toast to fly halfway across the room. (Indeed that happened frequently in the very early models!)

Manufacturers have devised various methods to perform each of these functions. There is no reason to delve into each method that has been used —there are too many. A general discussion of the more common methods probably will cover your model (Figure 2).

Generally speaking, when you push down the cradle-control lever, you cause the cradle to engage a mechanical latch. (In models in which bread lowers itself automatically, a motor is used. When bread is placed in the cradle, it causes a switch to close that starts the motor which lowers the rack by means of gears.)

At the same time that the cradle is lowered, a switch is closed that activates the heater-element circuit, allowing current to flow and elements to glow.

"Light," "medium," or "dark" toast commonly is achieved by a timing mechanism that winds itself up when the cradle is pushed down. A bimetal regulator (or compensator) is used in many toasters so the first slices of toast, which are made with a cold appliance, will be toasted the same as the second and subsequent slices, which are made with a hot appliance.

The bimetal strip is made of the same kind of material as a thermostat (see Chapter 14). It is affected by temperature.

When the toaster is cold, the bimetal regulator is straight and does not come into contact with the timing mechanism. The mechanism is allowed to wind down for the longest period of time, giving bread more time to toast.

However, with the toaster hot and subsequent slices of bread placed in

it for toasting, less time is needed. Heat affects the bimetal strip, bending it toward a speed-control lever. This lever controls the timing mechanism. When the lever is "pushed" by the bimetal strip, it causes the mechanism to speed up, which in turn results in a shorter period of operation of the timer.

The timing mechanism is set for light or dark toast, or any degree in between, by turning a knob or sliding a lever on the outside of the case. Actually, all you are doing is setting the position of the speed-control lever.

When the timer runs down, an auxiliary switch is forced open. It turns off the electricity going to the heating elements, allowing the elements to start a cool-down. At the same time, some kind of mechanism activates and trips the latching mechanism, allowing the cradle, which is spring-loaded, to pop up.

One type of latch release is called a hot-wire release, because it consists of a strand of wire that connects to the line voltage and is attached to the latch. As current flows through it, this wire gets hot and expands. But when current to the elements is shut off, it is also shut off to the hot-wire release. The wire cools down and contracts. As it contracts, it "pulls" the latch release with it, thus releasing the cradle.

Another interesting element in an electric pop-up toaster is a shock absorber, or snubber, that cushions the cradle as it springs up. This device is similar in operation to a pneumatic stop that is employed by storm doors to keep the door from slamming. The snubber puts the brake to the cradle, allowing it to ease up so the toast doesn't fly out.

Figure 3. A toaster should be kept clean! Dirt is enemy number one. From time to time, open the trap on the bottom and let loose crumbs fall out.

Figure 4. The insides of the toaster are delicate, so instead of a knife use a one-inch paint brush to dislodge crumbs that are hard to remove.

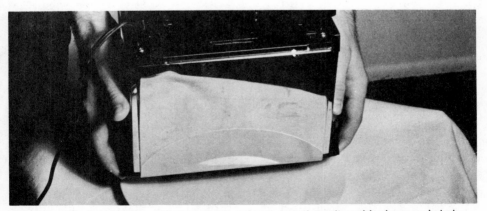

Figure 5. If the toaster doesn't have a clean-out trap, turn the unit upside down and shake. Admittedly, this is a messy job but it is a necessary one.

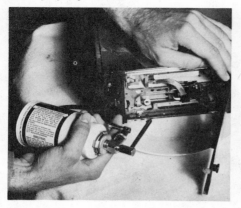

Figure 6. You can use compressed air to get rid of crumbs that can't be reached with the paint brush.

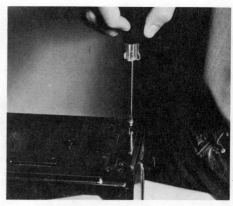

Figure 7. This photo and the two following help show you how to disassemble a pop-up toaster. First, remove all exposed screws.

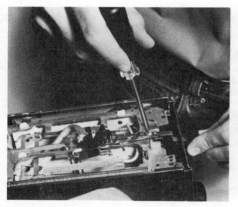

Figure 8. Take out all screws holding lever's, so they don't block disassembly.

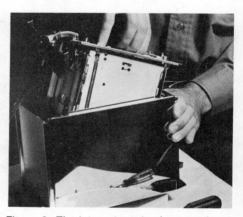

Figure 9. The internal mechanism can then be released from the shell.

the big foes: crumbs and crud

MOST PROBLEMS with an electric pop-up toaster are caused by food particles. Crumbs can affect both the mechanical and electrical operation of the unit.

For example, bread crumbs which drop inside the appliance can hamper the cradle latch, preventing the cradle from holding in a down position. This, of course, keeps the toaster from operating. In addition, contact points of switches can become coated with food matter, such as raisins. This can prevent electrical connections and thus toaster operation.

You should clean your toaster periodically and thereby avoid foreign-matter problems.

Most toasters have clean-out traps that permit you to reach inside and brush out dirt (Figure 3). First *detach the power cord.* Open the trap door and brush particles from all surfaces you can reach with a one-inch paint brush that is used only for this purpose (Figure 4).

If the toaster doesn't have a trap door, disconnect the power cord and turn the appliance upside down. Shake it vigorously (Figure 5).

If the unit develops a problem and

Trouble	Usual causes	How to correct
Toast is either too dark or too light	• Timer setting incorrect	• Check position of timer control knob or lever.
	• Timer mechanism has gone awry	• Replace
Bread doesn't toast evenly	• Heating element is open	• Check for loose connections; replace element if necessary.
	• Reflective surfaces are dirty	• Clean
Toaster doesn't work at all	• Damaged power cord	• Replace
	• Open switch	• Replace
	• Impediment between latch and catch	• Clean away foreign deposits and make sure tension of clutch is sufficient to make effective contact.
Toast burns	• Improper timer setting	• Check position of timer control knob or lever.
	• Bimetal regulator is distorted	• Replace
	• Auxiliary (cool-down) switch stuck closed	• Replace
Cradle doesn't pop up	• Bread, raisins or some other foreign matter impeding catch release	• Clean thoroughly and lubricate.
	• Bimetal regulator is distorted	• Replace
	• Hot-wire or some other catch release mechanism damaged or burned out	• Replace
	• Cradle spring broken or lacks tension	• Replace

has to be disassembled, make certain that you clean the parts as thoroughly as you can. It's still possible that crumbs, raisins, or jelly are the cause of the trouble.

The best "tool" to clean toaster parts is compressed air. You can employ it even if you don't have a compressor and air hose (Figure 6).

Visit a photography shop. Most such shops sell compressed air in a can with a nozzle. Photographers use it for cleaning dust from negatives. It is ideal for cleaning out the inside of a toaster.

When you are inside a toaster, examine all contacts and other parts carefully for burned matter which compressed air won't remove. This will have to be scraped off—carefully.

Take pains to make sure that the scraper doesn't slip accidentally and rupture a heating element.

After cleaning mechanical parts—springs, levers, catches and so forth—lubricate them lightly with a heat-resistant grease. This is available from hardware stores, but make sure that the tube stipulates that the lubricant may be used on toasters and other heat-generating appliances.

Caution: Do not apply lubricant to electrical components.

when crumbs aren't the cause

ESSENTIALLY THERE ARE five problems that can afflict an electric pop-up toaster. They are:

1. The toaster doesn't work at all.
2. The toaster burns the toast.
3. The toast doesn't pop up.
4. The toast is either too light or too dark.
5. The bread doesn't toast evenly.

The easiest repairs, strangely enough, are made if the toaster doesn't work at all, assuming that all elements don't suddenly burn out at once, which isn't likely to happen. Start, of course, by examining the power cord.

Next, to check the innards, make sure that the power cord is pulled from the wall outlet. Remove the light-dark control knob, which is usually only pressed into place (Figures 7, 8, 9).

Now look for a set screw holding the cradle-control lever in place. Remove it and the lever. Unscrew all the screws you can find holding the cover and whatever ornamental trim must come off so the cover can be lifted, revealing the inside of the toaster.

The first thing to do is to give everything a very close look. See if you can spot loose connections or broken wires. Make sure the toaster end of the line cord is okay and is held tightly by its terminals.

Now check voltage, using a voltmeter on both sides of the main switch. Replace a switch if there is a lack of voltage. Other than line-cord problems, a bad switch is the chief reason a toaster will refuse to function.

Important: To check voltage, you must depress the cradle to close the switch. Don't forget to connect the power cord to a wall outlet. *Be careful!*

Suppose your problem is uneven toast, which is a common thing. Chances are that one element is burned out or a wire has come loose, disconnecting the element from its conductor. You can buy a new heating element in many cases, but before you do, check the cost of repair against the cost of a new toaster. This should be done in every instance where a repair is a major one.

The best way to discover and correct the most common causes of electric pop-up toaster problems is to use the chart on page 139.

Chapter 21

Electric toaster-ovens

Consider this a transition chapter, because electric toaster-ovens are more roaster than toaster. This is why the chapter has been placed between the chapter on electric pop-up toasters and the one dealing with electric roasters

THE "TOASTER" FUNCTION of a toaster-oven allows you to toast bread. However, this is essentially the only resemblance between this appliance and an electric pop-up toaster. In fact, a toaster-oven resembles an electric roaster more than it does a toaster.

As you know, a regular toaster possesses wire-wound elements which are positioned vertically and are enclosed in a case. A toaster-oven on the other hand, possesses nichrome elements that are insulated in metal sheathing and are in the form of rods. These rods are exposed, just as they are in an electric roaster. They are not in an enclosure.

An electric toaster-oven has at least two and often more than two of these rod-type elements. One rod (or more) is located in the base of the unit, and the other rod or rods are attached to the top of the unit.

One set of rods, or both sets, may be activated at any one time. Thus, if you wish to make toast, both the top and bottom sets of rods are activated simultaneously. Bread is placed on the wire rack so that both sides receive heat.

Conversely, if you want to bake something—a frozen dinner, for example—the switch is set to activate the top set of rods only. Usually a pan is provided by the manufacturer of the unit. This pan is placed on the wire rack, and the tray of food is placed on top of the pan. Heat is applied from the top only.

facts about two switches

THE INTRICATE FEATURE of a typical toaster-oven, if any feature of this simple appliance can truly be called "intricate," is its switching devices. Practically speaking, the typical toaster-oven has two separate sets of switches—one for toasting and one for the oven part of the appliance. In most cases, however, the two switches are activated by one control.

The "toasting" switch is quite similar to the switch in a regular electric pop-up toaster. Essentially, it consists of two separate elements—a spring-loaded on-off switch and a thermostat.

When the on-off toasting switch is activated, a set of points is closed. This completes the circuit and permits electricity to flow through to both the top and bottom sets of rods. The rods heat up and the bread begins to toast.

The separate thermostat control for toast permits you to set the degree of toastiness—that is, "light," "dark," or in between. This control is nothing more than the conventional blade-type thermostat that we discussed in previous chapters. When heat causes the thermostat blades to part, the movable blade trips the on-off switch to "off." The toast is done.

In many electric toaster-ovens, the "on-off" switch is also turned off by just opening the oven door. This action causes a tang to trip the switch.

The switch which activates the oven function of an electric toaster-oven is a thermostat-type switch; that is, you can set the temperature for the amount of heat that is needed to cook the particular kind of food. Frozen foods, for example, usually require 450° of heat, while biscuits require about 350°. There is usually a setting as well for just keeping food warm or warming it up.

This type of switch works like the switching device of an electric blanket. When the oven reaches the temperature for which it is set, the thermostat opens so the food doesn't burn. The temperature is maintained at the set level by the thermostat switch opening and closing according to the "hotness" or "coolness" prevailing in the oven at any one time.

how to troubleshoot

THE WAY to troubleshoot a toaster-oven is to analyze what is and what is not happening. Suppose you turn on the toaster position and nothing happens. The rods do not heat up. The following might be at fault:

1. Wall plug.
2. Line cord.
3. Switch.
4. All the rods have burned out simultaneously, which is so farfetched

as to be ridiculous, so forget it.

You can immediately determine if the switch is at fault by switching from the toasting function to the baking function. If the top set of rods does not activate, the switch is probably not the faulty component. The trouble probably lies with the wall plug (house current) or line cord.

If the top set of rods begins to glow, then obviously electricity is flowing through the appliance, which means that the toaster switch has probably burned out and needs to be replaced.

Another problem that can hamper a toaster-oven is burning of food. The problem normally lies in one of two places:

1. An improper setting of the thermostat control by the person using the toaster-oven.

2. A faulty thermostat.

If the baking function does not work, the problem is probably the wall plug, line cord, switch or heating element. In this case, isolating the trouble involves continuity testing.

making repairs

ONCE YOU HAVE FOUND the cause of a malfunction, repairs can be made. As with many appliances, the biggest headache in fixing usually involves getting inside the unit. A careful examination of the outer case will reveal screws that have to be removed to take the unit apart. Take your time; be patient; proceed carefully.

After you repair a toaster-oven, don't forget to make a ground check before using the unit. When the line cord is plugged into a wall outlet, there must be no voltage on the case of the appliance. There is danger of serious injury if the appliance is grounded.

Chapter 22

Electric roasters

Other names for an electric roaster are "electric broiler" and "rotisserie."
Whatever you call it, this cooking appliance is quite similar to an electric
toaster-oven. The one obvious difference between the two is size.
And the rotisserie has a motor.

AN ELECTRIC ROASTER can be a very simple cooking appliance or it can possess several elaborate features.

Basically, a roaster is nothing more than an oven. In this respect, it works like the oven feature of an electric toaster-oven. It might surprise you to learn that both the electric toaster-oven and the electric roaster work like the oven of an electric range. The main difference among the three is size.

Inside its frame, the typical electric broiler has heating elements which in most cases are the same as those used in toaster-ovens and electric-stove ovens: they are encased in insulated rods. This type of unit is referred to very often by the name Calrod.

However, some units are designed with coiled nichrome wire heating elements.

A rotisserie also possesses a spit turned by a small electric motor. In some units, the motor is inside the appliance's frame. In other units, the motor is sold separately and attached to the appliance externally. When not in use, the external motor has to be detached and stored.

Heating elements and small motors to revolve spits are components of practically all electric broilers. However, some models have additional features with additional mechanical and/or electrical devices.

For example, some models have timers that can be set for a desired length of cooking time. At the end of this time, the timer automatically shuts the broiler off.

Some models bake as well as broil. This means that they have two elements—one in the top of the appliance and one in the base, so food can be cooked on both sides at one time.

Some newer-model broilers even clean themselves.

diagnosis and cures

THE FOLLOWING CHART sums up some problems that can strike an electric broiler, what causes them, and what you have to do to rectify them. Most of what can be said about troubleshooting and repairing a basic roaster has been said in connection with other appliances already discussed in this section (Figure 1).

143

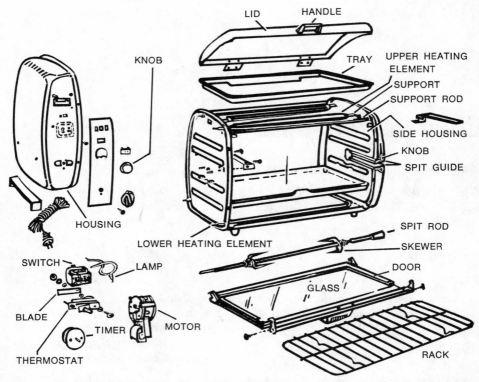

Figure 1. This drawing of a typical electric roaster will guide you in troubleshooting and making repairs. Heating elements are similar to those in toaster-ovens and range ovens.

Problem	Cause	Procedure
Roaster doesn't turn on	1. Bad switch 2. Open heating element	1. Replace switch with one manufactured for the unit. 2. Perform continuity tests to find the bad element and replace it with an element designed for the unit.
Roaster gets too hot or not hot enough	Bad thermostat	Replace the thermostat with a new one designed for the model.
Rotisserie feature doesn't work	Damaged motor	If you are able, disassemble the appliance and get to the gear train. Remove the gears, clean them in kerosene, replace gears that are damaged, reassemble and lubricate with light gear oil. If an externally mounted motor goes bad, buy a new one.
Roaster gives user a shock	Unit is grounded	Find the part which is grounded against the frame and repair or replace it. *Do not use the roaster until the fault is corrected.*

Chapter 23

Electric skillets, sauce pans and fry pans

This chapter deals with three appliances which are closely related.
They may differ somewhat in their makeup, but essentially all operate
the same way and are afflicted by the same problems.

ONLY A FEW MAJOR PARTS go into making an electric skillet, sauce pan and fry pan (Figure 1). They are: (1) the body of the appliance, which is usually aluminum; (2) a heating element that is built right into the body; (3) a handle that can usually be detached from the body; (4) a combination temperature control and thermostat; (5) a line cord.

If the most serious failure of all occurs—an open heating element— your "repair task" becomes a simple one. Throw the appliance away and get a new one. You cannot get inside the skillet, sauce pan, or fry pan to replace the heating element without completely destroying the unit anyway.

However, the likelihood of a heating element going bad is remote. Elements seldom, if ever, burn out if used in a normal manner. The only damage they are likely to suffer is if the appliance is dropped with sufficient force to break connections.

so what can go wrong?

OBVIOUSLY, THE LINE CORD won't withstand a heavy hand for long, and tugging on it will cause line-cord failure, which will affect skillet, sauce pan, or fry-pan operation. The line cord, then, becomes one of the components you should examine if a unit fails to function.

Another component that can malfunction is the temperature control, which may have a thermostat built into it. In other units, the temperature control and thermostat are separate. In any event, both are areas of possible failure.

One positive way to destroy the temperature control is to immerse the unit in water. Manufacturer's instructions regarding the cleaning of a temperature-control unit should be closely observed. These instructions usually tell you to wipe the control clean with a sponge that is hardly damp.

Other than line cord and temperature control and/or thermostat problems, the only other failure that can afflict an electric skillet, sauce pan, or fry pan is a broken part, such as a broken handle. Physical damage occurs usually when an appliance is accidentally dropped.

how these appliances work

OPERATION IS VERY SIMPLE. In

the typical unit, the temperature-sensing probe, which is the front part of the control unit, is inserted into a sleeve in a receptacle in the appliance. The line cord, which is integral with the temperature-control unit, is plugged into a wall outlet, and the knob of the temperature-control unit is turned on.

The sleeve in the receptacle intercepts two contacts of the heating element. This means that electricity flowing through the temperature-sensing probe has a complete circuit through the heating element when the probe

is snapped into the sleeve. The heating element gets hot. The sleeve and temperature-sensing probe also get hot. So does the skillet, sauce pan, or fry pan.

Let's suppose the thermostat is inside the temperature-control box, as it is in most skillets, sauce pans, and fry pans. It is connected to the temperature-sensing probe. When the probe reaches the desired temperature, which means that the skillet, sauce pan, or fry pan has attained the desired cooking temperature, the thermostat opens. This interrupts the

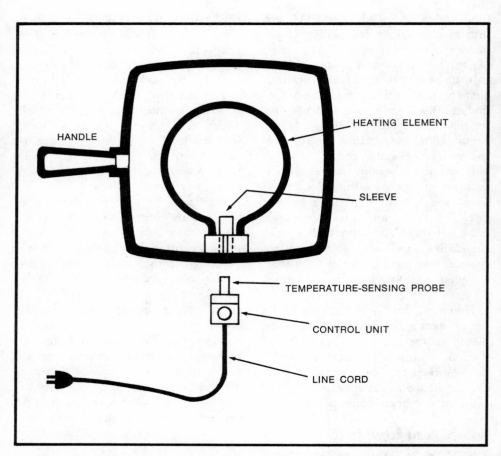

Figure 1. Electric cooking utensils discussed in this chapter are simple and easily checked.

flow of electricity through the appliance. Heating stops.

The degree of temperature—that is, the temperature at which cooking is to be done—is determined by the setting of the temperature-control knob. The knob actually controls the opening and closing of the thermostat. When the temperature-control knob is set at higher temperatures, more tension is placed on the thermostat, and more heat is required to open it. As an open thermostat cools down, it contracts so the thermostat points come in contact with each other again. This allows the flow of electricity (and heating) to resume.

Most electric skillets, sauce pans and fry pans possess a neon pilot light. As current passes to the heating element, a small amount diverts to the pilot light, allowing the light to glow. When the thermostat opens, cutting the flow of current, the pilot light goes out, which informs the cook that the vessel is ready for use.

how to troubleshoot the three

LET'S SAY you get no heat. Unless the heating element has failed, the cause of a "no heat" condition lies with the line cord, switch, or thermostat. To test the line cord and control box for continuity, proceed as follows:

1. Connect a jumper wire between the two connecting (female) terminals of the control box.

2. Connect the continuity tester or appliance test meter across the receptacles of the line cord.

3. Set the temperature-control knob at its highest setting, and plug your continuity tester or appliance test meter into a wall outlet.

4. If the line cord and control box are in sound condition, the bulb of the continuity tester will glow, or you will get a reading on the appliance test meter.

5. If there is no glow from the bulb, or you fail to get a reading on the test meter, flex the line cord over its entire length. This procedure is done to determine if a broken wire exists beneath the insulation. If the continuity test bulb suddenly glows, or you get a sudden reading on the appliance test meter, as the wire is flexed in a spot, it means that the wire is broken in that spot. Flexing simply has completed the circuit. The line cord is faulty and should be replaced.

But let's assume that no amount of flexing gives an indication of a complete circuit. There is just no continuity. The control box should be disassembled and each critical component—line cord, switch, and thermostat—tested for continuity separately. This involves, first of all, unscrewing the line cord from its terminals inside the control box. Twirl the ends of the line cord together and test line-cord continuity. Lack of continuity signifies a defective line cord.

If the line cord shows continuity, test the switch by reconnecting the line cord to its terminal connections and positioning a jumper wire across the switch terminals. Test continuity. Lack of continuity signifies a defective switch, which should be replaced.

You can usually determine if a thermostat is bad by looking at it. If the thermostat is pitted or corroded, it should be replaced. If it fails to feel "springy" as you activate the movable thermostat blade cautiously with your finger, the thermostat should be replaced.

Caution: When the line cord, switch, or thermostat has to be replaced, make certain you obtain identical replacement parts.

If the control box and its components prove to be in good condition, there might be one more defect which possibly can be repaired before concluding the worst—that the heating element has failed. Maybe the heating-element terminals are corroded or burned.

Examine the terminals. Look for pit marks and dullness. Terminals of some model skillets, sauce pans, and fry pans can be replaced, but first try to salvage the elements by polishing them with a piece of fine sandpaper.

When you have done everything possible to get an electric skillet, sauce pan, or fry pan heating again, but have failed, you may want to see if the heating element has gone bad before you discard the appliance. Connect the test leads of a continuity tester to the heating-element terminals. Plug the tester into a wall outlet. If the tester's light does not glow, the heating element is shot.

other problems you may meet

ANOTHER PROBLEM that may afflict an electric skillet, sauce pan, or fry pan is heating to an incorrect temperature. The appliance may overheat, or it might not reach the desired cooking temperature. One fact is certain: the heating element cannot be blamed, so the problem can probably be solved and the appliance saved from the scrap heap.

Let's assume that the appliance's temperature is believed not to be in accordance with the setting of the temperature-control knob. Obviously,

the first thing that should be done is to make a temperature test. There is no way of guessing whether temperature is correct.

There are special temperature-testing meters equipped with thermocouples that can be purchased, but one isn't really necessary. Buy an "area" type thermometer from a local department store, but make sure it registers to a minimum of 250° F. Set a grille on top of the skillet, sauce pan, or fry pan and place the thermometer on top of the grille.

You probably won't get an exact reading of the temperature that's on the surface of the appliance, but this isn't necessary. If the skillet, sauce pan, or fry pan is overheating or is not getting hot enough, you will be able to tell. All you are seeking is an indication.

Plug the appliance into the wall outlet and set the temperature-control knob at 200° F. Allow the appliance to cycle several times. This permits uniform heat to establish itself over the entire surface of the vessel.

After several minutes, the thermometer should read between 175° and 220° F. If the temperature doesn't fall within this range, the trouble is probably dirty thermostat contacts or a dirty temperature-sensing probe. Clean the thermostat and temperature-sensing probe with a piece of fine sandpaper. However, if there is an appreciable amount of burning or pitting, you probably will have to replace the control box.

Chapter 24

Hot plates and hot trays

This chapter is brief, because these two appliances are not at all complicated. It should take you only a few minutes to find and correct the trouble.

HOT PLATES AND HOT TRAYS consist of only two essential parts: a line cord and a heating element. Generally, the hot plate heats to a higher temperature than does a hot tray, because its heating element has greater resistance to electricity. You are able, therefore, to boil water and do some cooking on a hot plate, while a hot tray is used to keep prepared foods warm.

The elements used in these appliances can be of two kinds. One kind is the Calrod-type element which is similar to those used on electric ranges, for example. A Calrod, which is a trade name, is a nichrome wire element that is covered by a sheath to insulate it. This prevents foreign matter from coming into contact with the wire, which might possibly cause a short.

In other units, the heating element is a coil of nichrome wire. Nichrome wire, as you may recall from previous chapters, has resistance to electricity. The greater this resistance, the hotter the element will get.

In many hot plates and hot trays, a line cord is integral with the heating element to form a single unit. It might be difficult to get to the connection point between the two parts, which means that if the element fails you may have to discard the appliance. But if a line cord fails it may be possible to cut the cord and splice a new cord into place.

some variations you may find

THE SIMPLEST HOT PLATE OR HOT TRAY begins operating when you plug the line cord into the wall outlet. To shut the unit off, you just pull the line cord from the outlet. There is no switch.

Other models *are* equipped with a switch and temperature control (Figure 1). The line cord is plugged into the wall outlet, but the appliance will not operate until the switch is flipped on. Naturally, with switch-operated models, the switch becomes a candidate for testing if a failure occurs.

Some hot plates you encounter may have more than one heating element, with each element operated by a separate switch. Logically, if all burners fail to operate, the cause of the trouble is either in the line cord or with the house current feeding the line cord, so check the fuse or circuit breaker. It is very unlikely for all

Figure 1. Newer-model hot trays have more than one element, separately controlled.

heating elements to fail at the same time.

However, if one element fails to work, the trouble is being caused by the switch which controls the burner or by the element itself.

a simple check-out

ASSUME A HOT PLATE or hot tray doesn't work, and you are able to reach the connection points between the line cord and heating element. There is no control switch. To test this unit, just connect a test light between the two connections and plug the line cord into a wall outlet.

If the test light glows, the trouble is confined to the heating element. If the test light does not glow, the line cord (or house-current circuit) is to blame.

If possible, replace the faulty component.

If a unit is equipped with an on-off switch, the switch can be tested just as easily. Be sure the line cord is unplugged and attach a short jumper wire across the switch terminals. This takes the switch out of the circuit.

Plug the line cord into the wall outlet. If the appliance now proceeds to get hot, the switch is bad and should be replaced.

Section 3
Major Appliances

Chapter 25

Introduction

The chapters which follow tell how to repair a dozen big appliances. Although it's true that in certain cases you may need to call in a professional, remember that many problems of major appliances are minor and easy to fix.

REPAIRING a washing machine, clothes dryer, air conditioner or any one of the 12 major appliances we shall soon discuss is not always easy work. You aren't dealing with simple machines.

However, it is wasteful to call a professional serviceman every time a problem arises. Often, an ailment plaguing a major appliance is a minor one, so why should you spend $30 or more to have someone else perform a simple procedure?

But what is difficult for one is relatively easy for another, and vice versa. That is why the following chapters contain information for making repairs that range, in our opinion, from the most simple to the most difficult.

What constitutes a "difficult" repair? Generally, it requires extensive disassembly of a unit. Since appliances differ from one model to another in the way they are put together, it is not practical for us to explain here how to take apart your washing machine, dishwasher, garbage disposer, or whatever. And that is why some repairs may be difficult for you—because you have to take apart a unit without help.

Other repairs are "difficult" ("impossible" is a more appropriate word), because you lack tools. I am speaking specifically about repairing refrigerators, home freezers, and air conditioners. If a serious problem strikes one of these appliances, entailing the replacement of a part which requires purging refrigerant, you need special equipment. This equipment costs hundreds of dollars, and it would be foolish to buy it unless you are going to engage in repairing refrigeration systems on a full-time basis.

Since we told you what the following chapters cannot do, allow us to outline what they *do* do. First of all, information is provided to give you insight about the way in which the various major appliances work. You will quickly realize that they are not the mysteries they appear to be.

Secondly, the chapters provide detailed troubleshooting data which will guide you in putting your finger right on the cause of a problem. When you have found the trouble, you can decide whether you want to try making the repairs yourself or whether you should call in a professional. If you decide the latter is more desirable, at least you won't be dealing in the dark

introduction

ITEM	OLD	NEW	ITEM	OLD	NEW
Ballast			Terminal		
Adj. Thermostat			Timer motor		
Thermocouple			Plug connector		
Neon light	None		Starter (automatic)		
Transformer	None		Light (incandescent)		
Thermistor	None		Pressure sw.		
Transistor	None		Fluorescent		
Diode (rectifier)	None		Coil		
Rectifier (controlled)	None		Capacitor		
Double-throw thermostat			Resistor	500	500 Ω
Internal conductor			Centrifugal sw.		
Harness wire			Thermostat		
Permanent connection			Coil and switches		
3-prong plug			Motor, single speed		
Timer sw.			Motor, multispeed	1725 1140	1725 1140
Automatic sw.					
Manual sw.					
Double throw					
Crossover					
Heater (wattage shown)	2800	2800w.			
Ground					

. . . you will know or have a good idea of what's causing the difficulty, and you will be able to tell if the repairman is giving you a square deal.

However, if you decide to make repairs yourself, drawings and photographs accompanying the text will show you what to look for.

In preparation for troubleshooting the electrical section of the various major appliances, I suggest you keep this part of the book available since it illustrates the various symbols used on wiring diagrams (Figure 1). Practically every major appliance should have a wiring diagram glued somewhere to its housing. It serves as a road map through the complex arrangement of wires, switches, solenoids and the like.

Notice that two symbols are provided—"old" and "new." Symbols were revised in 1970. If your appliance is fairly new, its wiring diagram probably will possess the new symbols. If the appliance is an older model, its wiring diagram will possess the old symbols.

The following is the order in which the appliances discussed in this section are presented:

Good luck!

Chapter 26

Clothes dryers

They are big and heavy to maneuver, but once you have opened them up, you will find that clothes dryers are rather simple machines. There are two kinds: those that heat with gas, and those that heat with electricity.

ALTHOUGH ALL GAS-HEATED CLOTHES DRYERS work in generally the same way, manufacturers have incorporated various technical differences (Figure 1). The same is true of all clothes dryers that generate heat with electricity (Figure 2). This means that you may not be able to find the cause of a problem and fix it without the wiring diagram that is glued to the rear panel or somewhere on the inside of the chassis (Figure 3).

But since all gas clothes dryers work basically the same way, and all electric dryers work generally the same, knowing how they function is important to an understanding of what can go wrong with them. This knowledge leads to an idea of what faulty components to look for when a failure occurs.

Information in this chapter is organized along the following lines:

First is a discussion of operational functions that are common to both gas and electric units. We then explain functions relative to gas dryers, which is followed by a discussion of functions relative to electric dryers.

The final sections of the chapter discuss problems and their solutions. One section concerns problems relative to all clothes dryers, whether gas or electric. Another section is devoted to problems common only to gas dryers, and the final section deals with electric clothes-dryer problems.

what all dryers have in common

WHETHER GAS OR ELECTRIC, every clothes dryer has the same major components. These are: an **electric motor,** a **large drum,** a **blower unit,** and a couple of **belts** (Figure 4).

Every dryer, of course, also has a heat source, but this differs depending on whether the heat source is operated by gas or by electricity. Heat sources are discussed later in this chapter, but every dryer has a centrifugal switch that controls the heat source.

The job of the **centrifugal switch** is to keep the heat turned off until the drum has revolved for several seconds and is turning at full speed. This feature is incorporated to assure that failure of the drum to revolve won't result in heat being applied to one portion of damp clothes, damaging them (Figure 5).

Concerning motors, most are split-phase types that are rated at ⅓ horsepower. They operate on 115 volts AC.

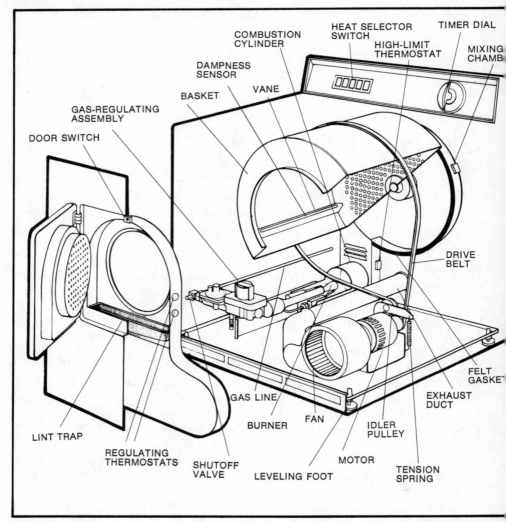

Figure 1. The components of a typical gas clothes dryer are illustrated here. Compare this drawing with that on the opposite page, which is of an electric clothes dryer.

For a discussion of split-phase motors, see the chapter on small electric fans.

The job of the motor is to drive the **drum and blower unit.** It does this in different ways, depending upon the dryer. In every case, however, drive belts are involved.

Belts: You may have a dryer, as in Figure 1, in which one large belt extends from the motor pulley right around the drum and is pulled so taut that when the motor revolves the drum revolves too.

In this installation, you may find a smaller belt extending from the motor pulley to a pulley on the blower housing. The blower's job is to blow moist, heated air through the drum and out through the vent that leads outside the home.

In another type of arrangement, there may be a relatively small drive belt extending between the motor pulley and a reduction pulley, and another small drive belt between the reduction pulley and a pulley on the

Figure 2. An electric clothes dryer has many of the same components as a gas dryer. Every dryer has an electric motor, a large drum in which the clothes are tumbled, a blower unit, and a couple of belts. Although the heat sources differ, every gas and electric clothes dryer has a centrifugal switch to control the heat source.

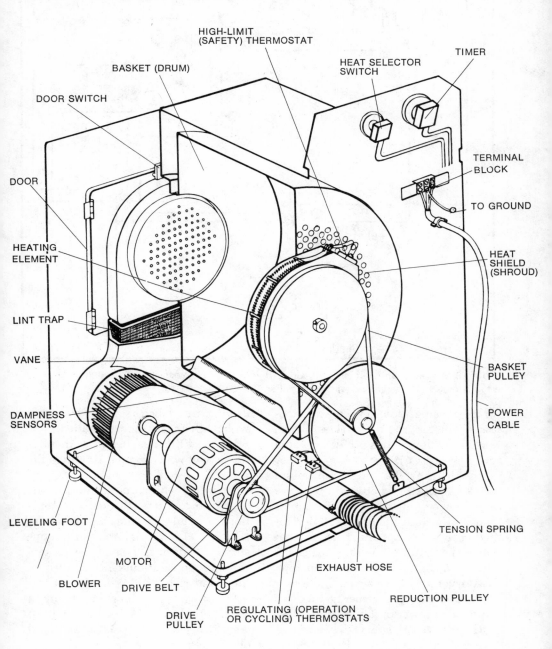

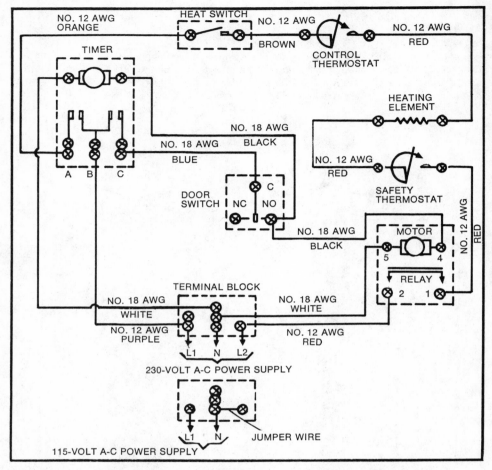

Figure 3. Above is an example of a wiring diagram for an electric clothes dryer. It is usually glued to the rear panel or somewhere inside the chassis.

drum housing. You can see what happens. The motor pulley drives the reduction pulley, which drives the drum pulley (Figure 6).

In this installation, there might not be a drive belt between the motor and blower unit. Instead, the motor and blower unit might be coupled together by a common shaft so that when the motor revolves, causing the shaft to turn, the blower will operate.

A dryer may have a combination of any of these arrangements to drive drum and blower unit.

Drums: A dryer may have one of two different types of drums. Some

drums are called shrouded drums, while others are non-shrouded. The primary difference between them is the way in which heated air enters the drum.

In dryers with shrouded drums, the heated air enters through perforations around the sides of the drum (Figure 7). In dryers with non-shrouded drums, heated air enters through perforations in the rear of the drum (Figure 8). This is not important when it comes to fixing a dryer problem. But I mention it to dispel any questions that sharp-eyed observers may have.

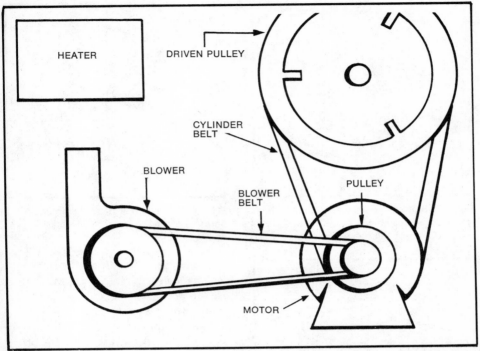

Figure 4. This simplified drawing shows the arrangement of the major components of a clothes dryer, and how they work in conjunction with each other.

Figure 5. The centrifugal switch is part of a heater delay circuit. It stays open until the drum is revolving at full speed, keeping the heat source from operating.

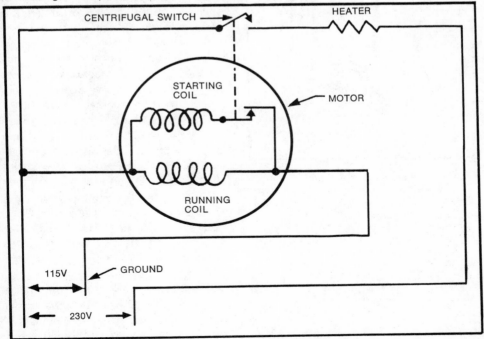

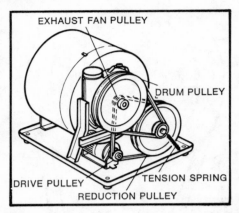

Figure 6. Some dryers have two belts which are arranged as you see here. The setup is called a reduction pulley basket drive.

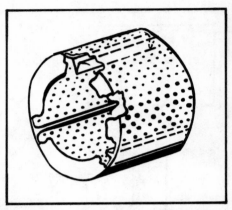

Figure 7. The drums of some dryers are perforated around the sides. Heated air enters through the holes.

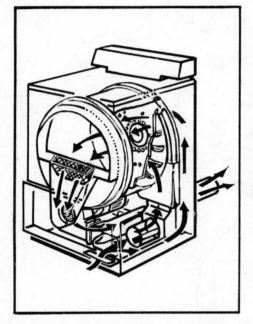

Figure 8. Heated air in other dryers enters through perforations in the rear of the drum. This drawing illustrates the airflow through a dryer with this type of drum.

Controls: All clothes dryers have certain controls in common. These *are* important when you have to troubleshoot a problem.

The primary control is a timer that is similar to the timer used by other major appliances, notably washing machines and dishwashers.

The **timer** is nothing more than an electric clock motor that runs at a set speed (Figure 9). It has on its shaft a series of cams, which are circular objects interrupted by projections.

These cams (the number depends on the number of functions the timer has to control) revolve at a set speed. As a projection comes around to a certain point, it strikes a switch to activate the particular function. When the projection slides away from the switch, the switch is deactivated, and the function ceases.

In the case of a clothes dryer, the timer has relatively little to do. Once you set it for the time desired, it simply winds itself back down to zero, at which point it trips a switch that turns the dryer off.

The timer works in conjunction with a heat-selector switch that turns heat on and off to control temperature in respect to the type of clothes being dried. For example, a normal (regular) drying selection permits heat to remain on, more or less, for the cycle duration.

However, about 10 minutes before the cycle ends, the timer activates a switch to turn the heating source off. This is done so the clothes will cool somewhat, making them easier to handle when the dryer stops.

A delicate fabric-drying selection, by contrast, is a low-heat setting to keep woolens, knits and synthetics from being damaged by excessive heat. The timer and heat-selector switch work together to cycle the heat, keeping it on for the proper duration and turning it off for the proper duration.

In addition to a timer and heat-selector switch, every dryer has several **safety devices** built into it. Some are in the form of thermostats, which function similarly to those we have discussed elsewhere in this book (see Index). Switches may also be used as safety features.

For example, every dryer has a

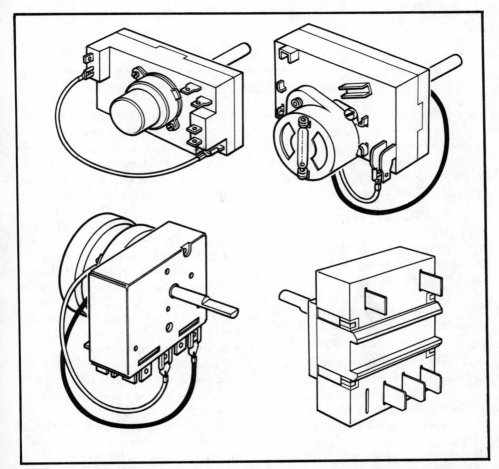

Figure 9. These illustrations will allow you to recognize the timer if and when it becomes necessary to replace one. The timer is similar to an electric clock motor. On its shaft are a series of projections which strike switches to activate various functions.

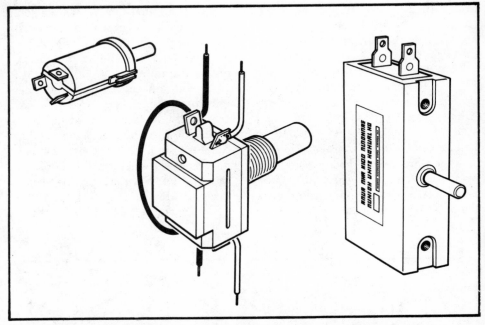

Figure 10. Clothes-dryer door switches come in various shapes and sizes.

door switch which is wired in series with the main power line coming into the dryer (Figure 10). The switch causes an interruption of electricity when the door is open, and therefore a cessation of dryer operation.

Another safety device in every dryer is a thermostat that keeps the dryer from overheating. When the inside of the dryer reaches a high heat (perhaps a buildup of lint is preventing normal air flow), this so-called high-limit thermostat opens and interrupts the electric circuit, causing the dryer to shut down (Figure 11).

Keep in mind that every dryer uses electricity—even models that employ gas as the heat source. Electricity is needed to ignite the gas and operate the motor. (Some gas models have a pilot light that burns all the time, similar to the pilot on a gas stove. These don't have electrically operated coils to ignite gas.)

An interesting feature of many newer-model clothes dryers is an electronic **dampness-sensor system.** What this does is "measure" the dampness in clothes, keeping the dryer turned on as long as the clothes need drying, but shutting the appliance off as soon as drying is completed. This prevents dryer operation when it is not needed.

Generally, these sensors are in the form of baffles located in the drum and wrapped with wire. Wired baffles are either positive or negative. When wet clothes are put into the dryer and lay across baffles, moisture completes the circuit between positive and negative, and the dryer operates.

When the clothes are dry, the moisture has dissipated and the circuit is broken. The dryer shuts down.

A sign that something is wrong with the electronic sensor system is when the dryer does not shut off automatically when clothes are dry. This is a complicated, delicate system, and its repair should be left to a factory-trained serviceman.

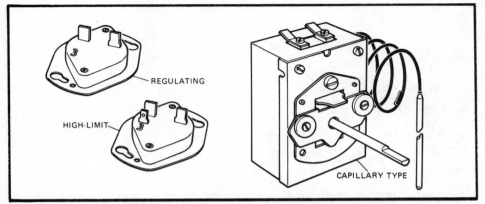

Figure 11. Thermostats in clothes dryers are bimetal types and capillary types. They control the regular functioning of the unit as well as a number of safety aspects.

the heat source in a gas dryer— and its controls

A CLOTHES DRYER that uses gas as the heating source can be compared with a gas stove, although the two are not alike. But comparison may make understanding easier.

A gas dryer has a main burner that resembles the burner on a stove (Figure 12). Just as gas is fed to the stove's burner, gas must be fed to the main burner of a dryer. The dryer's main burner is positioned in the airflow path so that heated air is circulated through the drum in which damp clothes are tumbling.

Just as with a gas stove, there has to be a means of igniting the gas coming from the main burner. In a gas stove, this is accomplished by means of a gas-fed pilot light that is burning constantly. There are some models of gas dryers that have a gas-fed pilot light, but they are few and far between, so for all intents and purposes the similarity between a gas stove and a gas clothes dryer ends here.

In most dryers that use gas as a heating source, the device that ignites the gas when the dryer is turned on is an electrically operated glow coil

(Figure 13). It works in conjunction with another part called a thermocouple control.

In essence, the **thermocouple control** is a safety device that will shut off gas going to the main burner in the event of an accidental flame-out. This prevents lethal gas from permeating the home.

Involved with the glow coil and thermocouple is a **solenoid** that is on the gas line. When the solenoid activates, it opens a valve to allow gas to flow to the burner. When the solenoid deactivates because gas (heat) is no longer needed, or there is a flame-out, or if a malfunction such as an excessive buildup of heat creates a hazardous situation, the valve seals the gas line.

A solenoid is an electromagnet consisting basically of a spring-loaded iron bar that moves freely into and out of a coil of wire. When electricity flows through the coil of wire, the coil becomes a magnet that has more force than the spring. It pulls the iron bar through the center of the coil. When voltage is interrupted, the spring controlling the iron bar has greater pull and returns the iron bar to its original position, out of the coil.

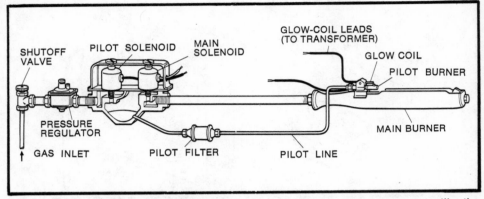

Figure 12. The main burner arrangement of gas dryers using glow coils is quite unlike the arrangement in a gas stove.

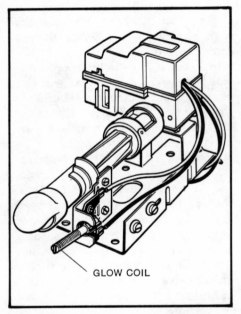

Figure 13. This illustration provides you with a close-up view of a typical glow-coil burner assembly.

Solenoids are used for various purposes in different appliances, because they can be hooked together with linkages, gears, plates (valves) or whatever. In a gas clothes dryer, the solenoid's job is simply to control a valve plate across the main gas line.

Another important part of the heating controls of a gas dryer is the centrifugal switch that was mentioned before. For all practical purposes, the entire gas-feeding process begins with this switch. Here is how all the parts work together:

When you turn on the dryer, the motor starts and the drum starts turning. As the drum reaches operating speed, the centrifugal switch (which is usually positioned on the motor) activates. It is wired in series with the gas-line solenoid, and allows the solenoid to open.

Once the centrifugal switch does "its thing," it lies dormant until the next time the dryer is turned on. The task of keeping the solenoid valve open is up to the thermocouple.

When the dryer is turned on, current is permitted to flow to the glow coil. This coil is a small unit that usually is made of platinum and is positioned right next to a pilot jet. When gas begins flowing from the pilot jet, it is ignited by heat from the glow coil, and gas flowing from the main burner is ignited by the flame of the pilot jet.

How does the thermocouple fit into all of this? The thermocouple is positioned right next to the pilot jet. A thermocouple is a device that produces a small voltage (less than one volt) when it is heated.

Thus, when the pilot jet lights, and heats the thermocouple, the thermocouple produces voltage, and this voltage is applied to the solenoid on the gas line. In other words, the thermocouple assumes the job of keeping open the gas line to the pilot and main burner. At this point, the glow coil is not needed anymore, and voltage to it is turned off.

At this point the pilot jet is on and the main burner is on, because the thermocouple is keeping the solenoid valve open, which is keeping the gas line open. But let's suppose that suddenly for some reason the flames blow out, and gas starts to escape.

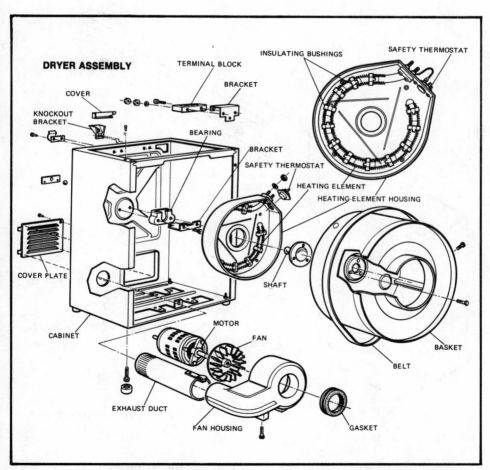

DRYER ASSEMBLY

TERMINAL BLOCK
INSULATING BUSHINGS
SAFETY THERMOSTAT
BRACKET
COVER
KNOCKOUT BRACKET
BEARING
BRACKET
SAFETY THERMOSTAT
HEATING ELEMENT
HEATING-ELEMENT HOUSING
SHAFT
COVER PLATE
CABINET
MOTOR
FAN
BASKET
BELT
EXHAUST DUCT
FAN HOUSING
GASKET

Figure 14. This breakdown of an electric clothes dryer shows the main parts. Notice the two heating elements that encompass the drum. The heating elements are fused separately, so if the dryer isn't providing enough heat, check to see if just one fuse has blown.

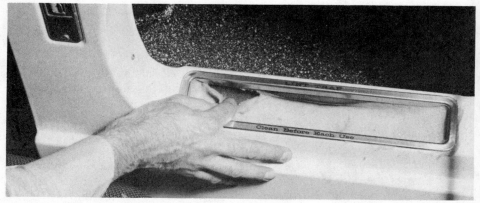

Figure 15. The most important maintenance function you can perform for clothes dryer is to clean the fuzz out of the lint trap after every load.

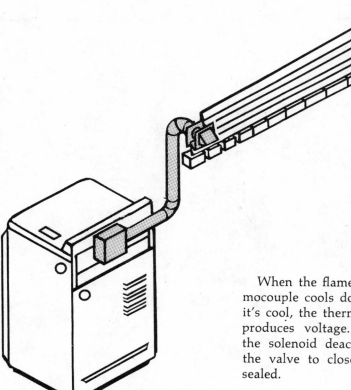

Figure 16. In time, the vent pipes of a dryer can clog with lint. Periodically take them apart and clean them.

When the flames go out, the thermocouple cools down rapidly. When it's cool, the thermocouple no longer produces voltage. Without voltage, the solenoid deactivates and allows the valve to close. The gas line is sealed.

the electric dryer's heat source

THE HEAT SOURCE for an electric dryer consists in most units of two heating elements that encompass the drum (Figure 14). These elements are made of nichrome wire that is the same wire used in room heaters,

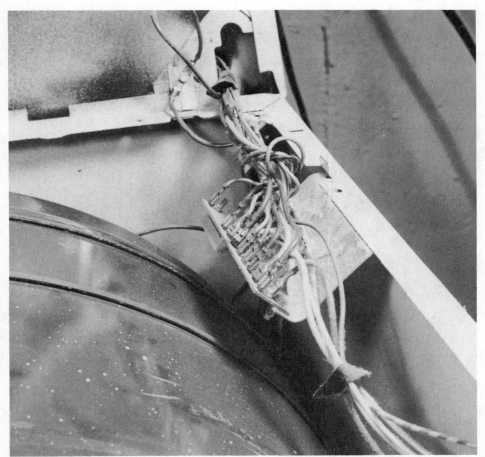

Figure 17. To get at the controls of most dryers you have to remove the top. This shows a timer exposed. Take off the rear or front panel to get at major assemblies like the motor.

toasters, and other appliances discussed in previous chapters.

The heating elements operate on a full 220-230 volts and produce approximately 5000 watts. The dryer motor works on 110-115 volts. This brings up an interesting point worth discussion, because it could save you a lot of time and aggravation if a particular failure occurs.

That failure is insufficient drying, because the dryer isn't providing enough heat. Keep in mind that each of the heating elements of an electric clothes dryer is fused *separately*. If the fuse of an element goes bad, but the fuse of the other element remains intact, the dryer will operate, but only with one heating element. Should this problem arise, check fuses before you do anything else.

Electric clothes dryers also have a centrifugal switch, which is wired in series with the heating elements across the 220-230 volt line. The switch turns on the heating element when the motor has assumed operating speed.

what to do when your clothes dryer goes on the blink

BEFORE OUTLINING specific repair

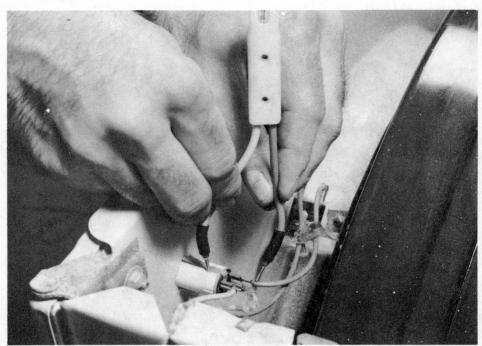

Figure 18. The ordinary troublelight (continuity tester) is the main instrument needed to troubleshoot most electrical parts of a clothes dryer.

Figure 19. A broken belt is the chief reason for the failure of a drum to revolve when the dryer motor operates. Take the broken belt to the dealer to get a replacement.

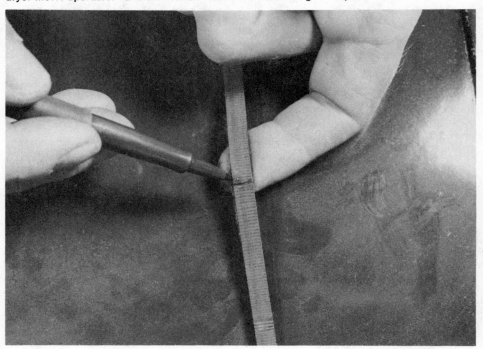

data relative to dryers, whether gas or electric, there are several important points that must be considered:

1. In most regions served by gas, the local utility company should be called in the event of a gas-dryer failure. Most companies have a policy (you can ask) of having servicemen repair any problem related to gas at no cost to the customer, with the exception of the cost of new parts. It is usually best to let gas companies do this. Gas can be lethal.

2. If a gas dryer fails for other than a gas-related reason and you insist on making repairs yourself, or for some reason the gas company won't do the work, make sure that you shut off the gas supply as well as the electricity before proceeding. Even if the trouble is not gas-related, you should first examine the setup with the idea that you may have to maneuver the dryer to get it into a better position for repair. Carelessness, such as moving the dryer without making certain that the gas feed line has sufficient room for movement, can cause a gas-line rupture.

The gas feed line to the dryer should have a valve on it. Turn this valve to shut off the gas supply to the dryer. If the gas feed line has to be disconnected so the dryer can be moved, use a wrench to unscrew the large coupling nut.

In reassembling a gas feed line, check for a gas leak coming from around the coupling nut after you have tightened it. Spread soapy water around the nut with a paint brush or some such applicator and watch to see if there is bubbling action in any spot. Bubbling signifies a leak. Using your nose to sniff around the coupling nut may also reveal a leak.

3. Don't forget to disconnect the line cord from an electric dryer (and also a gas dryer) before starting repairs.

4. Probably the only maintenance your dryer needs is cleaning of the lint trap after every use (Figure 15). However, consult the instructions that came with the appliance to determine if the unit requires any other servicing.

A buildup of lint probably causes more problems than do actual parts failures. If a dryer doesn't dry clothes fully, or if the unit builds up excessive heat, you should clean out not only the lint trap, but also the exhaust vent pipes (Figure 16).

After several years of operation, lint can clog up vent pipes, making it difficult for the dryer to "breathe." If the dryer is equipped with metal vent pipes, take them apart and clean them with a long brush or a vacuum cleaner attachment. If you have plastic vent tubing, which is relatively inexpensive, you may want to replace it every few years.

5. A leak in the venting system can cause insufficient drying and may also create a fire hazard in your laundry room. For example, if the sections of metal vent pipe are not sealed at the joints, lint and moist air can blow into the room. Lint is flammable.

All joints should be sealed with duct tape.

Check where the vent pipe comes through the outside wall. The opening should be equipped with a draft cover to keep wind from blowing back into the dryer. Drafts can cause the flame of a gas dryer to blow out. They also reduce drying efficiency.

The following troubleshooting charts apply to problems that afflict dryers in general. Keep in mind that the location of parts varies from model to model. You have to consult the wiring diagram for your dryer (Figure 17).

Problem	Causes	Procedure
Dryer doesn't run at all (no life)	1. Door is open	1. Make sure that the door is shut tightly.
	2. Main fuse blown or circuit breaker is tripped	2. Check main fuse or circuit breaker in home's main fuse box. If the malfunction keeps occurring, consult an electrician. There is probably a problem in the home's electrical system.
	3. Fuse that services the dryer motor is blown	3. Most gas and electric dryers have a fuse (frequently located in the doorway of the dryer) that will blow out if there is a motor malfunction. Check this fuse. If it is old, replace it, but if it goes bad again, there is an internal problem, probably motor-related, that should be traced and repaired.
	4. Defective door switch	4. The door switch is operated by a button (in the doorway) on which the door closes. Find the switch behind this button. Remove its wires and check continuity across the terminals (Figure 18). Don't forget to press the switch button when the tester is connected. If there is no continuity, replace the switch.
	5. Defective centrifugal switch	5. Consult the wiring diagram and find the switch terminals (probably on the motor). Test continuity. If there is no continuity, the trouble probably is a defective switch although it might also be a failure in the motor. Replace the switch. It's worth the gamble.
	6. Loose wiring at the motor	6. Make sure all wiring is tightly connected.
	7. Defective timer	7. Connect a testlight (115-volt) or volt-meter across the timer terminals. Turn on the timer. If you get a reading, the timer contacts have opened up. Replace the timer.
	8. Defective motor	8. Direct-test the motor by disconnecting wires from its terminals and hooking up a line cord you know is okay. Plug the cord in. If the motor fails to run, replace it.

Problem	Causes	Procedure
		Motors often give warning before they fail by emitting a strong odor of scorched insulation.
Motor runs, but drum doesn't revolve	1. Loose or broken belt	1. Check belts (Figure 19). Replace any that are broken. Tighten belts so there is no more than ¼ inch free play when pressing on the belt midway between pulleys.
	2. Loose pulley	2. Tighten all pulley set screws. If a pulley has slipped on its shaft, realign it in relation to its counter-pulley. Then tighten the set screw.
	3. Tension spring has broken	3. This is the spring that keeps the motor pulley properly aligned with drum and/or blower pulley. If the spring has fallen loose, replace it on the motor bracket. If the spring has broken or has lost tension (not likely), replace it.
	4. Motor idler pulley is defective	4. Check the idler pulley to see if it has sustained damage. A sign of a bad pulley is a glaze that has built up on the pulley groove. This will cause belts to slip. Replace a bad pulley.
	5. Drum binds	5. Turn the drum by hand. If it is very hard to turn, lint may have accumulated around it or some object may be caught between the drum and housing, causing the drum to bind. There is usually a baffle in the drum that can be removed. It is screw-held. Remove it and use a fabricated tool, such as a metal coat hanger fashioned to shape, to pull out lint or other binding matter.
Clothes do not dry or they dry too slowly	1. Lint buildup	1. Clean lint from all parts where it has accumulated, including the vent hose.
	2. Drum overloaded	2. Do not exceed the load specified for the machine by the manufacturer.
	3. Clothes are too wet	3. If the clothes are dripping wet when you put them into the dryer,

clothes dryers

Problem	Causes	Procedure
		there may be a problem with your washing machine. Clothes put into a dryer from a washing machine should be damp.
	4. Timer set improperly	4. Be sure the dryer is being operated in accordance with the manufacturer's instructions.
	5. Defective thermostat	5. Dryers for the most part contain several thermostats to control temperature at each setting. Usually these can be checked by placing a thermometer in the machine's vent duct and operating the unit through the cycle at which the problem is occurring. You will need the manufacturer's temperature rating for the thermostat. Write the company or call the company's local service representative. If the temperature recorded on the thermometer is not to specification, probably the thermostat is at fault and should be replaced.
Dryer does not shut off at end of cycle	1. Defective door switch	1. Test as described above under "dryer doesn't run at all".
	2. Defective timer	2. Test as described above under "dryer doesn't run at all".
	3. Defective thermostat	3. Test as described above under "clothes do not get dry or dry too slowly".
	4. Motor is grounded	4. Remove the wires from the motor terminals. Touch one lead of your continuity tester to one terminal and the other lead to ground on the motor housing. If the tester lights, the motor is grounded internally and should be replaced.
	5. Defective electronic dampness-sensor system	5. Consult a serviceman if your machine has this feature. There is probably a malfunction in the electronic control or with the sensors.
Dryer makes excessive noise	1. Loose objects flopping around in drum	1. Make sure all loose objects are out of the drum.

Problem	Causes	Procedure
	2. Loose fan in blower housing	2. Disassemble blower, if necessary, and retighten the fan-blade set screw.
	3. Worn, sloppy belt	3. Check belts for condition and play. Replace if necessary and tighten.
	4. Loose pulley	4. Check all pulleys for looseness. Tighten set screws.
	5. Something wedged between drum and housing	5. Turn the drum by hand until it binds. Remove impeding object.
	6. Out-of-balance condition	6. Check that all parts (pulleys and fan especially) are tight and that the machine is level. If it isn't level, level it (using a carpenter's level) by adjusting the leveling feet.
	7. Worn drum bearings	7. The drum revolves on bearings. These can wear. Many dealers sell replacement bearing sets. Replacement involves removing the drum.

troubleshooting heating sources

IF THE METHODS outlined above for the problem of "clothes dry slowly or not at all" do not give results, the cause of the problem probably lies with the source of heat. Checking an electric dryer is pretty simple, but a gas setup is far more intricate. However, keep in mind what we said concerning the role of the utility company.

The following procedures apply to gas dryers:

Problem	Procedure
1. Pilot light won't light or keeps going out	1. Look for draft blowback that extinguishes pilot; loose connections in the thermocouple circuit; a dirty pilot burner or orifice; a clogged pilot-line filter; a defective thermocouple; a defective magnetic valve; low gas pressure because of inadequate service; or a glow coil that doesn't get hot enough (see below).
2. Pilot light isn't burning properly (too low—too high)	2. Look for a clogged orifice; a pilot that isn't adjusted properly; a clogged pilot line filter; low

Problem	Procedure
	or high gas pressure; or an orifice of the wrong size.
3. Glow coil does not get hot	3. Look for an open coil; broken or disconnected coil leads; or an open circuit in the transformer, or in the circuit between the timer and transformer.
4. Glow coil does not get hot enough—pilot doesn't light	4. Look for low line voltage and for a loose connection or short circuit.
5. Main burner doesn't ignite	5. Look for a plugged main burner orifice; a defective solenoid; defective timer; or defective centrifugal switch.
The following procedures apply to electric clothes dryers:	
1. One element out of service	1. Check fuses in dryer to see if one of them has blown.
2. Inadequate electrical service	2. Standard 110-volt current is one-half the voltage that an electric dryer needs for efficient operation. Clothes take two or three times longer to dry. Consider the feasibility of installing a 220-volt outlet.
3. Defective heating element	3. Check heating elements for continuity. If either shows no reading, it has an open coil. Replace the element.

Chapter 27

Washing machines

The modern clothes washer comes in many styles, with a variety of features, and contains a myriad of components. But all washers have many things in common and are not that difficult to understand.

BOTH THE SIMPLEST automatic clothes washer and one possessing every conceivable feature perform *only four basic* functions (Figures 1 and 2). Every washing machine (1) washes clothes and (2) spins clothes damp dry. Interspersed between these two functions, every washing machine (3) fills itself with water and (4) drains itself of water.

Over the years, several different washing-machine designs have been

Figure 1. This automatic washer (at right; beside it is a dryer) has many settings.

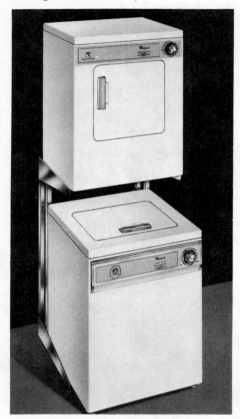

Figure 2. This washer-dryer setup is designed for homes where little space is available. The units set on a rack.

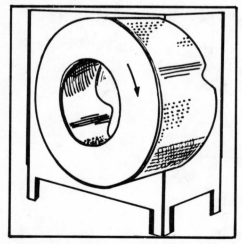

Figure 3. Some washing machines rotate clothes in large cylinders. These are in the minority.

offered to the public. For example, a drum type has been made whose interior looks like that of a clothes dryer. In washing clothes, the drum revolves, flopping the clothes over and over, into and out of the detergent wash water (Figure 3).

Although there have been several designs, one particular design has dominated. This has been the agitator-type washing machine. It has a large-bladed assembly that rotates on a center shaft in the middle of the clothes basket (Figure 4). The action of the agitator greatly stirs up the detergent wash water. It is this agitation of the water around the clothes that cleans the clothes. It is not, as many believe, that the agitator "beats" the clothes.

We will discuss only the agitator-type washing machine in this chapter. However, the mechanisms it uses are similar to the mechanisms employed by machines of other design.

consider the control devices

FOR THE SAKE of simplicity, think of your washing machine as consisting of two main systems: a water system and a mechanical system. But governing the operation of these systems are a number of electrical components. They are the timer and various switches.

Timer. The timer is the heart of the machine (Figure 5). Its job is to control the time at which each function is to occur so that a correct sequence of events is maintained.

A timer consists of several contact points ganged together which are controlled by cams. Each set of contacts has its own individual cam. The cams are turned by a gear-spring-shaft mechanism called an escapement. This

Figure 4. Most washing machines contain an agitator which moves water around the clothes to clean them, as in this unit.

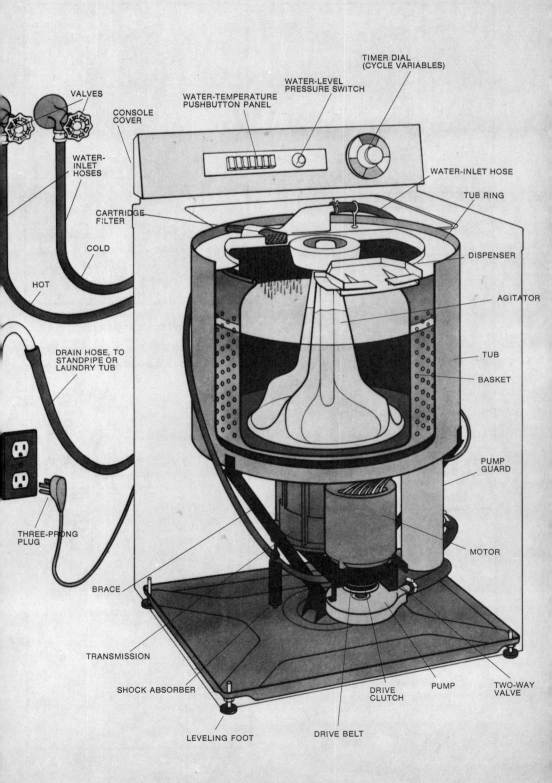

VALVES

CONSOLE COVER

WATER-INLET HOSES

WATER-TEMPERATURE PUSHBUTTON PANEL

WATER-LEVEL PRESSURE SWITCH

TIMER DIAL (CYCLE VARIABLES)

WATER-INLET HOSE

TUB RING

CARTRIDGE FILTER

COLD

HOT

DISPENSER

AGITATOR

TUB

BASKET

DRAIN HOSE, TO STANDPIPE OR LAUNDRY TUB

PUMP GUARD

THREE-PRONG PLUG

MOTOR

BRACE

TRANSMISSION

SHOCK ABSORBER

LEVELING FOOT

DRIVE CLUTCH

DRIVE BELT

PUMP

TWO-WAY VALVE

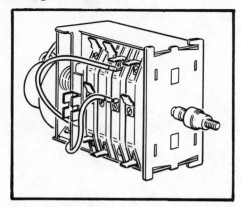

Figure 5. If you ever have to locate the timer, look for a part like this.

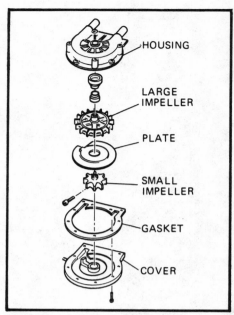

Figure 7. Use this diagram to disassemble and repair a faulty water pump.

HOUSING

LARGE IMPELLER

PLATE

SMALL IMPELLER

GASKET

COVER

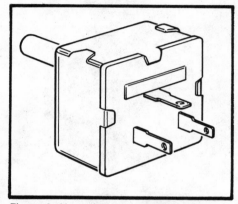

Figure 6. No matter what other features your automatic washing machine contains, it has a water-temperature switch (above) and a water-level pressure switch (below).

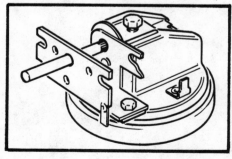

Figure 8. Water valves in a washing machine can fail. But the chief problem lies in clogged screens, which can be cleaned.

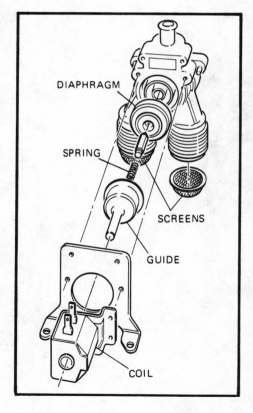

DIAPHRAGM

SPRING

SCREENS

GUIDE

COIL

escapement, in turn, is driven by a synchronous motor which is the same as that used in an electric clock. Naturally, the motor runs at a constant speed since its operation is governed by house current which delivers, in most areas, a constant 60 cycles per second.

Each cam has high and low points. As the cam rotates on its high points, the contact terminals it controls are open. The terminals resemble the points in a car's distributor. One terminal is movable—the other is stationary. The cam activates the movable terminal. When the cam presents its high point, it makes contact with a little lever called a cam follower. This lever pushes the movable contact terminal off the stationary contact terminal.

Now, all this does is prevent a circuit from being completed. No electricity can flow through the particular circuit, and the function doesn't take place.

When the time comes, though, the cam is snapped into position by the escapement so its low point is presented. This allows the contact terminals to snap together, permitting completion and activation of the circuit.

Notice that cams *snap* into place—they do not move into position gradually. Gradualism would cause arcing, because a narrow gap would be created between the terminals. Arcing is a sustained discharge of electricity across a gap, and it can destroy the set of terminals, and therefore the timer.

Switches. Automatic clothes-washing machines possess switches that control water temperature, water level, motor speed, spin-stop and several other functions. Switches are activated by various means (Figure 6). For example, some switches are

manually operated. One is the door switch that may be a pushbutton or toggle. When you open the machine's door while the machine is operating, the switch opens and the circuit is broken. The machine shuts off. Closing the door on the push-button, or whatever, causes the switch to activate.

Other switches are pressure switches that are actuated by pressure reacting on a diaphragm, float switches that turn on and off according to the level of water, centrifugal switches that are actuated by the force established by a spinning shaft, and thermal switches that are actuated by temperature.

Another kind of switch which is used in all washing machines is the solenoid switch. A solenoid is an electromagnet that transforms electrical energy into mechanical motion.

The basic components of a solenoid are a coil of wire and an iron bar which is set up to move freely through the center of the coil of wire. The iron bar is referred to as the core.

The core is connected to a spring. The coil of wire is connected into a circuit so it can receive voltage. When no voltage is applied to the coil of wire and everything is de-energized, the core is kept at rest by the spring. But when voltage is applied, the coil becomes a magnet that pulls the core into another position. By attaching a solenoid to various linkages, or whatever, it can be made to perform various functions. One of these functions is to service the washing machine's water system.

in the deep

THE WATER SYSTEM of a typical automatic clothes washer consists of a water pump, water-pump guard, water valve, water filters, and hoses. Each has its own job to do, as follows:

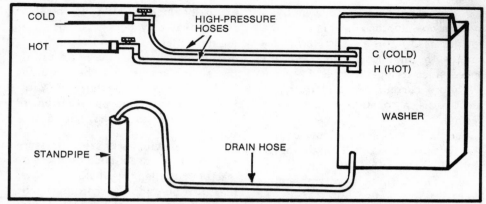

Figure 9. This diagram shows the usual hookup of a washing machine to its water sources.

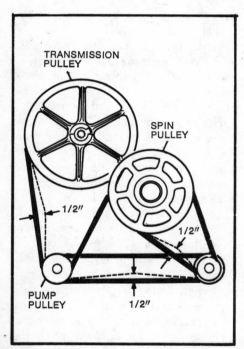

Figure 10. Belts are properly tight when you can deflect them ½-inch at midpoint. Check belts if tub fails to drain.

1. **The water pump** has two tasks. During the wash and rinsing phases, it recirculates water from the tub to a filter and back again. Its other job is to discharge water from the machine at the completion of the wash phase. Some washing machines have a feature called a suds-saver. This device "stores" suds between washing phases so they can be reused. If your machine is equipped with a suds-saver, its pump draws suds from the sud-saving device back into the machine for re-use.

When a water-pump problem occurs—let's say the machine won't drain—the trouble is very often caused by a foreign object getting into the pump and causing a sticking or binding condition. It is usually possible to disassemble the pump, remove the foreign object, reassemble the pump, and put the unit back into service (Figure 7).

The one time when a pump should be replaced rather than repaired is when its bearings have seized. The cost involved in replacing a bearing assembly is normally almost as great as replacing the bearings.

2. **The pump guard** has the job of doing exactly what its name says it does. It is supposed to see that no foreign object gets into the pump.

The pump guard in a typical installation is placed between the tub and pump. The unit is usually made of plastic and can be removed for cleaning, if necessary. Keep in mind that the pump guard will trap large for-

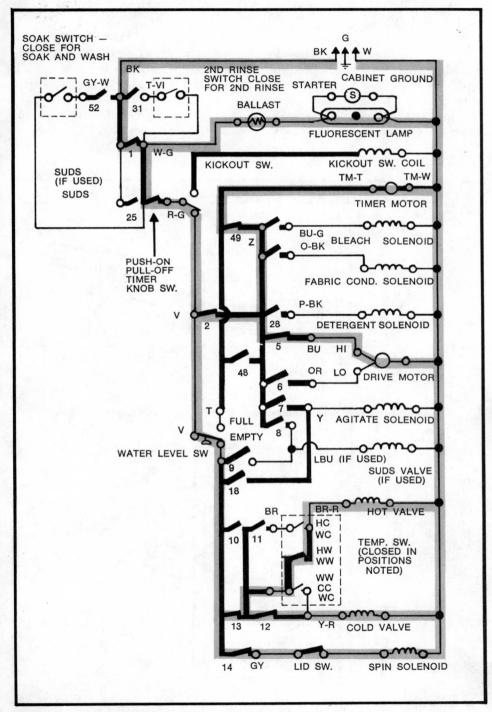

Figure 11. This is an example of a washing machine's wiring diagram. Refer to the illustration in chapter 25 for the meanings of the symbols.

eign objects, but it may not be successful in blocking the passage of smaller things.

There's another fact to remember regarding pump guards. Suppose suddenly your washing machine doesn't drain completely. One common cause for this is that the vent hole in the pump guard clogs up, which causes an air lock. The pump guard should be removed and this bleed hole cleaned.

3. **The water (mixing) valve** has the task of letting water into the tub (Figure 8). In this, it is assisted by solenoids.

The water valve of a typical automatic washing machine has two in-

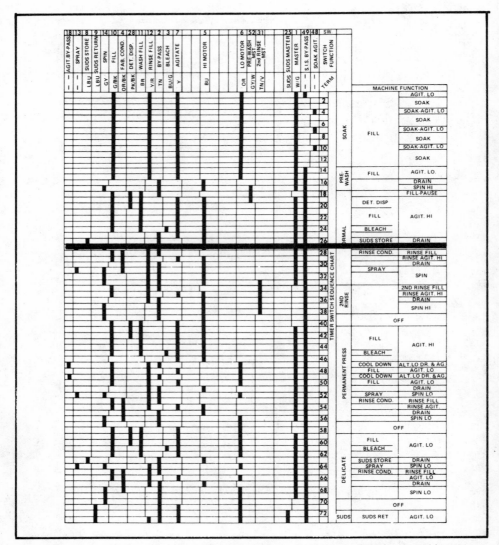

Figure 12. Accompanying the wiring diagram which is glued to the chassis of washing machines is a chart that looks like this. It is a timer cam chart.

lets. One is connected by hose to a hot-water faucet, and the other is connected by hose to a cold-water faucet (Figure 9). This permits the selection of three water temperatures: hot, cold, and warm.

Important: It is important to stress something that has been implied throughout this chapter. We are dealing here with a *typical* washing machine, but there are several variations. For example, we discuss what occurs in a water valve controlled by two solenoids. However, some washing machines are equipped with a single-solenoid valve, while others have three valves. Nevertheless, the principles involved are basically the same for all.

In a washing machine in which the selection of three water temperatures is possible, one solenoid controls the cold-water inlet of the water valve and another solenoid controls the hot-water inlet. When both solenoids are energized, both cold-water and hot-water inlets are open, permitting cold water and hot water to flow together and provide warm water.

To obtain the desired water temperature in a typical washing machine, the user operates a water-temperature control on the panel of the appliance. The knob (or pushbutton, or whatever) is turned to either "cold," "hot," or "warm." What this does is set a switch which will activate the particular solenoid(s) when the machine is turned on.

When the timer knob is set and the machine is turned on, the switch closes and the solenoid(s) is activated. Remember what was said in the previous section about the makeup of a solenoid?

When the solenoid is activated, the core is pulled by the magnetic force created in the core of wire away from the water inlet of the valve. This un-

blocks the inlet, and water is allowed to flow into the machine. At the completion of the "Fill" phase, when water reaches the desired level, water activates another switch called the "water level switch" that deactivates the solenoid. Spring pressure causes the core to close over the water inlet, and water flow into the machine ceases.

The typical washing machine allows the user to select a water level —either low, medium, or high. All this does is determine at what point the water-level switch will deactivate the solenoid. The water-level switch in many cases is a pressure-type switch, which, as we pointed out before is controlled by a buildup of pressure on its diaphragm.

4. **A filter** that catches lint is part of most washing machines. Two basic types are in use: self-cleaning and manual-cleaning.

During the wash and rinse phases, water is drawn from the tub by the water pump through the filter where lint is filtered out. The water is then recirculated back into the tub.

Manual-cleaning filters come in various forms, but primarily either as stainless-steel screens or plastic material which has a series of bristles that trap lint. The plastic-type filter resembles a hair brush. Manual-cleaning filters are positioned in an accessible area and should be removed periodically by the operator for cleaning.

Self-cleaning filters, obviously enough, clean themselves. One type traps lint in a pebble- or marble-like assembly of plastic. This filter is cleaned out as the machine drains. Cleaning is accomplished by water reversing itself through the filter to flush the filter and carry lint out the drain pipe with the water.

5. **Hoses** are used to connect fau-

cets with the water-inlet valve so the washing machine can be filled. Other hoses are used to connect the various components of the water system— for example, the water pump to the drain discharge pipe.

Hoses seldom give problems, but if one fails and begins leaking only the hose size and type specified by the machine's manufacturer should be used as a replacement. Failure to do this will lead to complications.

For example, the hoses used for supplying hot and cold water to the water-inlet valve from faucets must withstand relatively high pressures. One manufacturer recommends that the hot-water hoses be able to withstand 600 pounds of pressure per square inch at 200° F, and that the cold-water hose be able to withstand a pressure of 80 pounds per square inch at 60° F.

In the hoses connecting the faucet to the water-inlet valve, the parts which give the most trouble are the small stainless-steel filter screens which are inserted inside the hoses' ferrules at the faucet end. In hard-water areas in particular, these filter screens can clog with calcium and restrict the flow of water into the machine.

An indication that this may be happening is a reduction in the flow of water or abnormal water temperature. For example, if you set the water-temperature control for warm water and get cold water, it indicates that the flow of hot water is being restricted.

To clean out filter screens, shut off the water and unscrew the brass ferrules. Carefully remove the washer in each ferrule and then the screen.

Clean the screen out in a commercial cleaning solvent, if possible. But if calcium deposits do not dissipate, replace the screen.

Take care in attaching the hose back on the water faucet, or for that matter onto the water-inlet valve if the hose had to be replaced. Avoid cross-threading and overtightening.

To tighten, run the ferrule up finger tight and turn on the water. If water drips from around the ferrule, turn the fitting slowly with a properly fitting wrench until the drip ceases.

A common problem afflicting water systems is premature siphoning of water from the machine. This is caused most often by an improper relationship between the drain hose leading from the pump and the so-called standpipe (water drain pipe). In most installations, the standpipe should be positioned higher than the tub.

However, if the installation is correct and siphoning action continues, ask a dealer who sells your make of machine whether the manufacturer has issued an anti-siphon kit. With some machines, siphoning is a common problem that can be corrected by installing one of these kits.

Caution: The water-inlet valve is not immune to failure. It is possible for the valve to open up and let water flow into the machine although the machine is not in use. Because of this possibility, the faucets serving washing machines are usually outfitted with a shut-off valve(s). Whenever the washing machine is not being used, this valve(s) should be closed. Otherwise you may return from a day's outing to discover a laundry room flooded with water.

all about motors and transmissions

IN ADDITION TO control devices and a water system, a washing machine possesses a mechanical system.

This consists of several components, but the major ones are the motor and transmission.

Drive motors used in washing machines may be one-, two-, or three-speed. Almost always they are ½-horsepower, 115-volt, 60-cycle, split-phase, single-extension-shaft devices.

Which doesn't mean too much to the average person. Really, though, the one important thing to keep in mind about the motor is that it has the job of driving, via drive belts, other components, such as the transmission and water pump. If the motor burns out, which rarely happens, judge the cost of replacement against the age of the machine and the cost of a new machine. The motor and transmission are the most expensive parts of an automatic clothes-washing machine.

The motor and transmission are connected together by means of a belt, and the transmission (or gearcase assembly) drives the agitator—first in one direction and then in the other (Figure 10). The amount of travel that the agitator moves in each direction, and the number of oscillations it makes in a minute are determined by the design of the gears, the size of the pulley, and the motor speed. A "normal"-stroke gearcase is considered to be one that drives the agitator in a 195° arc at about 70 oscillations per minute.

In the typical agitator-type washing machine, the gears in the gearcase are driven by a large pulley that is screwed to the gearcase housing. The transmission possesses several braking and clutching devices that allow disconnecting of one set of gears and the meshing of others. Thus, the agitator oscillates during one phase of a cycle. The gears causing oscillations are then disconnected. This allows the tub to spin and water to drain during another phase.

As with a motor, the transmission will seldom fail, but if it does, cost of repair and cost of replacement of the machine should be compared.

some hints and tips concerning washing-machine repair

IF YOU ARE GOING to get involved in doing more than cursory repair, you should know how to read a schematic wiring diagram (see Chapter 25). This diagram should be glued somewhere on the machine's chassis. It possesses a number of symbols that may be foreign to you, but which you have to understand if the diagram is to be used for what it's meant: as a "road map" to repair (Figure 11).

The troubleshooting charts provided in this chapter will allow you to determine what can cause the various washing-machine failures and what actions must be taken to overcome them. The only repair we wish to emphasize right now is testing the timer. You do it in the following manner:

1. Turn the timer dial slowly from the "off" position to the place in the cycle where the machine is not working normally. Count the number of increments (clicks) it takes to arrive at this point.

2. Count the corresponding number of increments on the timer cam chart which is usually included as part of the wiring diagram (Figure 12). The chart will then tell you the terminals of which switch should have been activated at the particular spot on the dial.

3. Remove the panel which reveals the timer (Figure 13). Connect a 115-volt test light to the terminals determined by counting clicks and turn on the machine. If the test light fails to glow, the timer is faulty at this one

spot, but that doesn't matter. The whole unit should be replaced. If the test light glows, then the cause of the trouble is elsewhere in the circuit.

troubleshooting and repairing automatic clothes washers

THE CHARTS BELOW outline the problems you may encounter with your automatic clothes washer, how to troubleshoot them, and then how to repair the cause. Procedures proceed from the most likely (or easiest to fix) cause of trouble to the least likely (or most difficult).

Cautions: The combination of water and electricity can be lethal. In doing troubleshooting and repairs, where necessary, be sure to pull the line-cord plug from the wall outlet before doing the procedure; then reconnect the line cord if you need electricity, but keep as far away from electrical danger as possible.

So there can be no mistake when it comes to safe practices, here is a list of precautions that should be followed:

1. Make sure that electricity is turned off before you handle components.

2. Shut off water valves when you have to work on components that carry water, such as the water-inlet valve.

3. Before you replace an electrical part that you have diagnosed as being faulty, see if a loose connection is causing the problem instead.

4. After you replace an electrical component, make sure that the terminals are tightened.

5. Before reconnecting electrical service to the washing machine, check to see that ground wires are connected and tightly secured.

6. Make sure that water connections are secure. If they aren't, water will leak.

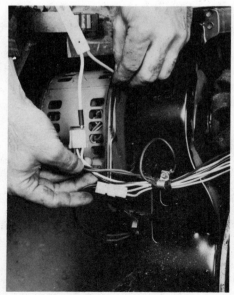

Figure 13. The control panel on a washing machine can be removed and a testlight used to find a faulty timer or switch.

Figure 14. Filter screens are found both in hose ferrules and at water valve inlet as seen here. Screens may need cleaning.

Problem	Causes	Procedure
Clothes washer fails to fill with water	1. Water faucet(s) is closed	1. Open faucet(s).
	2. Water hoses are kinked	2. Straighten the hoses. If the hoses won't stay straight, replace them with new ones.
	3. Clogged water screens	3. Remove the screens as described in the text, and flush out sediment or replace them (Figure 14).
	4. Damaged water-valve solenoid	4. Find the water-valve solenoid(s) and remove its leads. Connect a 115-volt test light across its terminals, turn on electricity, and move the control knob to "Fill." If the light does not glow, the solenoid is faulty, Replace it.
	5. Defective timer	5. Test the timer as was described in the text above.
	6. Defective water-temperature switch	6. Locate the switch by consulting the wiring diagram. Remove its leads and connect a 115-volt test light across its terminals. Turn on the electricity and move the control knob to "Fill." If the light does not glow, the switch is bad. Replace it.
	7. Defective water-level pressure switch	7. Locate the switch by consulting the wiring diagram. This switch usually has three terminals. With the washing machine set in "Fill" position, there is contact between two of the terminals—the third terminal is "open." Make sure you determine which terminals are active with the control dial in "Fill" and connect a test light (115-volt) across these two. Turn on the electricity and move the control knob to "Fill." Failure of the light to glow means that the switch is bad. Replace.
	8. Water-inlet valve has an internal malfunction	8. Remove the valve from the washing machine and take it apart. Examine each part for damage, but pay particular attention to the guide assembly and diaphragm. Replace a bad part if you can get a

Problem	Causes	Procedure
		replacement. If not, replace the water-inlet valve.
	9. Open circuit	9. With the control knob in the "Fill" position, and using the wiring diagram as a guide, probe each wire connection with a 115-volt test light to determine if a loose connection or bad wire is the cause of the trouble.
Clothes washer fails to drain	1. The drain hose is kinked or clogged	1. Straighten it out (or replace it); clean it out.
	2. The drain is clogged	2. Clean out the drain.
	3. Broken or slipping pump drive belt	3. Replace or tighten the drive belt.
	4. Defective water pump	4. Remove the pump from the machine and first test its bearings for easy revolving. If the bearings are frozen, replace the pump. If not, take the pump apart and check for an obstruction or a bad impeller. If you can get a replacement impeller, replace the bad one. If not, the pump probably will have to be replaced.
	5. Defective timer	5. Test the timer as was described in the text above.
	6. Open circuit	6. Test the circuit as described under "Clothes washer fails to fill with water," but make sure the control knob is in the "Drain" position.
Clothes washer fails to agitate	1. Broken or slipping drive belt (motor-to-transmission)	1. Replace or tighten the drive belt.
	2. Defective drive clutch	2. Take off the drive belt and turn the clutch by hand, but make sure the control knob is in the "Wash" (agitate) position. If the clutch doesn't hold (grab), it is defective and should be replaced.
	3. Defective transmission	3. Disconnect the drive belt and rotate the transmission pulley by hand in the direction of agitation, which is usually clockwise. Make sure the

Problem	Causes	Procedure
		control knob is in the "Wash" (agitate) position. If this action doesn't drive the agitator, there is a malfunction in the transmission. To check on this, you should consult a professional unless you are knowledgeable about automatic clothes-washer transmissions.
	4. Defective timer	4. Test the timer as was described in the text above.
	5. Defective water-level pressure switch	5. When water has filled the tub, contact reverts to the third terminal of this switch and to one of the other two terminals (see above under "clothes washer fails to fill with water." Connect the test light to the proper terminals and check this switch in the same manner as above, except turn the control knob to "Wash" (agitate) position.
	6. Open circuit	6. Test the circuit as described above under "clothes washer fails to fill with water," but make sure that the control knob is set at the "Wash" position.
Clothes washer fails to spin or spins too slowly	1. Broken or slipping drive belt (motor-to-spin pulley)	1. Replace or tighten the drive belt.
	2. Loose motor pulley	2. Tighten the pulley.
	3. Defective drive clutch	3. Test as described above under "Clothes washer fails to agitate," but make sure that the control knob is in the "Spin" position.
	4. Spin brake fails to release or transmission is frozen	4. The spin brake and transmission are separate units, but since they are attached and work together, they are inspected as a unit. Set the control knob to "Spin" position and remove the drive belt. Turn the brake stator. It should move freely, but if it doesn't, the brake assembly or transmission is defective. Both units should be taken apart by a professional for possible repair.
	5. Defective timer	5. Test the time as described in the text.

Problem	Causes	Procedure
	6. Open circuit	6. Test the circuit as described above under "Clothes washer fails to fill with water," but make sure the control knob is in the "Spin" position.
The motor won't run	1. Line cord is not plugged in	1. Check the line cord.
	2. Fuse is blown or circuit breaker has tripped	2. Check fuse or circuit breaker. If the problem recurs, there is an electrical malfunction that should be traced and repaired.
	3. Defective timer	3. Test the time as described in the text.
	4. Defective lid switch	4. Connect a 115-volt test light across the lid switch, close the door and turn the machine on. If the light fails to glow, replace the switch.
	5. Defective motor	5. Most motors are protected by an internal overload circuit breaker that halts operation if the motor overheats. If the circuit breaker stops motor operation, but the motor can be started again after about 30 minutes, consider the following: (a) If the motor trips off when the machine goes into the "Spin" cycle, the cause of the problem may be in the clutch, brake, or transmission—and not in the motor. Determine this by removing the drive belts and allowing the motor to operate. Now, if it does not trip off, the motor is in sound condition. Look elsewhere for the trouble. (b) If the motor operates in the "Wash" position, but will not operate in the "Spin" position, or vice versa, check the timer and the lid switch, and look for broken wires, before concluding that the motor has gone bad.
	6. Open circuit	6. Test the circuit as described above. Do this before you take the motor out of the washing machine.

Chapter 28

Dishwashers

In most cases, a problem with a dishwasher is not the fault of the machine. However, if a mechanical or electrical malfunction hits your unit, the information in this chapter will help you cope.

THE BIGGEST COMPLAINT that people have against their dishwashers is that dishes fail to get clean. In practically every case, this is caused by incorrect stacking of dishes, the use of a non-dishwasher detergent or an old detergent, water temperature not hot enough for thorough cleanliness, or improper preparation of dishes prior to washing.

But of course dishwashers can fail because of a mechanical or electrical reason. There are certain definite common malfunctions, and no esoteric causes, which means that troubleshooting a dishwasher is fairly cut-and-dried.

On the other hand, some dishwashers are not so simple to repair. It depends on the model of dishwasher you own, and how easy (or difficult) it is to get at working mechanisms.

Unfortunately, this book cannot be specific when it comes to disassembling a dishwasher to get inside. Models vary, so you will have to proceed by yourself in examining component layouts and determining how to get at the working parts. In some cases, you may have to slide the appliance from its position beneath a countertop.

Caution: Before going further into this discussion, heed one very urgent warning. A dishwasher uses both water and electricity, which is a combination that easily can kill you under certain circumstances.

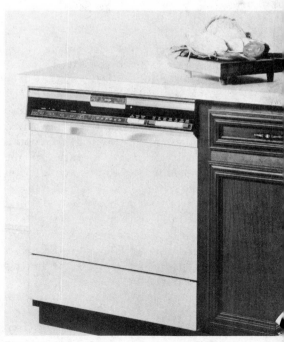

Figure 1. A dishwasher performs four basic functions: fills with water, washes, lets water drain off, and dries dishes.

Figure 2. Replacement of front panels enables some dishwashers to be fitted into various kitchen decorative schemes.

Thus, before you so much as remove a screw from your unit, turn off the electricity to the machine. This can be done by finding the fuse or circuit breaker in the home's main fuse box which services the dishwasher, and opening the circuit at this point.

When you have to turn off the water—suppose, for example, you have to "break" a water line to replace a valve—probably you will find a shut-off valve on the water inlet leading to the machine. Turn it off. If you find no water shut-off valve, you can always turn off the home's main water valve.

Portable dishwashers, naturally, are easier to disconnect. To turn off electricity, simply pull the line cord from the wall outlet. To turn off the water, just disconnect the water line from the sink tap.

a dishwasher is a simple machine

DESPITE ITS SIZE and the variations from model to model, a dishwasher *is* a simple machine (Figures 1 and 2). Understanding how it functions will allow you to make accurate troubleshooting analyses.

The major parts of a dishwasher are one or more motors; an impeller, or one or more spray arms; a pump; a water-inlet valve; a water drain valve; a heating element; and a cup that holds detergent (Figure 3).

And a timer! The timer automatically controls every phase of the washing cycle. Basically it is an electric clock motor that runs at a constant speed.

The exact length of time it takes the timer to make a complete revolution dictates the exact time that the dishwasher functions. This time is built into the appliance by the arrangement of various gears, which in itself is not important to troubleshooting and repair.

But what is important is the fact that the timer possesses various terminals to which wires are attached. Wires are connected to various switches that control the on-off functioning of the different phases of a washing cycle (Figures 4 and 5).

Timers are extremely reliable devices, but they can go bad. When one does, a particular phase of a cycle, or the entire cycle itself, will not take place.

Because of its general reliability, however, a timer is usually the last thing to check when troubleshooting. If you find it to be bad, the timer must be replaced. You cannot repair it.

Figure 3. Illustrated at right are the basic parts of a typical dishwasher. There are also top-loading dishwashers.

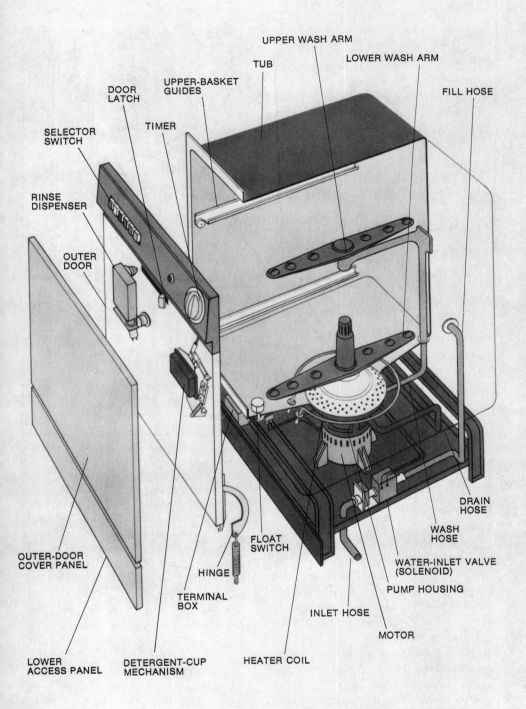

UPPER WASH ARM

TUB

LOWER WASH ARM

FILL HOSE

DOOR
LATCH

UPPER-BASKET
GUIDES

TIMER

SELECTOR
SWITCH

RINSE
DISPENSER

OUTER
DOOR

OUTER-DOOR
COVER PANEL

HINGE

FLOAT
SWITCH

TERMINAL
BOX

DRAIN
HOSE

WASH
HOSE

WATER-INLET VALVE
(SOLENOID)

PUMP HOUSING

INLET HOSE

MOTOR

LOWER
ACCESS PANEL

DETERGENT-CUP
MECHANISM

HEATER COIL

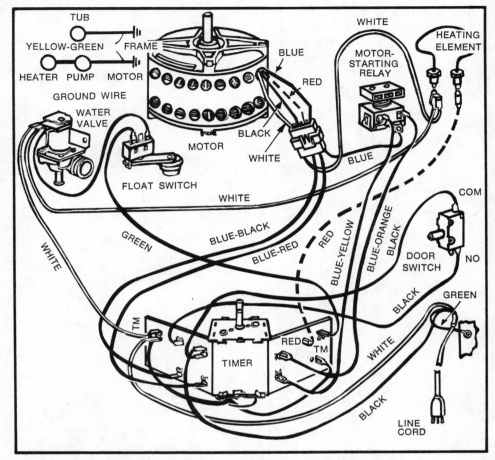

Figure 4. The timer is the device that controls functions. This drawing will give you an idea of how the timer is connected to the various components.

the cycle goes 'round and 'round

THE TYPICAL CYCLE of a dishwasher includes an initial draining, filling, first washing, draining, initial rinsing, second washing, draining, two or more rinsings, and drying (Figure 6). Not every dishwasher engages in every one of these functions, but they all engage in some, so let's discuss each one so you will understand whatever happens. Throughout the discussion, keep in mind that the timer controls the on-off phase of each function.

1. **Initial draining.** When you turn

on a unit, there is a brief period (of less than one minute) when the drain valve opens and the pump operates to drain whatever water may be left in the machine from the last washing.

2. **Filling.** The drain valve closes, the pump shuts off, and the water-inlet valve in the hot-water line opens (Figure 7). Water enters the tub. During this phase, the motor (or motors) is not operating.

The water-inlet valve remains open for the length of time set for it by the timer. This is very important to remember. The amount of water that eventually enters the tub depends not

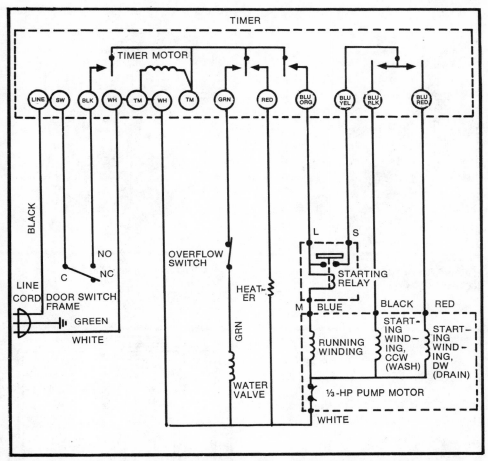

Figure 5. This is a typical wiring diagram for a typical dishwasher. Such a diagram is very helpful to you when you are troubleshooting electrical components.

only on the amount of time that the valve remains open, which is constant, but on the water pressure in your home.

If the water pressure is too great, there is a possibility that too much water can enter the tub and leak from around the door. Most manufacturers install a float valve in series with the water-inlet valve to keep this from happening. When water reaches the permissible high mark, the float valve closes and is strong enough to prevent water from entering the tub although the water-inlet valve may still be open. But what if the float

valve fails, which may happen? This is an important point to consider if you should find water on the floor.

3. **First washing.** The water-inlet valve closes. The way in which the washing phase takes place depends on whether the dishwasher is equipped with an impeller or spray arm(s).

An impeller resembles an agitator in a clothes washer, but it is driven with much greater force, and it revolves rather than oscillates. In a dishwasher that uses an impeller, usually there is only one motor. It is a "common" unit in that it drives not

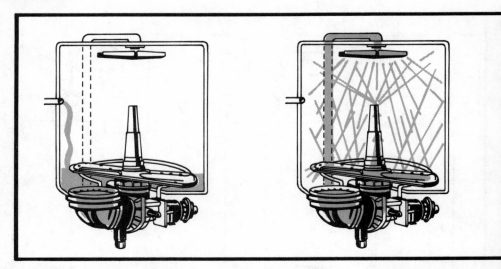

Figure 6. The diagrams above and on the next page each illustrate one of the four basic functions of a dishwasher—from left to right: filling, washing, draining, drying.

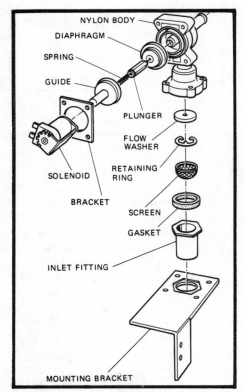

NYLON BODY

DIAPHRAGM

SPRING

GUIDE

PLUNGER

FLOW WASHER

RETAINING RING

SOLENOID

SCREEN

BRACKET

GASKET

INLET FITTING

MOUNTING BRACKET

Figure 7. This drawing shows the makeup of the water inlet valve. Refer to it if you need to repair the valve.

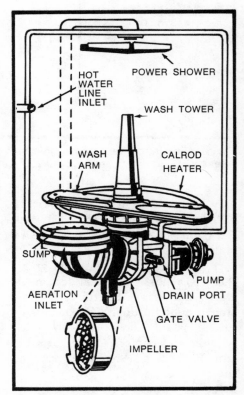

POWER SHOWER

HOT WATER LINE INLET

WASH TOWER

WASH ARM

CALROD HEATER

SUMP

AERATION INLET

PUMP

DRAIN PORT

GATE VALVE

IMPELLER

Figure 8. This view of the driving components of a dishwasher shows the relation of one part to another.

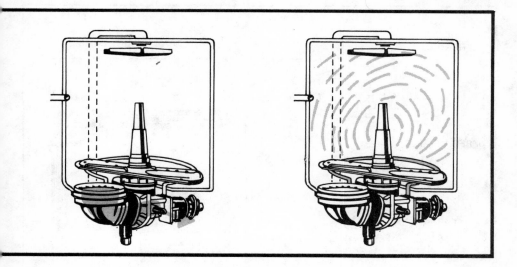

only the impeller, but also the drain pump.

The motors in dishwashers in most cases are split-phase units although some use shaded-pole motors.

In an impeller-equipped dishwasher, the amount of hot water permitted to enter the tub is sufficient to rise above the top of the impeller. The impeller is driven with great force to throw water up onto the dishes and clean food particles from them. As the water is circulated, it mixes with detergent.

The detergent function of a typical dishwasher is interesting to note. In most models, there are actually two phases.

Detergent used during the first washing is the detergent not normally placed in the detergent cup that has the spring-loaded cover. It is the detergent put into the open cup (or similar device). The second phase of detergent action, as you will see soon, takes place during the second washing. This phase uses the detergent that is placed in the cup that has the spring-loaded cover.

In a dishwasher that has a spray arm (or spray arms), the amount of hot water permitted to enter the tub usually is kept below the top of the spray arm in the base of the tub. Some dishwashers also have a spray arm in the top of the tub. In these, sufficient hot water enters the tub to permit both arms to do an adequate job.

A dishwasher equipped with a spray arm(s) usually has two motors. One motor drives the spray arm and the pump which permits wash water to recirculate (Figures 8 and 9). The other motor, which drives the drain pump, is at rest during the washing phase (Figure 10).

The recirculating pump drives water up the spray arm and out the holes in the arm. These holes are offset to each other so that the force of the water being ejected from them causes the spray arm to revolve, spraying water with great force over the entire interior of the tub.

In both impeller and spray-arm-equipped dishwashers, the initial washing phase takes five or six minutes.

4. **Draining.** After the timer signals that the initial washing phase is complete, the impeller or recirculating

dishwashers

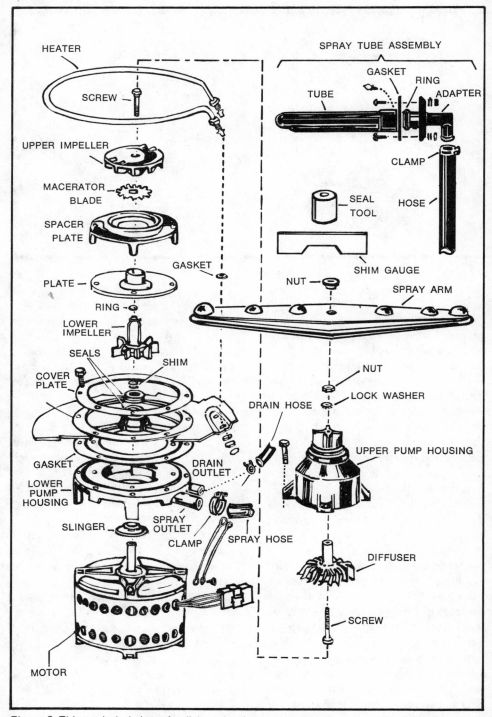

Figure 9. This exploded view of a dishwasher is presented to give you an idea of how to take the driving elements apart if you need to do so.

pump shuts off and the water drain valve opens. The motor that drives the drain pump switches on, and water drains from the tub.

5. **Initial rinsing.** The drain valve closes, and the water-inlet valve opens. Clean hot water fills the interior of the unit, but there is no detergent for it to mix with. The detergent in the open cup has been used and has drained, and that in the sealed cup is still not permitted to enter the tub.

When the tub has filled, the water-inlet valve closes, and the hot water is impelled or sprayed over the dishes as it was during the initial washing step. This first rinsing lasts for from three to five minutes. When the period has elapsed, draining occurs.

6. **Second washing.** The only difference between the first washing phase and this second washing is the length of time. At the beginning of this washing step, the sealed detergent cup springs open and introduces fresh detergent into the machine. This washing step can last as long as 15 minutes, with the exact time varying from one model to another. At its conclusion, draining takes place as before, followed by two or more fresh-water rinses as before.

By two or more "fresh-water rinses," I mean that at the conclusion of each rinse, water drains from the tub and fresh water for another rinsing is introduced.

7. **Drying.** With all water now drained from the dishwasher, and dishes clean, the timer switches on the heating element. This element is the same nichrome-wire unit used in appliances such as space heaters. However, there is a difference.

In other appliances, the nichrome-wire element is an exposed unit. In a dishwasher, the nichrome-wire element is insulated with a metal sheath.

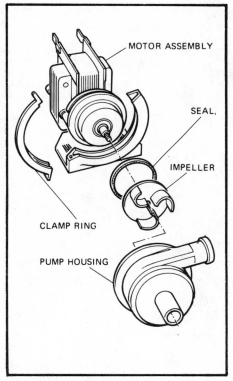

Figure 10. The drain pump of a spray-arm dishwasher has its own small motor. It is not used during the washing phase.

MOTOR ASSEMBLY

SEAL

IMPELLER

CLAMP RING

PUMP HOUSING

This is necessary because the nichrome wire would otherwise be exposed to water.

You may have heard the term "Calrod." This is a trade name for one type of insulated nichrome-wire heating element. Insulated nichrome-wire heating elements are used not only in dishwashers, but also in electric ranges, table ovens, and other appliances.

The heating element in a dishwasher is replaceable. Usually it is connected to its terminals by screwoff bolts. If you have to replace a heating element that has burned out, make sure the replacement has the same electrical rating and is the same size as the damaged unit.

The drying phase lasts 10 to 20 minutes.

You should be aware of one more point regarding dishwasher operation. Most dishwashers, especially built-in

Problem	Causes	Procedure
Dishwasher fails to go on	1. Door is not locked	1. Open the door and lock it again, making sure it is shut and the latch handle is pushed all the way to "start".
	2. Cycle-selector button is not fully depressed	2. Make sure the desired cycle button is pushed in all the way.
	3. Electric failure	3. Check the fuse or circuit breaker of the circuit servicing the dishwasher. If the circuit breaker keeps tripping or the fuse keeps blowing, you probably have a malfunction in the home's electric wiring. If the dishwasher is a portable model, determine if the failure is caused by a faulty line cord. Also make sure that the wall outlet is "live".
	4. Defective door switch	4. If there is a button on the doorway, press it. You should hear an audible "click." If not, replace the switch. Some models have the switch beneath the lower-access panel doorway. Remove the panel and latch the door to see if this switch is activated.
	5. Wires have come loose or are parted from terminals	5. This is possible in time, because a certain amount of vibration is created when a dishwasher operates. Check all wire terminals to see that they are tightly capped or taped. Most dishwashers have wires terminating at a junction box. This may be beneath the door panel or

models that have front-opening doors, are equipped with interlock switches in their handles. Such a switch shuts off the appliance if the door is opened.

let's troubleshoot

THE CHARTS BELOW will lead you through troubleshooting procedures for problems that hamper dishwashers. The procedures take you from the most likely (or easiest to check) cause of trouble to the least likely (or most difficult).

Incidentally, manufacturers place a wiring diagram somewhere on the chassis of the particular dishwasher or in the instruction manual that comes with the unit. This diagram is a big help in locating parts and figuring out the wiring setup. If you don't have a wiring diagram, write the manufacturer for one, but be sure to tell him which model you have.

Problem	Causes	Procedure
		beneath the lower access panel. Generally, both panels can be unscrewed and removed.
	6. Defective timer	6. You can check the timer for continuity, but if the trouble has not been uncovered up until this point, usually you can assume that the timer is bad.
Dishes do not get clean	1. The water is not hot enough	1. Check water temperature at a hot-water tap with a thermometer. The temperature should be 140°–160°F. If the temperature is too low, raise it if possible by increasing the setting on the thermostat of your hot-water heater. If you live in an apartment where you have no control over water temperature, you will have to complain to the janitor.
	2. Dishes not properly prepared	2. Some foodstuffs, such as cooked egg, are not soluble in hot water. These should be rinsed from dishes before they are placed in the dishwasher. It is also a good practice to scrape particles of food from dishes prior to placing them in the unit. If your appliance is equipped with a filter screen that catches food particles, see that it is clean.
	3. Dishes not stacked correctly	3. Dishes should face the direction of spray for thorough cleaning. See that they don't touch each other. Proper spacing assures that water will spread itself over the whole

Problem	Causes	Procedure
		dish. Make sure that no dish blocks the detergent from the water.
	4. Insufficient detergent, old detergent or the wrong kind of detergent	4. Use only an approved dishwasher detergent. Detergents for clothes washers won't work. Detergent that has been kept too long loses potency. Use fresh detergent. If you live in an area that has "hard" water, you will probably have to use more detergent than otherwise.
	5. Spray arm is blocked	5. Check to see if a dish or utensil is preventing spray-arm movement.
	6. No water in tub	6. See below under "dishwasher fails to fill".
Dishwasher fails to fill	1. Defective water-valve solenoid or water valve	1. Use the wiring diagram to locate the water-inlet valve and solenoid. Manually turn the timer to "Fill" position and check voltage at the solenoid terminals with a 115-volt test light or voltmeter. If there is no voltage, check the wiring and the source of electricity. If there is voltage, but the water valve does not open, replace the solenoid or the valve assembly. The valve and solenoid may be an integral unit, and you may not be able to replace one without the other. If you do replace the solenoid only without response, replace the valve.
	2. Dirty water valve	2. Water-inlet valves usually are outfitted with filters that can get clogged with deposits. Clean and also check for foreign matter at the valve's diaphragm and pin.
	3. Defective float switch	3. In machines with float switches, if there is an interruption of current to the switch, the float may stay closed. Check for a loose wire. Lift up the float arm and let it drop. You should hear a definite click. If not, replace the float assembly.
	4. Defective timer	4. See above under "diswasher fails to go on".
Water doesn't shut off	1. Water-inlet valve is stuck open	1. Disassemble and clean, or replace the water-inlet valve.
	2. Timer is defective	2. The timer does not advance off the

Problem	Causes	Procedure
		"Fill" phase, which lasts about one minute normally. If there is no advancement (you can tell by watching the timer dial), replace the timer.
	3. Defective float switch	3. See above under "dishwasher fails to fill," except now the float is stuck in the open position.
Water doesn't drain	1. Drain hose kinked or clogged	1. Look for bends and straighten them. If the hose won't stay straight, buy a helical spring which is a bit larger than the outer diameter of the hose and place it around the hose to keep it straight. If the hose is straight, disconnect and blow through it to see that it is clear.
	2. Pump motor defective	2. Advance the timer to the "Drain" phase. If the motor hums, disassemble the pump and look for obstructions that are hampering impeller operation. If vanes of the impeller are broken off, replace the part. But if the impeller moves freely and is in good condition, the pump motor winding is defective, and the motor should be replaced.
	3. Timer sticks in "Wash" phase	3. If the timer doesn't advance from the "Wash" to the "Drain" phase, the timer is defective and should be replaced.
Detergent-cup lid fails to spring open	1. Dish or utensil is blocking the lid	1. Make sure dishes and utensils are positioned so they can't possibly jam against the detergent-cup lid.
	2. Detergent put into a wet cup or left in the cup too long	2. The cup should be dry when the detergent is put into it, because the detergent will harden in a wet cup and may cause the lid to jam. If the detergent remains in the cup for too long a period, it may cake.
	3. Hard-water deposits (calcium) are hampering lid operation	3. Clean the cup and lid with vinegar.
	4. Detergent-cup lid solenoid valve is defective	4. Consult the wiring diagram and locate the solenoid. Place a continuity tester across the solenoid

Problem	Causes	Procedure
		terminals and advance the timer through the appropriate "Fill" phase during which the lid is supposed to open. If you get light, the solenoid is stuck and should be replaced. If you don't get light, there is a defect in the circuit leading to the solenoid.
	5. Timer defective	5. See above under "dishwasher fails to go on".
Dishes do not dry	1. Improper placement	1. Air space should be left around the dishes to permit free passage of heat.
	2. Calcium deposits have built up on heating element	2. Examine the element and clean off deposits with vinegar.
	3. A wire has come loose from the heating element	3. Be sure wires are tightly attached.
	4. Heating element has burned out	4. Test the element for continuity by placing a tester across its terminals. If there is continuity, the element has failed. Replace it.
Dishwasher leaks water	1. Defective or mis-positioned door gasket	1. See that the gasket is properly clipped to the door. If it is flattened or torn, replace it.
	2. Broken door hinges	2. Replace.
	3. Door out of alignment	3. Loosen door hinges and readjust the door so it fits tightly.
	4. Defective pump-motor seal	4. Check around pump motor for evidence of leaks (rust, calcium). If the motor is leaking, replace the motor seal.
	5. Loose hose clamps	5. Check around the hoses for signs of leakage. If the hose clamp is loose, tighten—if deformed, replace. If the hose is split, replace.
	6. Loose heating-element fasteners	6. Check the heating element for tightness—water can leak around a loose fastener and drip onto floor. Tighten.
	7. Defective float	7. See above under "dishwasher fails to fill".

Chapter 29

Room air conditioners

Room air conditioners frequently are difficult or impossible for the home handyman to repair, and central air conditioning systems are even more so. But here's help with several malfunctions that you can fix.

TO BE HONEST about it, repairing a room air conditioner (Figures 1 and 2) is not easy. If a problem requiring discharging the unit occurs, as is often the case, the home handyman probably would be at a loss since special tools are needed. These tools permit the system to be discharged so repairs can be made, and then vacuumed prior to recharging.

It really doesn't pay to buy these tools unless you are going into the air-conditioner repair business. They are expensive, and for what they cost, you could pay a professional for many repair jobs.

However, failures are not always major ones. Sometimes a malfunction occurs which is within the scope of the home handyman. Even if you can't fix the trouble, it's nice to have an idea of what is wrong when dealing with a serviceman. That is what this chapter will give you—a way to repair the trouble if it's within your capability and/or information that will let you know what is causing your problem.

To understand what can go wrong, you have to understand what makes an air conditioner tick. The principles discussed here apply to any air conditioner—room, central or automobile.

Figure 1. Above is a standard-size room air conditioner.

Figure 2. Below is a small unit for a small space. Excess capacity wastes money.

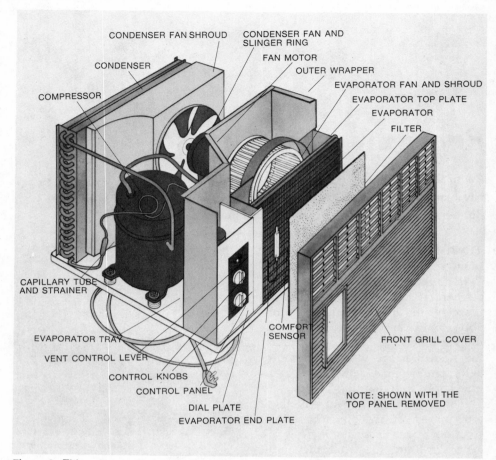

CONDENSER FAN SHROUD
CONDENSER FAN AND SLINGER RING
CONDENSER
FAN MOTOR
OUTER WRAPPER
COMPRESSOR
EVAPORATOR FAN AND SHROUD
EVAPORATOR TOP PLATE
EVAPORATOR
FILTER
CAPILLARY TUBE AND STRAINER
EVAPORATOR TRAY
COMFORT SENSOR
FRONT GRILL COVER
VENT CONTROL LEVER
CONTROL KNOBS
CONTROL PANEL
DIAL PLATE
EVAPORATOR END PLATE
NOTE: SHOWN WITH THE TOP PANEL REMOVED

Figure 3. This cutaway shows you the various components of a typical room air conditioner. The trouble with air conditioners is that special expensive tools are needed to repair them.

how an air conditioner operates

AN AIR CONDITIONER not only cools. It also removes moisture from the air, filters out dirt, and circulates air. The result is a room, rooms or a car that is cool, comfortable, and relatively dust-free on hot, humid days.

The typical air conditioner consists of several major components, including a compressor, condenser, evaporator, and expansion valve (Figure 3). An air conditioner works on the principle of evaporation. Evaporation is a process that creates "coolness" by changing a liquid into a vapor and vapor back into a liquid (Figure 4).

In an air conditioner (and refrigerator and home freezer, too) the fluid that does this chameleon act is called *refrigerant*. One trade name that has become synonymous with the generic term is Freon.

Refrigerant is contained totally inside the air-conditioning circuit. This is a completely sealed unit—at least, it should be. If the circuit should spring a leak around, say, a fitting, the air conditioner will lose its refrigerant, and with it its ability to cool. This is a common problem.

When refrigerant absorbs heat, its boiling point is exceeded, and it reverts to vapor form. When the va-

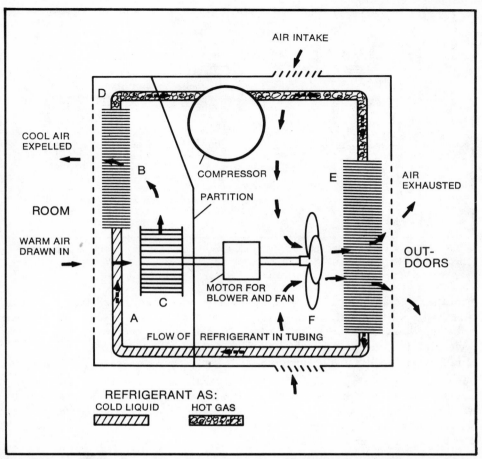

Figure 4. In air conditioner, 45° refrigerant (A) chills evaporating coils (B) which absorb heat from room air drawn in by blower (C). Heat from room air and pressure action of compressor make refrigerant boil (D). It flows into condenser coils (E) where it expands, causing gas to lose heat to air blown outdoors by fan (F). Cooled refrigerant recycles.

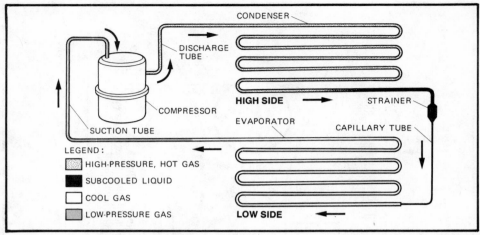

Figure 5. Vapor/refrigerant cycle is the same for air conditioners, refrigerators, freezers. The amount of refrigerant used controls the temperature.

orized refrigerant gives off heat, it changes back to a liquid. This process is called the vapor (or refrigerant) cycle, and it is the basis on which air conditioners work (as do refrigerators and home freezers) (Figure 5).

Let's start at the compressor, which is merely a pump that circulates refrigerant through the system (Figures 6 and 7). The outlet side of the compressor is the high-pressure side of the system. The inlet side of the compressor is the low-pressure side.

The compressor is run by a built-in electric (capacitor-start) motor. A capacitor-start motor, which is discussed in detail in the chapter on garbage disposers (see Index) is basically a split-phase motor to which a capacitor has been added. The capacitor is wired in series with the starting coil to provide more torque for starting under a heavy load.

The motor permits the refrigerant to circulate through the various valves and galleries of the compressor and through the tubes of the system. When it leaves the compressor under high pressure, the temperature of the vaporized refrigerant is about 210° F.

The hot gas is forced from the compressor through a tube to the outside of the house where it enters the tubing of the condensor.

The job of the condenser is to do exactly what its name implies—to allow the gas to condense, thereby cooling down. Assisting the condenser in this task is a fan that blows air across the condenser coil.

This cooler air blown across the condenser by the fan drops the temperature of the vaporized refrigerant to about 115° F., which is sufficient to let the vaporized refrigerant revert to liquid form.

At 115° F., refrigerant even in liquid form is not able to cool any area except one exceeding 115° F. It is a law of physics that warm air travels toward a cooler area. To make a hot room cool, then, heat has to be drawn toward the coolness of the air conditioner, and when we speak of the coolness of the air conditioner we really mean the refrigerant. But at 115° F.?

To get the refrigerant to a temperature at which it will be an effective cooling agent—specifically, to about 45° F.—the liquid refrigerant leaving

the condenser is forced through a small pipe or capillary tube. Then it enters an expansion valve where it expands rapidly.

When a warm liquid is permitted to expand suddenly (when pressure on it is relieved), its temperature drops. Assisting the refrigerant in dropping its temperature even further is another fan that is blowing across the evaporator coil.

The liquid refrigerant enters the evaporator coil from the expansion valve at the lowest temperature it can

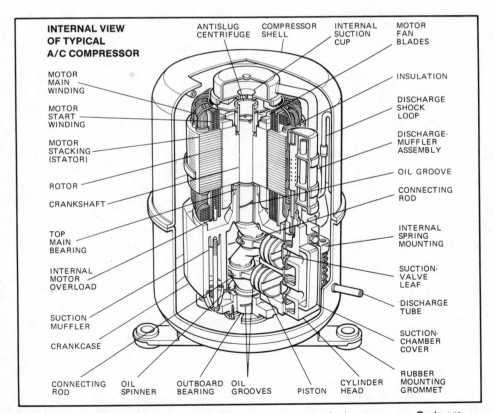

INTERNAL VIEW OF TYPICAL A/C COMPRESSOR

ANTISLUG CENTRIFUGE
COMPRESSOR SHELL
INTERNAL SUCTION CUP
MOTOR FAN BLADES

MOTOR MAIN WINDING
MOTOR START WINDING
MOTOR STACKING (STATOR)
ROTOR
CRANKSHAFT
TOP MAIN BEARING
INTERNAL MOTOR OVERLOAD
SUCTION MUFFLER
CRANKCASE

INSULATION
DISCHARGE SHOCK LOOP
DISCHARGE-MUFFLER ASSEMBLY
OIL GROOVE
CONNECTING ROD
INTERNAL SPRING MOUNTING
SUCTION-VALVE LEAF
DISCHARGE TUBE
SUCTION-CHAMBER COVER
RUBBER MOUNTING GROMMET

CONNECTING ROD
OIL SPINNER
OUTBOARD BEARING
OIL GROOVES
PISTON
CYLINDER HEAD

Figures 6, 7. Cutaway pictures show the interior parts of a typical compressor. Parts are the same for air conditioners, refrigerators, and freezers.

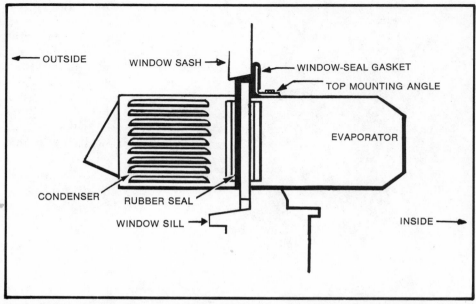

Figure 8. Room air conditioners should be sealed in properly to prevent air leakage, which reduces the efficiency of the unit and wastes energy.

attain, and the hot, humid air in the room moves toward it. The humidity of the air drops, and the air cools. The moisture that condenses on the evaporator coil is carried off by a drain tube and is ejected outside the house.

The liquid refrigerant absorbing all this heat gets very hot again and vaporizes. Back it goes to the compressor, and the whole cycle starts all over.

maintenance: a task for even the non-handyman

YOU MIGHT NOT BE ABLE to make air-conditioner repairs, but you can forestall breakdowns by taking care of your unit (Figure 8). The following maintenance procedures are suggested:

1. Keep the air filter clean (Figure 9). A dirty filter restricts the flow of air, reducing cooling efficiency and adding to the cost of operating the unit. An air conditioner has one of two types of filters: fiberglass or a permanent, germicidal sponge-type. Fiberglass filters should be replaced. The permanent-type filter may be washed in soapy water, rinsed in fresh water, and squeezed dry.

The U.S. General Services Administration recommends that air-conditioner filters be cleaned or changed once a month during the cooling season.

2. Every year, the air-conditioner compartment should be cleaned. The most complete way of doing this is to slide or remove the unit from its chassis so all parts can be reached.

There are two types of room air conditioner chassis. One type allows you to slide the unit out like a drawer. The other type requires that the unit be removed from its position in the window or wall.

With the system exposed, remove dirt and lint from the condensor and evaporator by vacuuming them. Wipe crusted dirt from the compressor, fan motor and blades, and tubing with a solvent such as trichloroethylene, which you can purchase in hardware stores or paint-supply stores.

Important: When you reinstall the unit, make sure that it is slightly tilted (⅛ to ¼ inch) toward the outside of the house. This angle is needed to allow condensate to drain.

3. Examine the outside case (which is usually metal) for rust every year or two. Scrape rust off with a putty knife and touch up the spot with a metal primer and paint.

4. Protect your air conditioner during winter by covering it with a dust-proof and moistureproof cover. A plastic sheet will do nicely. A cover keeps windblown dust from getting inside the unit, and helps to stop damage caused by snow and rain.

troubleshooting a room air conditioner

THE FOLLOWING CHART lists the most common room air-conditioner problems and their causes. It will assist you in deducing what might be wrong with your unit, and dealing with a serviceman if you have to consult one.

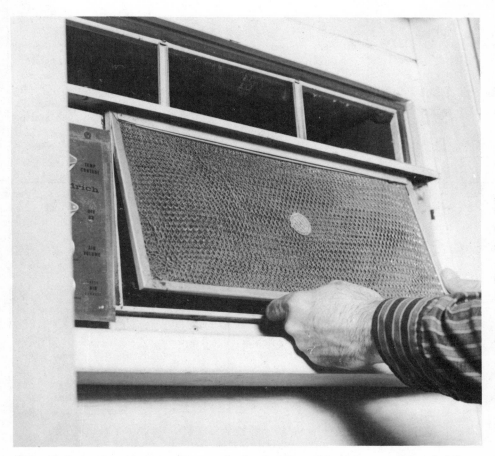

Figure 9. On most room air conditioners, the front of the unit has to come off to get at the filter. Keep filters clean. The work and money involved are less than having to make repairs.

Problem	Causes	Procedure
Air conditioner will not run at all	1. Blown fuse or tripped circuit breaker	1. Turn off the air conditioner. Replace the fuse or reactivate the circuit breaker. If the problem recurs, refer below to "air conditioner continually blows a fuse or trips its circuit breaker"
	2. Broken or loose wire connection	2. Make sure that the line-cord plug is tight in the wall socket. Examine the line-cord connections at the control (on-off) switch for tightness and integrity
	3. Thermostat is defective	3. Pull the line cord from the wall. Turn the temperature-control knob (thermostat) to "Cool" and check continuity across the thermostat terminals. If there is no continuity, replace the thermostat
	4. Starter capacitor is defective	4. Remove the control panel. Behind it you should find two capacitors (if not, consult the schematic wiring diagram for the unit). One is the starter capacitor; the other is the running capacitor. The starter capacitor is the smaller one. Wtih the line cord unplugged, remove the starter capacitor and replace it with one of the same rating
Fan runs, but the compressor does not	1. Thermostat is defective	1. Connect a jumper wire across the thermostat terminals, turn the thermostat (temperature control) to "High Cool" and switch the unit on. If the compressor now comes on, the thermostat is defective. Replace it
	2. Wiring is loose or broken	2. Examine all wiring and terminals. See that connections are clean and tight
	3. Overload switch is defective	3. The compressor is equipped with an overload switch that may be inside the component or attached outside. Test the switch for continuity. Lack of continuity indicates overload switch failure. Replace
	4. Running capacitor is defective	4. Find the running capacitor, which is usually behind the control panel. It's the larger of the two capaci-

Problem	Causes	Procedure
	5. Compressor is defective	tors. Unplug the line cord and replace the running capacitor with one of identical rating 5. If the air conditioner is a 117-volt unit, hook up the compressor directly to a power line for a *few* seconds. If the compressor fails to start, repair or replace it. Compressors serving 220-volt units have to be tested on a bench
Air conditioner continually blows a fuse or trips its circuit breaker	1. Incorrect operation	1. The unit is being restarted too soon after it's been running and has been shut off. You should allow about five minutes for system pressure to equalize before restarting an air conditioner
	2. Circuit is overloaded	2. The air conditioner should be on a line reserved for it alone. No other appliances or lights should be served by the line. Also make sure that the fuse in the main fuse box is of the proper rating as recommended in the instruction manual provided by the manufacturer
	3. Wiring is shorted or grounded against the frame	3. Examine all electric connections to the compressor and control panel. See that connections are tight and that no wire is exposed or touching any metal part
	4. Stuck or defective compressor	4. See above under "fan runs, but the compressor does not"
	5. Running capacitor is defective	5. See above under "fan runs, but the compressor does not"
Air conditioner does not cool	1. Thermostat is not set properly	1. Turn the thermostat to a cooler setting
	2. Air filter is dirty	2. Wash or replace the air filter
	3. Condenser is dirty and dirt in the chassis is hampering air flow	3. Vacuum out the unit and wash off parts with solvent
	4. Unit is undersized for job it's being asked to do	4. Replace with a unit that has the needed cooling capacity. Generally, a medium-sized bedroom requires an air conditioner with a capacity of 5000–6000 Btu/hr; a medium-

Problem	Causes	Procedure
		sized livingroom requires an air conditioner of 8000–12,000 Btu/hr; if several rooms are connected that you wish to cool, the air conditioner should have a 15,000–20,000 Btu/hr capacity. A valuable booklet that discusses how to choose the right air conditioner for your needs, as well as other topics, is "Room Air Conditioners." It is published by the U.S. General Services Administration and may be ordered from the Superintendent of Documents, U.S. Government Printing Office, Washington, D.C. 20402
	5. Compressor does not run	5. See above under "fan runs, but the compressor does not run"
	6. Air is leaking in from the outside	6. Caulk or seal all joints around the air conditioner. See that windows are shut and that drapes or furniture are not blocking the front grille
	7. Refrigerant is leaking	7. Slide out or remove the unit from the case. With the air conditioner running, carefully apply soapy solution to tubing and joints. Bubbles indicate a leak
Air conditioner cycles on and off too often (short cycling)	1. Improper operation	1. See above under "air conditioner continually blows a fuse or trips its circuit breaker"
	2. Thermostat is short cycling	2. The evaporator is probably dirty and should be cleaned. See that the thermostat sensing bulb is touching the evaporator and is tightly clamped against it
	3. Condenser is dirty	3. Clean the condenser fins. You should be able to see light through them.
	4. Condenser fan is not operating properly	4. Check the operation of the fan motor. If it gets hot and stops, replace the motor
	5. Overload switch is defective	5. See above under "fan runs, but the compressor does not"

Problem	Causes	Procedure
Evaporator builds up frost	1. Air flow over the evaporator is restricted 2. Thermostat is not set in relation to outside temperature 3. Refrigerant is leaking	1. See that the air filter is clean. Then clean off the evaporator and all parts inside the case 2. The critical temperature outdoors is 70°. If the temperature drops below this, turn the air conditioner off or operate it on "Low Cool" 3. See above under "air conditioner does not cool"
Air conditioner operates too noisily	1. Tubing is vibrating 2. Loose parts 3. Fan blades are loose on shaft or are bent	1. Tubing should not rub against other tubing or against other metal parts. Carefully bend tubing away from metal. 2. Tighten up all screws and bolts. See that the grille cover is tight. Pay particular attention to the fan motor, which may be loose on its mounts 3. With the air conditioner turned off, try to move the fan blades on their shaft. If the assembly moves back and forth (in and out) appreciably, motor bearings are probably worn and should be replaced. Make sure the blades are not hitting against another part
Compressor operates, but the fan does not run	1. Fan switch is defective 2. Fan capacitor is defective 3. Fan motor is defective	1. Disconnect the line cord and test the fan switch for continuity across its High, Medium and Low operating terminals. Refer to the schematic wiring diagram to find terminals. Replace the switch if it fails the test at any setting 2. The fan capacitor and the running capacitor are usually one and the same, but check the wiring diagram to be sure. Replace the capacitor with one of the same rating 3. The motor may be tested for continuity across each wiring terminal (High, Medium and Low). If no reading is obtained at any setting, replace the motor

room air conditioners

Problem	Causes	Procedure
Water drips from the air conditioner	1. Pitch is not correct	1. The unit should have a slight pitch toward the outside. Do not exceed a pitch of ¼-inch, however
	2. Drain holes are clogged	2. Clean out the drain holes
	3. Slinger ring is out of adjustment	3. Many units have a small ring on the condenser that slings water from the base pan. The clearance between the ring and the base pan should be 1/16 inch. If clearance is excessive, water pickup will be reduced

Chapter 30

Refrigerators and home freezers

These two appliances are essentially the same and in principle both resemble air conditioners. Although they are employed for different purposes, refrigerators and home freezers include basically the same components.

THE BASIC DIFFERENCE between a refrigerator and a home freezer is in their operating temperature, and the degree of operating temperature depends upon the amount of refrigerant which is being delivered to the unit (Figures 1 and 2). In refrigerators, obviously the amount is less than in comparably sized freezers. Since it possesses a greater charge of refrigerant, a home freezer can generate a lower temperature than the same size refrigerator.

The two, though, work on the same principle, and both operate like air conditioners. For this reason, I suggest you read the previous chapter to gain insight into functioning. This information will help you understand how and why a refrigerator or home freezer fails.

When it comes to repairs, the home handyman's role is a limited one. Lacking the tools necessary for discharging and recharging the refrigeration system, and for cutting and flaring tubing, you can only act against "exterior" causes of trouble.

However, knowing what can go wrong with a refrigerator and freezer, and understanding the possible causes will put you in a better position to deal with a professional serviceman.

refrigerator and freezer maintenance

DEPENDING ON THE KIND of units you possess, there are three things you can do to keep a refrigerator and freezer in good shape. These maintenance procedures will assure that the appliance operates at maximum efficiency and will help keep failure to a minimum:

1. Clean the condenser coils periodically if they are exposed. Dirt on an exposed condenser blocks circulation and drastically reduces refrigerating efficiency. You can use a long-handled bristle brush or vacuum cleaner (Figure 3).

2. If your model is non-self defrosting, defrost it regularly, especially in hot weather. Frost builds up on the evaporator coils twice as frequently in hot as in cold weather.

Defrost the refrigerator and/or freezer before the frost gets thick. Frost reduces the transfer of heat, which impairs the efficiency of the unit. Frost also traps and retains odors.

3. Try to keep the number of times that the refrigerator and freezer doors are open to a minimum, and reduce the length of time you keep doors

Figure 1. A typical refrigerator has a refrigerator food compartment below and a small freezer compartment above.

open. The more frequently doors are open, the faster frost builds up (Figure 4).

troubleshooting refrigerators and freezers (figure 5)

HOW FAR CAN YOU GO? That depends mostly on how far you feel confident in going. That is why the troubleshooting charts presented below are fairly detailed. At least, the list of possible causes for failure will give you a good idea of what a serviceman, if one is consulted, should check.

Keep in mind, though, that the home repairman is capable of doing some checking for himself. For ex-

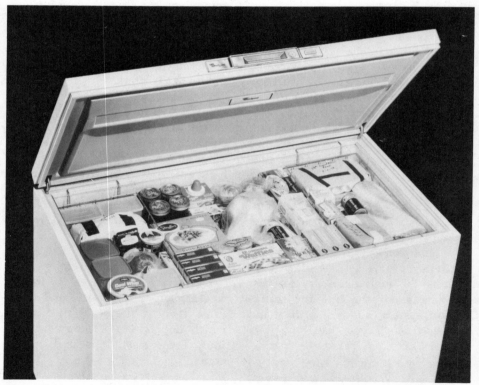

Figure 2. Home freezers are available in chest-type and upright models. Both work the same, and both work on the same principle as refrigerators and air conditioners.

ample, let's say the compressor in a unit runs continually or for unusually long periods, and the temperature inside the box rises. The major reason for this is that the refrigerant system is undercharged, and undercharging is most commonly the result of a leak.

To find a leak, look for oil stains at joints. You can determine where the leak exists by brushing a solution of soapy water over joints on the system's high side (that is, on the side containing the compressor, condenser and capillary) while the unit is running, and on joints on the low side (evaporator and suction line side) while the unit is idle. "Bubbly" soapy water signifies the area of leakage.

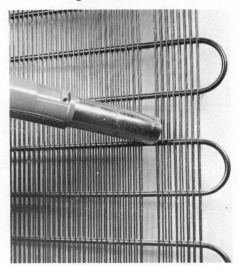

Figure 3. Cleaning the condenser coils frequently helps maintain a unit's efficiency, reduces chance of failure.

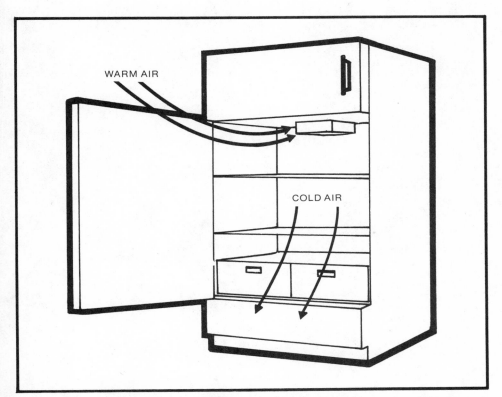

Figure 4. When a refrigerator door is open, cold air pours out and warm air pours in. For maximum efficiency and less frosting, open the refrigerator as little as possible.

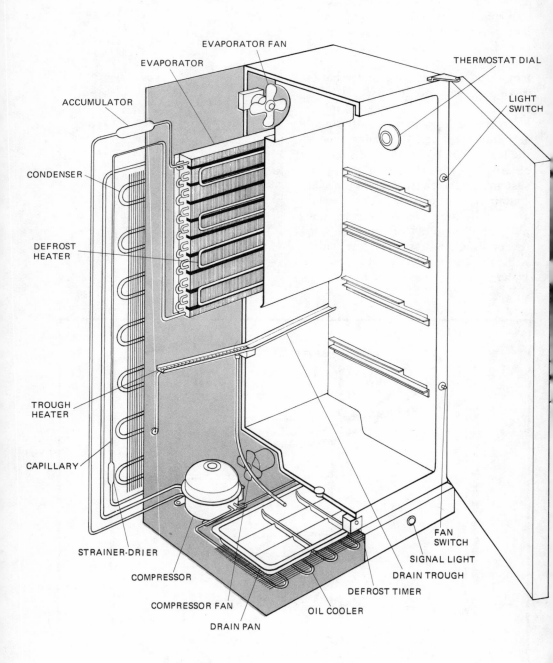

Figure 5. This cutaway drawing of a typical home freezer will assist you in locating the components of the freezer or refrigerator on which you are working.

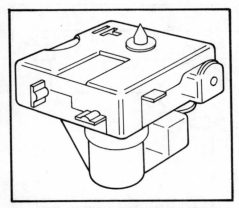

Figure 6. A typical compressor relay looks like this. The relay is replaced under circumstances noted in chart.

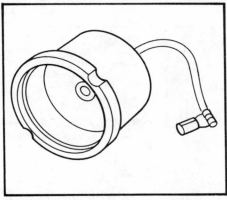

Figure 7. The compressor overload protector looks like this and is generally in the area of or on the compressor.

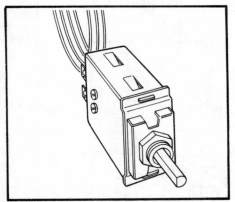

Figure 8. The shapes of thermostats differ from model to model. The one in your unit may possibly look like this one.

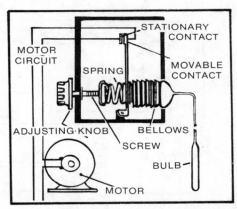

Figure 9. On the other hand, many units employ the so-called bellows thermostat, which is shown here.

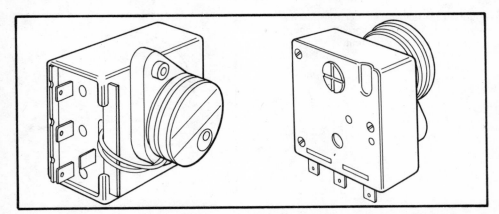

Figure 10. If the compressor will not run, it may mean that you have a defective defrost timer. The timer should be tested for continuity, and replaced if defective.

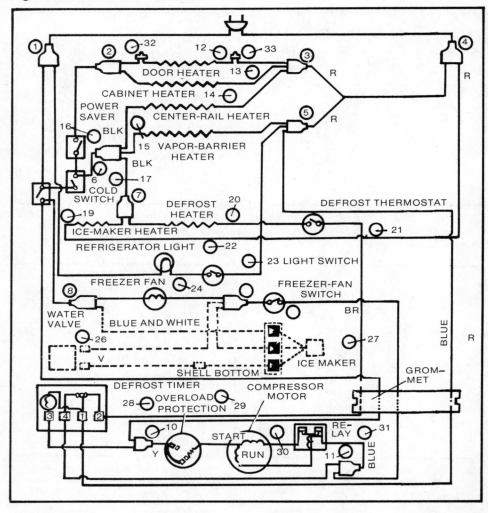

Figure 11. Above is typical refrigerator wiring diagram. There should be one glued to the chassis of your unit.

Figure 12. This is a compressor. If it burns out, check the price of a new one against the price of a new refrigerator.

Problem	Causes	Procedure
Compressor will not run	1. Blown fuse or tripped circuit breaker	1. Replace fuse or reset circuit breaker
	2. Defective compressor relay (Figure 6)	2. Test continuity between terminals L and R, and between S and L. Replace the relay if there is no continuity between L and R, or if there *is* an indication between S and L.
	3. Defective compressor overload protector (Figure 7)	3. Remove the wires from the protector and test for continuity across the terminals. Replace if there is no continuity. *Note:* This test should be done at room temperature
	4. Defective thermostat (temperature control) (Figures 8 and 9)	4. Remove the wires from the thermostat, turn the control indicator to the coldest setting, and check for continuity across the terminals. Replace the part if there is no continuity.
	5. Defective defrost timer (Figure 10)	5. Remove the wires from the timer. Test for continuity across terminals for the timer motor, and for the defrost and compressor circuits consult wiring diagram) (Figure 11). Replace the timer if an open circuit is indicated.
	6. Defective compressor (Figure 12)	6. Test compressor with jumper. If it fails to operate properly, replace.
Compressor cycles on-off too often	1. Low voltage	1. Test voltage at the wall outlet with a voltmeter. It should be within 10 percent of normal. If too low, call the utility company.
	2. Blocked air circulation over condenser	2. Clean the condenser coil and surrounding area.
	3. Defective compressor relay	3. See above under "compressor will not run."
Compressor runs constantly or too much	1. Thermostat is set too high or sensor bulb has worked loose	1. Adjust thermostat to a warmer setting. Make sure that the thermostat's sensor bulb is secure in its setting.
	2. Blocked air circulation over condenser	2. See above under "compressor cycles."

Problem	Causes	Procedure
	3. Poor door seal	3. Insert a dollar bill in the doorway and close the door. Pull the bill out. There should be a slight tug. If not, check hinge alignment and/or replace the door gasket.
	4. Undercharged system	4. Find and fix the leak, and recharge the system
Food compartment is too warm	1. Thermostat set too high	1. Reset thermostat to lower setting.
	2. Poor door seal	2. See above under "compressor runs constantly."
	3. Door is opened too often	3. Cut the number of trips to the unit.
	4. Unit is overloaded with food	4. Remove some food, if possible. Keep down the content.
	5. Defective fan	5. Test fan motor for continuity. Replace if there is no continuity.
	6. Defective defrost heater	6. Test heater for continuity. Replace if there is no continuity.
	7. Defective defrost timer	7. See above under "compressor will not run."
	8. Interior light remains on	8. Push light-switch button. The light should go out. If not, replace the switch.
Automatic unit will not defrost	1. Defective defrost timer	1. See above under "compressor will not run."
	2. Defective defrost heater	2. See above under "food compartment is too warm."
Moisture condenses on compartment's sides	1. Poor door seal	1. See above under "compressor runs constantly."
	2. Door opened too often	2. Reduce the number of trips to the unit.
	3. Faulty thermostat setting	3. Thermostat is set too cold. Turn to a warmer reading.
Noisy operation	1. Unit is not level	1. Level the unit.
	2. Tubing vibrating	2. Adjust the tubing slightly so it isn't rubbing against an adjacent part.
	3. Compressor is loose in its mounting	3. Tighten the compressor's leg mountings.

Chapter 31

Garbage disposers

Most are strong and rugged, but even so they aren't able to grind up all wastes. If long, troublefree service is to be expected, care should be taken in the type of garbage stuffed into the hopper

THE BIGGEST TROUBLE with garbage disposers is caused by those using the appliance. An operator should be thoroughly familiar with manufacturer instructions regarding what can and what can't be placed in a disposer.

Any garbage disposer will grind and get rid of soft food wastes, such as meat particles, bread scraps and soft vegetable leftovers. However, only the more expensive models—specifically, those equipped with capacitor-start motors—also can handle bones, seafood shells, corncobs and other heavy food matter.

No garbage disposer is designed to handle non-food wastes. They are not built to grind glass, pottery, broken dishes, bottle caps, rubber, plastic, silverware, string, cardboard, paper or rags. Placing this stuff into a food disposer will damage the unit and can clog the drain.

A garbage disposer can be installed in homes served by septic systems as well as those served by municipal sewers. However, there could be a problem if the drainfield is not adequate to accommodate the extra load placed on it by the unit.

A garbage disposer uses about six

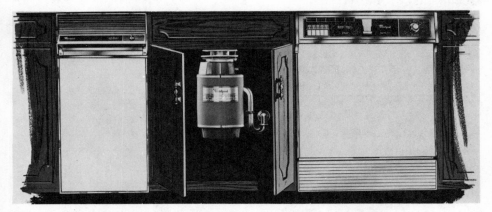

Figure 1. A garbage disposer is a handy hidden servant that fits into a sink drain and grinds up all kinds of soft food wastes so they can be rinsed away to the sewer.

Figure 2. Motor turns revolving table. Hammers fling wastes against shredders which pulverize garbage.

Figure 3. Continuous-feed model garbage disposers have a rubber baffle which covers the opening of the unit.

gallons of water per day. To be on the safe side, then, your drainfield should meet the following minimum requirements:

Number of Occupants In Home	Size of Septic System
4	750 gallons
6	900 gallons
8	1000 gallons
10	1250 gallons

If the septic system is smaller than this, vis-à-vis the number of occupants, installation of a garbage disposer might overload the field.

the secret is rotary action

BASICALLY, A GARBAGE DISPOSER is a simple machine (as are so many other appliances) (Figure 1). It consists of two chambers—an upper and lower—that are bolted together with a gasket between them to prevent water from leaking.

Garbage is placed down the throat of the upper chamber. The only other part in the upper chamber is a round metal ring that has teeth cut into it. The ring, which is called a shredder, is attached to the sides of the upper chamber and extends around the entire circumference (Figure 2).

When you drop garbage into the upper chamber, it falls on a round disc which is the flywheel or table. The flywheel may or may not have a disc attached to its top onto which the garbage falls, but this is immaterial. However, the flywheel *is* equipped with two or more impellers or hammers that move freely on pivots. When the flywheel is at rest, the impellers lie flat. But when the flywheel

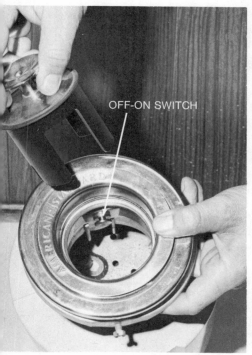

Figure 4. Batch-feed model garbage disposers have a cover that must be placed in position to trip the on-off switch.

Figure 5. Some garbage disposers have a button, on the housing, that is pushed to relieve an overload.

revolves, the impellers fly outward and also revolve, tossing garbage against the shredder. Garbage is ground into bits and is washed down the drain by cold water, which should be running during the entire cycle.

Caution: **Never use hot water.** Heat melts fat, allowing it to flow down along the sides of the drain pipe where it could solidify and eventually cause a blockage. Cold water causes fat to harden, which allows the impellers and shredder to grind it into bits.

The motor that drives the flywheel in models that are able to do heavy work is a capacitor-start motor. The motor used in other models is a split-phase motor (see the chapter on small electric fans for a discussion of split-phase motors).

Capacitor-start and split-phase motors are similar to each other, with one notable exception. The capacitor-

start motor has a capacitor which assists in starting the motor, giving the motor substantial starting torque that allows it to handle heavier loads.

A capacitor-start motor is equipped with two field coils; so is a split-phase motor. One coil is the starting coil, and the other is a running coil. In a capacitor-start motor, the starting coil is wired in series with the capacitor.

This means that when the appliance is turned on the capacitor gives the starting coil a boost to start the motor with sufficient torque to overcome the load imposed on it by heavier foodstuffs. A garbage disposer equipped with a capacitor-start motor is able to handle two quarts of all kinds of food waste, while one equipped with a split-phase motor can handle only one quart of food wastes that are limited in bulkiness.

Once the motor is started and at

229

operating speed (about 1750 revolutions per minute), the capacitor and starting coil are no longer needed. Their continued operation could overload the motor. Thus, a centrifugal switch is included in the mechanism, as it is in a split-phase motor. This switch opens up to take the capacitor and starting coil out of the circuit, and the operation of the motor is assumed by the running coil.

a matter of switches

THE NUMBER AND TYPE of switches from one garbage disposer to another may vary. However, every disposer has an on-off switch.

Some disposers have the on-off switch mounted on a wall above the sink. The switch resembles an ordinary light switch. The type of garbage disposer that uses this switch is called a continuous-feed model, because you can stuff garbage into the disposer while the appliance is running (Figure 3).

This, however, is not necessarily a desirable feature, especially with youngsters in the home. They could stick their hands into the disposer while the unit is operating. Adults are not immune from accidents either.

For this reason, the other method of switching is considered by many to be more desirable. The on-off switch is positioned in the mouth of the disposer and is controlled by the stopper. The type of garbage disposer using a switch of this sort is called a batch-feed model (Figure 4).

When the stopper is loose or out of the unit's mouth, the switch is deactivated, and the unit can't run. After you fill the hopper with garbage, you have to install the stopper, turn and lock it in place. The locking action trips the switch, turning on the machine. When the stopper is relieved, the switch flicks off.

Some garbage disposers also have an on-off switch in the cold-water line that works in conjunction with the other on-off switch. The cold-water switch assures that the disposer won't operate until cold water is flowing into it even though the other on-off switch is "on."

Many garbage-disposer motors are equipped with an overload switch. This shuts off current if too heavy a load is imposed on the motor. The units have a button that can be pressed to reactivate them once the load has been lessened.

troubleshooting garbage disposers

MANUFACTURERS CLAIM that a garbage disposer has a life expectancy of five to ten years, and that once one fails it is more economical to buy a new unit than repair the old one. This is sound advice if the motor burns out or if the unit begins leaking.

However, if other failures occur during the life of a garbage disposer it is often possible to repair them and restore the appliance to service. The following troubeshooting charts tell you how to do this.

Caution: Never work on a garbage disposer while it is running. Always disconnect the fuse or trip the circuit breaker on line, if the garbage unit is not plugged into a wall outlet that you can get to. If the latter situation prevails, pull the cord from the wall plug. This safety step assures that someone won't accidentally turn on the disposer while you are working on it.

Problem	Causes	Procedure
Motor hums, but disposer doesn't operate	1. Garbage is jamming the unit	1. If your unit has a reversing switch that switches flywheel direction, causing the unit to spin in an opposite direction and dislodge particles, use it. If not, reach into the hopper and try to turn the flywheel counterclockwise by grasping an impeller and using it as a handle. If you have a special wrench that some manufacturers supply to help clear jams, use it. If nothing works, unscrew the bottom housing from the upper housing, but be careful not to let the bottom half drop. It is heavy. Remove obstructing particles from below.
	2. Bearings are frozen	2. Remove the bottom housing and try to turn the flywheel. If it binds (not because of jamming waste), replace the flywheel and motor bearings if they are accessible. If they aren't accessible, you will have to take apart the entire unit, including the motor, to reach them.
Motor shows no life	1. Tripped overload	1. Relieve the heavy load and press the overload reset relay.
	2. On-off switch of batch-feed model has shifted	2. See that the stopper engages the switch when it is locked. If it doesn't, reposition the switch so it is in its proper place.
	3. Burned-out switch	3. Check all switches for continuity with the switch turned on, but make sure the disposer is not connected.
	4. Burned-out motor	4. Direct-test motor with a line cord. If it doesn't show life when the cord is connected to its terminals and plugged in, dispose of the disposer.
Disposer won't shut off	1. On-off or cold-water switch is stuck	1. Replace the switch.
Disposer shuts itself off	1. Tripped overload switch	1. Relieve the heavy load and press the overload reset relay.
	2. Defective overload switch	2. Remove the lower housing to get at the motor and replace the switch.

garbage disposers

Problem	Causes	Procedure
Lengthy grinding time	1. Impeller is stuck	1. Reach into the hopper and try to move the impellers. If one doesn't move, pry it up with a small screwdriver.
	2. Shredder is worn	2. Replace the shredder if it is replaceable and if a replacement part is available. If not, consider replac-the disposer.
Disposer leaks	1. Worn bearings and seals	1. Disposer requires a complete overhaul. It will probably be more economical to buy a new unit.
Offensive odors		Fill the disposer with ice cubes and run it for 15–30 seconds while keeping the unit shut off unless there is a cold-water switch. Follow with a good flushing of the unit with cold water—then give it a minute. Now, put two lemon halves down the tube and run the unit for 30–60 seconds with the water off, if possible. Follow with a water flush for another 30 seconds. With the disposer turned off, fill the sink with cold water. Turn the disposer on, force-flushing the water through the disposer.

Trash compactors

A recent innovation, the trash compactor dramatically reduces the volume of household waste. And it is generally trouble-free. Learn here how it works and what to do in case you encounter a problem.

TO GET AN IDEA of just how much trash, including bottles, cans, cartons and paper, a trash compactor can compact, visualize two over-flowing 20-gallon garbage cans holding, say, 40 pounds. The trash compactor can take this junk and reduce its volume (not its weight) into a neat package of approximately 9 inches by 16 inches by 17 inches. This package, which in most cases is also deodorized, is then placed out for the trash collector.

Electrically, a trash compactor requires no more than any other major appliance. A grounded 120-volt electrical supply is needed that conforms to local electrical codes. The unit should be plugged into its *own* 15-ampere circuit.

Most units are designed to slip beneath standard kitchen countertops (Figure 1). Or, if you wish, you can leave the compactor free-standing. The unit must be level, however. This is accomplished by turning leveling legs screwed into the base of the compactor until the bubble of a carpenter's level zeroes itself, telling you that the compactor is straight.

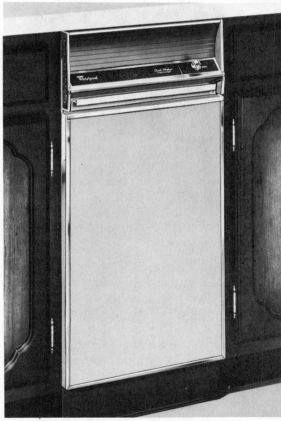

Figure 1. The trash compactor may be built into a kitchen-cabinet setup. It is a relatively narrow unit.

Figure 2. This trash compactor has an elaborate switching system, with an on-off switch and start and stop switches.

Figure 3. This gives you an idea of what's inside the housing. The unit which does the compacting is the belt-driven ram.

how a trash compactor is operated

THE TYPICAL TRASH COMPACTOR has two controls. One is a start switch. The other is a safety switch. In some models, the safety switch is actually a key-operated lock. If there are small children in the house, this permits you to turn the machine off by locking it with a key. After all, you don't want Junior "compacting" the family cat.

Some trash compactors incorporate a "stop" feature with the start control (Figure 2). The start and stop switches are combined into rocker-type switches, allowing you to flip easily from one to the other. The "stop" side of the switch, when engaged, opens up a contact in the feed line of the motor to stop the ramming cycle immediately and at any point.

Why would this be necessary? Suppose your phone rings. A trash compactor does make some noise. Whatever, you can stop the ramming at any time you wish.

After the "stop" side of the switch has been depressed, depressing the switch to "start" does *not* automatically allow the ram to continue on its

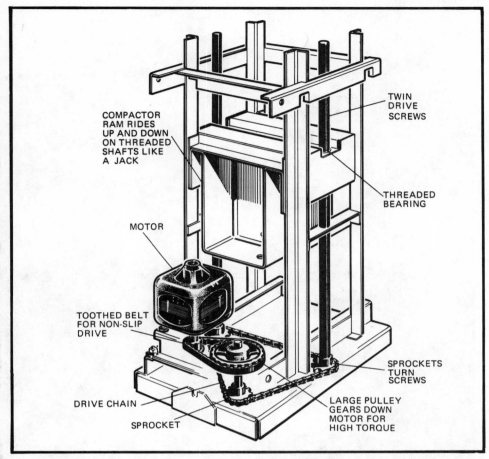

COMPACTOR
RAM RIDES
UP AND DOWN
ON THREADED
SHAFTS LIKE
A JACK

TWIN
DRIVE
SCREWS

THREADED
BEARING

MOTOR

TOOTHED BELT
FOR NON-SLIP
DRIVE

SPROCKETS
TURN
SCREWS

DRIVE CHAIN

SPROCKET

LARGE PULLEY
GEARS DOWN
MOTOR FOR
HIGH TORQUE

Diagram illustrates the operation and components of a typical trash compactor. The sturdy unit compacts trash with some 2,000 pounds of pressure to create a neat package of approximately 9 inches by 16 inches by 17 inches out of 40 gallons of trash.

cycle to compact garbage. Instead, the ram returns to its retracted position so that full force can be applied. If you now want to compact the garbage, you must once more depress the "start" switch.

When the trash compactor is turned on, it automatically goes through one cycle only. A ram moves down on the trash with a force equal to approximately 2,000 pounds of pressure. At this point, when compression can no longer be done, the motor "stalls" and the ram reverses itself, returning to its original "retracted" position (Figure 3).

Complete instructions for operating a trash compactor are attached, usually to the inside of the door. I suggest you read them carefully, especially how to emplace the heavy, plastic-lined bag (Figure 4). Misplacement can lead to trouble.

It is important that the bag be positioned as stated on the instructions to keep it from being drawn into the compactor during operation, leaving you with a mess. Generally, bags are held in place by spring retainers. When trash has been compacted, the typical trash compactor has latches on one side of the con-

Figure 4. Trash is dropped into the bag, and the unit is closed and started. The heavy, plastic-lined bag must be positioned carefully to prevent it from being drawn into the compactor during operation.

tainer to permit you to swing the side open and remove the compacted trash without difficulty.

how deodorization takes place

THIS IS NIFTY. With the drawer of a typical trash compactor open, you can hinge down the upper access door. There is a clamp inside the door of the typical unit that holds an aerosol can of trash-compactor disinfectant.

When the drawer is closed, an actuator roller comes into contact with two cams, one behind the other. Through this arrangement, the aerosol valve is pressed twice, allowing the spray can to give two metered bursts of deodorant.

Furthermore, each part of a typical trash compactor that comes into contact with garbage can be reached easily for washing. By depressing the latch stop pin of some units, for example, you can hinge down one side of the container to gain access to all recesses. Also, the ram cover of some units can be detached for washing in detergent.

The entire container assembly of a trash compactor rolls out on guides and bearings. Keep this in mind, because occasionally this area will require some lubrication.

If rollers begin making noise or the container becomes hard to roll, apply a drop or two of SAE 30 weight oil to each guide and slide the container back and forth to spread the lubricant.

what happens inside a trash compactor

TRASH-COMPACTOR OPERATION is not very difficult to understand. But working on the "guts" of a unit is something else again. I don't mean to dissuade you from making repairs. Some can be done easily. What I am going to do, though, is leave the extent of repair entirely up to you. If you think you can tackle it yourself after looking inside the unit, go to it.

One consolation: trash compactors have proven to be extremely reliable. Malfunctions seldom occur.

The heart of a trash compactor is a motor-drive assembly that consists of a powerful split-phase motor which drives a sprocket by means of a gear belt. This belt resembles the gear belt used on snowmobiles.

The geared end of the drive sprocket is engaged by a drive chain that's just like the drive chain of a motorcycle. This chain also engages two driving screws that drive the ram. It's obvious what happens.

The motor is started. It drives the drive sprocket by means of its geared belt. The drive sprocket under tremendous torque drives the drive chain, which drives (again with tremendous torque) the turn screws which push the ram home.

The one part of a trash compactor that may give some problem is the drive chain. Luckily, it is no more difficult to handle than the drive chain of a bicycle.

If the chain wears and has to be replaced, you simply remove a master link. The chain drops off. The one difficulty may be in locating the chain. Typically, it is "hidden" beneath a cover that is removed by removing screws. This is normally in the base of the unit.

Incidentally, unlike the chains of bikes and motorcycles, the drive chain of a trash compactor seldom, if ever, requires lubrication. This is because it isn't used that often and so doesn't receive the wear and tear of cycle chains. However, if the chain does seem a bit binding, apply a drop of ordinary chain lubricant. You can buy some in a bike or cycle shop.

how to troubleshoot and repair a trash compactor

THE FOLLOWING CHARTS explain what can go wrong with a trash compactor and what can be done to fix it:

trash compactors

Problem	Causes	Procedure
Unit won't work	1. Appliance isn't plugged in	1. Make sure the line cord is plugged into its outlet.
	2. Circuit breaker or fuse is "open"	2. Replace a faulty fuse or reset a tripped circuit breaker.
	3. Safety lock in the "off" setting	3. Make sure the safety switch (lock) is deactivated.
	4. Drawer is open	4. Most units have a door switch that keeps the compactor from operating if the door isn't closed. Perhaps something is keeping it wedged open.
	5. Motor overload (ram in the "down" position)	5. Wait 10 minutes for the motor to cool down. With the line cord pulled from the wall plug, check for low voltage, a tight drive belt and chain, or broken parts.
	6. A defective switch	6. The typical trash compactor contains several switches, as follows, any one of which can keep the unit from working if it goes bad: a start/stop switch, safety switch, door switch, and drawer safety switch. Check switches for continuity. Replace a faulty one.
	7. Loose connections or broken wires	7. Check all connections to make sure they are tight. Make sure that there are no broken wires.
Compactor begins to cycle and then stops	1. Circuit breaker or fuse suddenly fails	1. Check it out.
	2. Drawer open	2. See above under "unit won't work."
	3. Drive motor goes out because of an overload	3. See above under "unit won't work."
Drive motor runs, but the trash won't compact	1. Drive belt is broken	1. Replace.
	2. Drive chain is broken	2. Replace or repair the broken link, which is possible to do with some chains.
	3. Motor pulley is loose on the motor shaft	3. Tighten pulley.
	4. Drive pulley is loose on the drive shaft	4. Tighten pulley.
	5. Drive sprocket roll pin is sheared	5. Replace the broken roll pin.

Problem	Causes	Procedure
	6. Drive shaft is broken	6. Replace.
	7. Ram power nuts are stripped	7. Replace.
Compactor operates too noisily	1. Drive chain not adjusted properly	1. Proper chain deflection is ¼ inch. See below for advice on adjusting the drive chain.
	2. Drive belt not adjusted properly	2. Proper belt deflection is ⅛ inch. See below for advice on adjusting the drive belt.
	3. Ram power nuts need lubrication	3. Lubricate with SAE 30 weight motor oil.
	4. Loose parts	4. Check all parts for tightness.
Aerosol disinfectant doesn't work	1. Aerosol spray can is empty	1. Replace with a full can.
	2. Spray can nozzle is plugged	2. Try unplugging the nozzle with a thin piece of wire or replace the nozzle with a new one.
	3. Aerosol can actuating mechanism is defective	3. Check to see that the actuating mechanism "hits" the spray button as it should. Replace or repair parts as necessary.
Drawer won't open	Ram is part way down and won't retract	• Check to see that the unit hasn't come unplugged from the wall outlet. • Make sure that the drawer is closed —maybe the door switch has caused a shutdown. • Unplug the appliance and look for a broken belt, chain or pulley. • Motor overload (see above under "unit won't work").
Compactor keeps running	1. Defective top-limit switch	1. Push the start/stop switch to "stop" or turn the safety switch to "off." Check the continuity of the top-limit switch. If there is no continuity, replace the switch.
	2. "Start" side of a start/stop switch remains closed because of fused contacts	2. Turn the safety switch to "off." Check the start/stop switch for continuity. If continuity is indicated, it means contacts are fused. Replace the switch.
	3. Defective directional switch	3. If the ram continues to run up and down without stopping at the top of the cycle, the directional switch contacts have failed. Replace the switch.

when adjustments are needed

ON OCCASION, the drive belt and drive chain of a trash compactor may need to be adjusted. In addition, the directional switch and top-limit switch of many units may also require adjustment. The following information describes in general how to do these. The actual procedure differs from unit to unit, of course:

1. Adjusting the drive belt. Loosen the nuts holding the motor mount. Pull back on the pulley until you get a deflection in the center of the belt of about ⅛ inch. Tighten the nuts securely.

2. Adjusting the drive chain. Loosen the bolts holding the motor-mount assembly. Pull back on the pulley until you get a deflection in the center of the chain of about ¼ inch. Tighten bolts securely.

3. Adjusting the directional switch and top-limit switch. Loosen the screws holding the switches to their mountings. Generally the top-limit switch should be adjusted so it will open when the ram is about ½ inch below the top of the ram guide posts. The directional switch should actuate ¼ inch lower than the top-limit switch—that is ¾ of an inch from the top of the ram guide posts.

Chapter 33

Oil and gas furnaces

It's a cold, snow-snarled day and your gas or oil furnace is dead.
You call one serviceman after another, but all are busy or can't get through to
your house. Here's what you'll need to know to fix the furnace yourself.

MOST FURNACE PROBLEMS result from minor causes that homeowners generally can fix themselves—if not permanently, then at least temporarily so they can get some heat into the home to tide them over until help arrives. Before we discuss the ways to approach the problem, here are some basic facts you need to know.

A furnace is only one part of a typical home heating system. It is the place where heat is produced. But heat must be delivered to rooms. Otherwise, it is wasted. Thus, a delivery system constitutes the other part of the system.

Regardless of whether your furnace burns oil or gas to make heat, that heat is delivered by hot water, steam, or forced air. In a hot-water system, the oil- or gas-fed fire heats water to a temperature below its boiling point. Heated water is delivered to a convection system in each room, and heat is radiated.

A steam system works in a similar manner. However, water is heated in a boiler to above its boiling point so that steam is created. This steam, rather than hot water, is then delivered to each room of the house.

With a forced-air system, the oil or gas flame heats air which is blown through ducts into the rooms of the house by means of a blower.

Obviously, when you troubleshoot a home heating system you must consider the type of furnace (oil or gas) and the type of delivery system (hot water, steam or air).

how to get a stopped oil burner going again

SUPPOSE YOUR OIL BURNER stops working. The temperature in the house keeps dropping, and you don't hear that "rushing" sound coming from inside the furnace cabinet which signifies that oil is being burned. Here is what to do, and in the proper sequence:

1. **Check the thermostat.** Observe the indicated room temperature on the thermostat thermometer. Set the thermostat at least five degrees above that. The burner should go on.

In other words, if the thermometer tells you that the room temperature is 65°, turn the thermostat pointer to the mark indicating the 70° setting.

Important: If the thermostat is an automatic day-night control, make certain that the cycle setting has not been reversed so that the night-time setting, which is generally cooler, is prevailing during the day and the day-time setting is prevailing at night.

Open the thermostat cover. If the dial control is a sealed capsule full of mercury, close the thermostat cover. A mercury control seldom gives trouble.

However, if the control consists of a set of contact points, dirt between the points may be preventing them from meeting. Lack of point contact keeps the thermostat "open," and prevents the furnace ignition system from starting.

Pass a fresh, crisp dollar bill, business card, or tag that is the thickness of a business card between the points to remove dirt. If the furnace still fails to start, then the cause of the problem is not the thermostat.

2. **Make sure** that someone hasn't accidentally turned off one of the emergency switches. Most oil burners are equipped with two emergency switches, but there may be more. Usually one switch is on the furnace itself, while a second one is often located at a distant spot. You may find this second switch at the head of the basement stairway or above the basement door that leads to the yard.

Emergency switches that are at the head of basement stairways are particularly susceptible to inadvertent shut-off when someone in the house, intending to turn the basement lights on or off, switches the burner emergency switch instead.

Reminder: It would be a good idea to locate emergency switches *now* so you will know where they are before a problem occurs.

3. **See if the safety switches have tripped.** Most oil burners possess a motor-overload switch and a stack-control relay switch that will trip if an overload develops in the furnace

or motor electric circuit.

The motor-overload switch, which is normally painted red, is found on the motor housing (Figure 1). Usually the stack-control relay switch is located on the smoke pipe or burner housing (Figure 2).

It is possible for one of the safety switches to trip because of a momentary alteration in electric current, so you should reactivate each switch, but with caution. If the burner fails to start after pressing each switch *one time only*, or if the burner starts and stops again, do *not* re-activate the safety switches. There may be a serious electric malfunction that should be left to a professional serviceman. Reactivation of switches only increases the chance of a more serious oil-burner breakdown or, worse yet, a fire.

The correct way to handle safety switches is to press the overload switch on the motor first. If the motor does not start, activate the stack-control relay switch once only.

Before we leave the subject of safety switches, we must emphasize that some furnaces are controlled by a photoelectric cell. Check literature that applies to your model oil burner to see if it has this control device.

If the face of a photoelectric cell gets dirty, the burner may refuse to operate. An indication of a dirty photoelectric cell is burner cycling—that is, the burner will turn on when you press the stack-control relay, but will shut down after running about 30 seconds.

Locate the photoelectric cell housing and remove the small screw or screws that will allow you to gain access to the inside of the housing. Carefully pull out the cell.

Using a clean cloth, wipe the face of the cell clean and place it back in its housing. Now, activate the safety

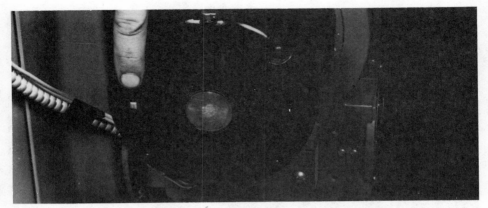

Figure 1. The motor overload switch is a safety switch that should be pressed once only if an oil-burner shutdown occurs. Usually it is colored red.

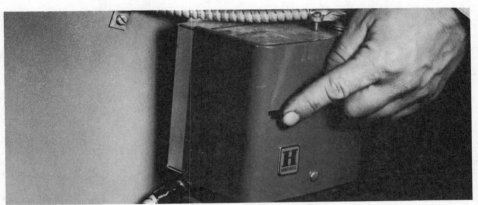

Figure 2. The stack control relay is another safety switch on most oil and gas burners; but press motor overload switch first. Stack switch is on the smoke pipe or burner housing.

switches one more time.

4. **Examine the fuse** or circuit breaker that is protecting the furnace electric circuit. The fuse or circuit breaker, of course, will be found in the main electric box.

If the circuit breaker has tripped, reset it, but if it trips again, do *not* reset it. A circuit breaker that keeps tripping signifies a serious electric problem that the homeowner should not pursue himself unless he is a licensed electrician.

Fuses are more devious than circuit breakers. Vibration can loosen a fuse and interrupt the circuit, so make certain that the fuse protecting the furnace is tight in its socket (Figure 3).

An old fuse can "blow," but you can't always see that the fuse is bad by looking in through the small window. The link may seem to be in one piece, but may actually be separated in a spot hidden from observation. Replace the fuse with a new one just to be sure.

As with a circuit breaker, if a new fuse blows out, do not replace it again. Consult a service technician.

5. **Check to see if the oil valve is malfunctioning.** Especially those furnaces having photoelectric cells usu-

Figure 3. Don't let a fuse fool you, just because it looks okay. It may be loose in its socket, or it may have blown although its link may seem to be in one piece.

ally are equipped with delayed oil valves that control the flow of oil to the burner. If the valve gets clogged with dirt, or its electric supply is interrupted, the valve will remain closed and no oil will flow to the furnace's firebox.

In an emergency, you can get the furnace to operate by taking the oil valve out of the system. Disconnect the input and output oil lines at the valve. Remove the valve, and connect the input line right to the output line. Oil will now flow, and you will be able to get heat, but be sure to have the valve serviced and put back into the system as soon as possible.

6. **Make sure** that there is an ample supply of oil. This is not as obvious as it seems to be. After all, you have seen many people run out of gas on the highway.

Don't always trust the gauge of an indoor tank. It can stick. Tap the gauge to see if the needle remains in place.

If the cap of an outside tank is accessible—that is, if you are able to shovel away the snow to get to it— check out the supply with a dipstick. Naturally, if there is no oil in the tank, there will be no heat.

7. **Determine the condition** of the nozzle-and-electrode assembly. If the problem has not been rectified up until this point, probably its cause is centered in the oil-nozzle-and-electrode assembly, which is inside the burner. To remove the assembly for service, you must turn off *all* emergency switches.

Caution: Never do any work inside an oil burner unless all emergency switches are turned off. You could be seriously injured.

Some nozzle-and-electrode assemblies are fairly easy to get at by simply removing an access cover. Others are more difficult. You may have to detach and drop the transformer.

In any event, once you can reach inside the burner, loosen the oil-line connection with a wrench and disconnect the transformer and electrode wires. Usually these wires are held by snap-on connectors.

Take the nozzle-and-electrode assembly out of the burner, but be careful that you don't bang the electrodes and upset their setting. If the electrode setting is disturbed, ignition of

the oil will not take place. Instead, the oil will "puff," which does no damage to the furnace, but which can scare the pants off you.

Lay the assembly on a clean surface and unscrew the nozzle (Figure 4). Use two wrenches—one to hold the assembly steady and the other to unscrew the nozzle.

You will probably find a small filter inside the nozzle. Remove it and wash it in warm water (Figure 5).

Probably you will also find a small set screw inside the nozzle. Take this out, too, and wash it in warm water. A clogged filter or dirt-covered set screw will hamper the flow of fuel.

Blow through the nozzle. If the nozzle is clean, air will pass through it freely. If it is not clear, you have found the reason for furnace failure, but there is not much you can do about it unless you have a spare nozzle around. A nozzle is preset and should not be widened with a piece of wire or some such probe. Widening a nozzle will result in furnace "puff"— not in furnace operation.

Clean off the electrodes carefully with a rag or piece of fine steel wool.

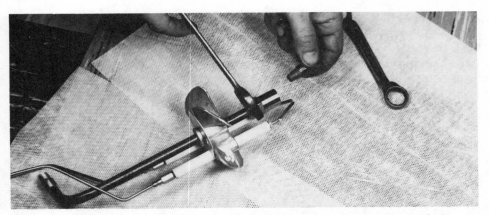

Figure 4. Many times a clogged nozzle causes oil-burner failure. Remove the nozzle to clean it, using one wrench to steady the assembly and the other to unscrew the nozzle.

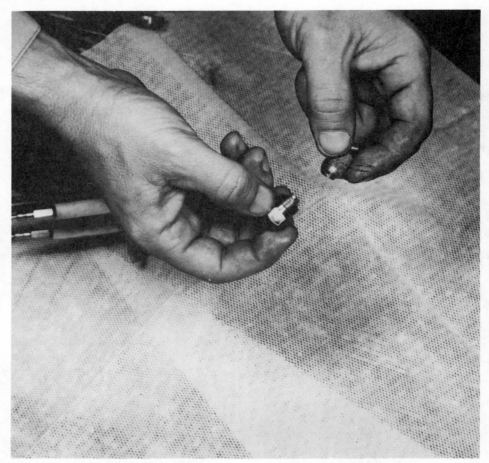

Figure 5. Remove the small filter if there is one inside the nozzle, and wash it in warm water. Also remove and wash the small set screw inside the nozzle.

A reminder—don't upset the setting.

Place the assembly back into the burner and connect all wires. Turn on the emergency switches and press the stack-control relay switch. Hopefully, the furnace will start up and run.

Important: Rotary-type oil burners do not have nozzles. To service the electrodes, turn off the emergency switches, reach inside the burner with a rag, and wipe the electrodes clean without upsetting the electrode setting.

what to do if the gas burner doesn't light

GAS IS MORE DANGEROUS to handle than oil. That is why troubleshooting is limited. If for some reason the flow of gas is shut off in your neighborhood, there is nothing that you can do to get your furnace operating. Otherwise, follow this procedure:

1. **Check the thermostat.** The exact same method described above for a thermostat that controls an oil burner should be followed for a thermostat that controls a gas burner.

2. **Check the safety switch** to see that it hasn't been turned off accidentally. This switch is usually mounted right on or right near the furnace.

3. See if the main fuse has blown or the circuit breaker has tripped. The same data given above that apply to fuses and circuit breakers protecting oil burners also apply to gas burners.

4. See if the gas pilot light is functioning. If the pilot is not burning, attempt to light it as outlined on the instruction plate which is attached to the furnace. A pilot light that refuses to light probably is clogged with dirt or carbon.

Turn off the safety switch and the gas valves that control the main burner and pilot. Tap the pilot burner with a screwdriver in an attempt to dislodge dirt or carbon.

Now, turn the control valve for the pilot back on and try to light the pilot. *Do not open the control valve to the main burner until the pilot is lit.*

If the pilot lights, turn on the control valve for the main burner and switch on the electricity. Set the thermostat.

Caution: Do not try to light a main burner by hand. A flare-up could result that could cause injury.

If the pilot does not light, forget the whole thing. Turn off the pilot control valve, and wait for a service technician.

when the furnace works but heat doesn't get through

IF YOUR OIL BURNER or gas furnace is functioning, but heat is not being delivered to the rooms, there is a malfunction in the delivery system. Let's run down each of the delivery systems to see what you can do to overcome the problem, and at least get some heat into the house.

• **Steam system**—Check the boiler gauge. A burner will shut off automatically if the water level in the boiler gets below a certain level. However,

do not refill the boiler if it is hot. Cold water flowing into a hot boiler may cause the boiler to crack.

Let the boiler cool down. Then, let the water run. The burner should begin operating when the boiler's gauge shows that the boiler is about half-full of water.

• **Hot-water system**—Inspect the circulator. One that needs lubrication will not circulate hot water although the burner will continue to operate.

Caution: Lubricate the circulator only with the grade of oil and/or cup grease recommended on the instruction plate attached to the circulator's body. Any other type may cause a complete breakdown.

If the circulator has stopped working whether for lack of lubricant or some other reason, press the reset button on the device one time only. If there is no reset button, slap the housing with your hand.

A circulator will not deliver heat if one of its couplings is broken. However, the unit will continue to run, so put your ear close to the housing and listen for a sharp, rapping sound.

You may be able to repair the break temporarily. Remove the access cover. If you can get at the broken coupling, wire the broken cross-pieces together.

If you cannot repair the circulator, but the burner is operating, you should be able to get some heat through the house. Most hot-water systems have a flow valve on the water line that runs from the furnace to the heat-radiating components. Open the valve. This will feed hot water through the system by gravity.

Important: Don't forget to close the flow valve after the circulator has been repaired.

• **Forced-air systems**—One reason for a reduced heat condition in a forced-air system is a clogged air filter (Figure 6). If you have a spare

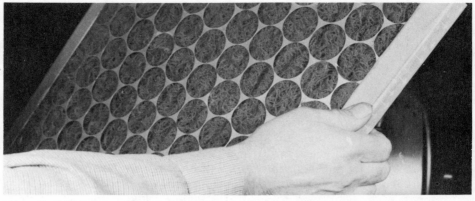

Figure 6. If the furnace filter clogs with dirt, delivery of heat will be curtailed. It is best to replace a dirty filter; at least take it outside and knock some dirt out.

around, install it. If not, remove the old filter (some furnaces have more than one), take it out-of-doors, and knock it against a hard surface to loosen dirt.

Another reason for little heat delivery is a broken blower-motor belt. The best solution is to replace the belt, so you should keep a spare on hand. You can buy a belt for your blower motor from a hardware store or gasoline station. Make sure it is the right size.

Place the belt on the blower-motor pulleys and tighten the adjusting nut, which is usually found behind the motor, until the belt has about ½-inch free play.

If you do not have a spare belt, try wrapping some strong rope around the pulleys as a temporary measure.

A final reason for failure of a forced-air system to deliver heat is a short in the blower motor. A short is indicated by on-off cycling of the motor in short spurts or complete refusal to run.

Shut off the switch controlling the blower motor and remove all filters from the furnace. Some hot air will rise and permeate through the ducts to the registers so that minimum com-

fort may be attained until a service technician arrives.

how to get heat when there is a power failure

IF A POWER FAILURE strikes your area, you can get some heat into the house if you have a gas-fired furnace. You cannot do anything if you have an oil burner since electricity is needed to pump oil from the storage tank to the furnace.

You will experience no difficulty if your gas furnace has a self-energized steam or hot-water delivery system. The system will function normally, because it does not rely on external electric power.

However, a forced hot-water or forced-air system is another story. It depends on a pump or blower motor for delivery of heat.

An obstacle to overcome in a system which has a main gas burner that is not self-energized is lack of ignition, because there is no electricity to send an impulse from the thermostat.

But these are not insurmountable drawbacks. You can get the gas burner going if it has a manual control on the motor control valve. The control is operated by a pushbutton,

Figure 7. During an annual inspection, a serviceman should clean or replace the oil filter. He should also clean out the system and check stack pressure.

timing device, or lever that protrudes from the housing of the motorized valve. Activate whatever device is on your furnace until the burner is ignited by the pilot.

With the main burner operating, open the flow valve on the water line if you are working with a forced hot-water system. This allows hot water to feed through the system by gravity.

With the main burner of a forced-air delivery system operating, remove the air filter from the cold-air return duct to induce circulation and permit warm air to feed by gravity to the registers.

If you use one of these methods during a power failure, *you must keep your eye on the main burner to make sure that excessive pressure and heat don't build up.* Some gas burners have a throttling device similar to that on a kitchen range for raising and lowering the flame.

Lower the flame every half-hour and allow the burner to cool down. If there is no throttling device, shut off the manual control every half-hour for about 10 minutes.

Important: When electric power is restored, return everything to normal operation.

maintenance that will assure efficiency

ONCE EVERY THREE YEARS, you should have your gas furnace inspected by a professional serviceman. In most areas, the professional serviceman you call is an employee of the local gas company, and in many areas there is no charge for this service.

Call the gas company and speak to the service department, requesting a serviceman. The best time to do this is in the early summer when gas companies aren't as busy as they are at the start of the heating season.

EVERY 12 MONTHS, an oil burner should be checked by an expert. He should perform several services, including changing the oil filter, cleaning out the system and checking stack pressure which tips him off to any problem in the stack that could cause a fire (Figures 7 and 8). Unfortunately, the same benefit is not available as with a gas furnace. Probably you will be charged for this service.

Between inspections, there are several maintenance tasks you should perform yourself to assure adequate performance and long-lasting service.

Figure 8. Stack pressure should be checked annually. If clogging or a leak occurs, a fire hazard is present.

They are as follows:

1. If you have a forced-air system, inspect the filter(s) frequently. Hold them up to a light. If you cannot see through the filter for the dirt, replace it.

Make sure that the arrows on the filter's holder point in the direction of air flow. If there is no arrow, the oily side of the filter should be placed nearest the return duct opening.

2. If you have a forced-air system, inspect the blower motor for an oil cup. If an oil cup is present, lubricate the motor as instructed on the plate attached to the furnace. Lubrication instructions differ from furnace to furnace, and you should follow yours to the letter to avoid damaging the motor by over-lubrication or lack of lubrication.

If a motor has no oil cup, it possesses self-lubricating bearings. Usually, these should be repacked by a serviceman every 15,000 to 20,000 hours of operation. If you reside in a cold climate, this works out to about once every five years. Figure on once every 10 years if your house is in a moderate-climate area.

3. Inspect the fan belt of a blower motor every year for cracking. Don't take a chance with a weak belt. It's likely to break on the coldest day of the year, perhaps when snow prevents driving and you have to hike through drifts to the hardware store or gasoline station.

Buy a belt of the correct size for your unit. Usually size will be inscribed on the old belt's outer edge.

Make sure that the belt is properly adjusted by pushing in on its center. The belt should give way about ½ inch. To tighten a loose belt, tighten the adjusting bolt you will find somewhere on the side of the motor housing.

4. When you start up a steam or hot-water system at the beginning of the heating season, check the radiators, if you have radiators, to make sure they heat up and don't knock. If a radiator doesn't heat, see if the shutoff valve is turned on.

Lack of heat is often caused by an air valve that has failed and is preventing steam or hot water from entering a radiator. Test the air valve of a nonfunctioning radiator by unscrewing the valve and placing it on a radiator that is working. If the good radiator cools down, the air valve is bad. Replace it.

If the test shows that the air valve is in working order, probably the nonfunctioning radiator is water-logged. This happens if the radiator is out of balance. Level it with a carpenter's level by inserting wood shims beneath the radiator legs.

5. If a radiator shut-off valve is leaking from around the packing nut, tighten the nut. If the leak persists, remove the packing nut, wrap some fresh packing around the stem, and retighten the nut.

6. Radiator hammer signifies that water is trapped in the pipe, because the radiator is not level. Level is explained above.

Chapter 34

Electric and gas water heaters

**The chief complaint you are likely to hear about a hot water heater
is that it doesn't provide enough hot water. This may be because it simply isn't
big enough. However, there are various other common problems you can fix.**

BASICALLY, THERE ARE TWO TYPES of water heaters: electric and gas. How they work is so simple that we can sum it up in one paragraph:

A water heater, whether electric or gas, has two main parts: a tank that holds water, and a heating source. Water enters the tank through a pipe called a dip tube. The dip tube directs the water flow almost to the bottom of the tank. Electric heating elements or a gas-fired burner heat the water. Hot water rises to the top of the tank where it enters a pipe that directs it to the various hot-water faucets in the home. That's it.

The most serious trouble that can afflict your water heater is if the tank springs a leak. This is caused by a buildup of rust on the sides of the tank, especially around seams.

It is often claimed that one way to prolong the life of a tank is to draw off a pail full of water every month or so to rid the tank of sediment. Maybe so, but there really isn't any proof we have been able to uncover that substantiates this theory. The only thing that drawing off water may do is drain off sediment buildup in the bottom of the tank that may cause noise when it's stirred up by incoming water (Figure 1).

In time, every tank will fail. It may take 5 years—10—15—maybe even 20. That depends primarily on the quality of the tank.

When you see a small puddle of water beneath your tank, you can expect that within a few days or so the flood will start. Make plans for replacement accordingly. There is no effective way to repair a *leaking water tank*.

The second major problem with water heaters involves the heating source. It can be repaired.

what you should know about electric heating sources

THERE ARE TWO TYPES of electric heating source. One is called an induction source, and the other is an immersion unit.

A water unit heated by induction is equipped with a heavily insulated heating element that is strapped around the outside of the tank (Figure 2). Heat is directed inward through the wall of the tank to the water (induction). Because of the heavy insulation, none (or very little) passes out to the atmosphere.

A water heater that uses an immersion heater usually has two heating

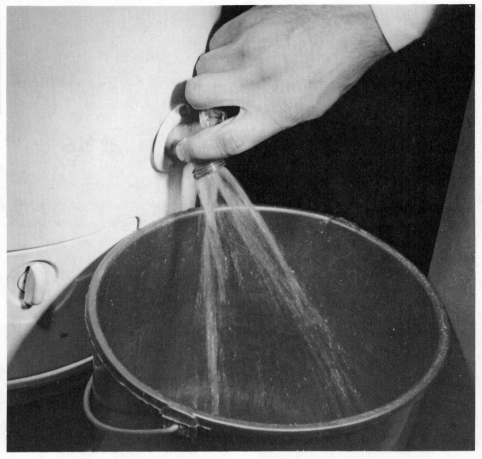

Figure 1. Whether or not draining a water heater prolongs the life of the tank is questionable. However, draining does permit the drawing off of sediment.

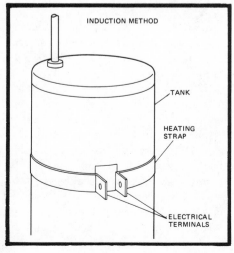

INDUCTION METHOD

TANK

HEATING STRAP

ELECTRICAL TERMINALS

Figure 3. Illustration on opposite page shows the components of a typical water heater with immersion-type elements.

elements which pass right through the wall of the tank and come into contact with the water inside (Figure 3). The holes through which the elements pass are well sealed with gaskets, offset flanges and sealer.

Figure 2. An electric water heater may have an induction system; a heavily insulated heating element is strapped around tank.

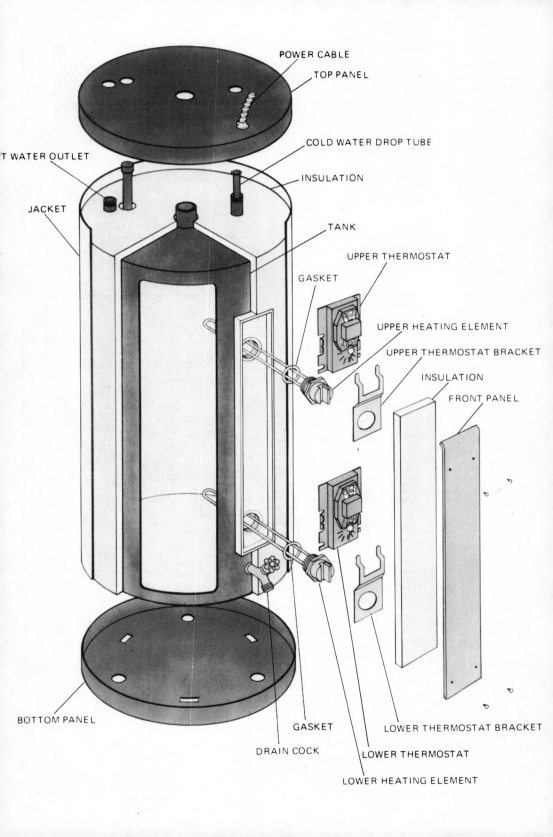

POWER CABLE

TOP PANEL

COLD WATER DROP TUBE

INSULATION

T WATER OUTLET

JACKET

TANK

GASKET

UPPER THERMOSTAT

UPPER HEATING ELEMENT

UPPER THERMOSTAT BRACKET

INSULATION

FRONT PANEL

BOTTOM PANEL

GASKET

DRAIN COCK

LOWER THERMOSTAT BRACKET

LOWER THERMOSTAT

LOWER HEATING ELEMENT

electric and gas water heaters

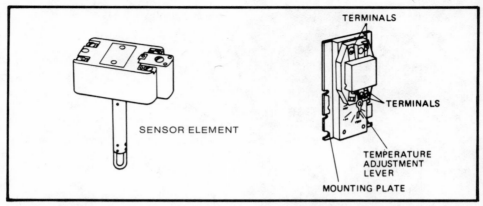

TERMINALS

SENSOR ELEMENT

TERMINALS

TEMPERATURE
ADJUSTMENT
LEVER

MOUNTING PLATE

Figure 4. These drawings show the thermostats of a typical immersion-type water heater. At left, notice the sensor element of the unit.

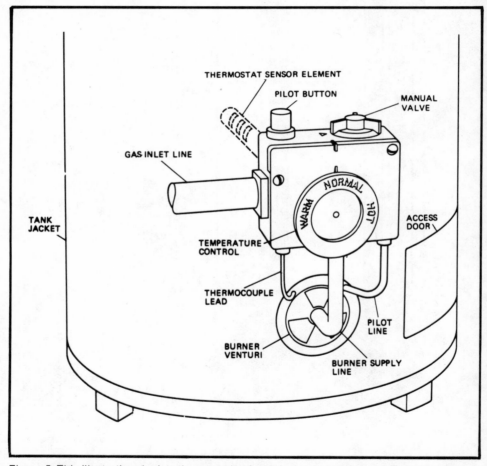

THERMOSTAT SENSOR ELEMENT

PILOT BUTTON

MANUAL VALVE

GAS INLET LINE

TANK JACKET

TEMPERATURE CONTROL

THERMOCOUPLE LEAD

BURNER VENTURI

ACCESS DOOR

PILOT LINE

BURNER SUPPLY LINE

Figure 5. This illustration depicts the controls of a typical gas water heater. Temperature can be controlled by turning a dial that adjusts the spring tension on the thermostat.

Practically every water heater that employs immersion heaters is also equipped with a load-limiting circuit which prevents both elements from drawing current at the same time. Doing so would overload the circuit.

Essentially, a load-limiting circuit is nothing more than a thermostat—two thermostats actually, one serving each element (Figure 4). When the tank is full of cold water, the thermostat controlling the upper heating element allows that element to turn itself on. This element generates heat until approximately 25 percent of the total volume of water is heated. This water is in the top of the tank (and is the first to be drawn off; heating it first enables the user to get hot water quicker).

At this point, the upper thermostat senses the "heat" and opens up to break the electric circuit going to the upper element. The element shuts off.

Now, the thermostat controlling the lower heating element, which is made of a metal that is less sensitive than the upper thermostat, responds and allows current to flow to the lower element. When all water in the tank is finally heated, the thermostat breaks and the element turns off.

The lower thermostat and element are the ones that heat water when cold water enters the tank as long as the top 25 percent of the water in the tank is hot.

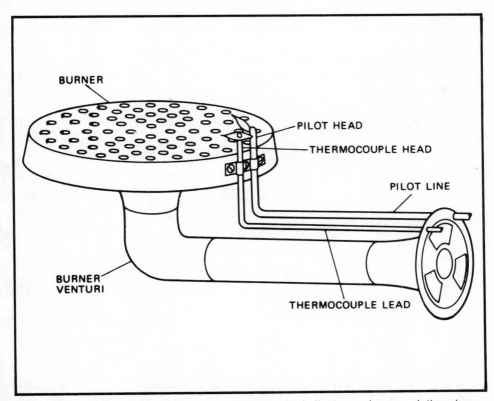

Figure 6. The gas-burner assembly in a water heater is similar to one in a gas clothes dryer. Let the gas company handle repair of this unit.

some facts about
gas-fired water heaters

GAS-BURNER UNITS in water heaters consist of a thermostat that is positioned inside the tank in contact with the water, an ordinary gas burner, and a pilot light that is controlled by a thermocouple. Thermocouple-controlled pilot lights are discussed in Chapter 26 (clothes dryers).

You are able to control the temperature of the water, as you are with electric-element water heaters, by turning a dial that manipulates the spring tension on the thermostat (Figure 5). Normal hot water temperature is 140°-150° F. When the dial is set on "warm," the temperature is about 120° F. When the dial is set on "hot," water temperature gets up to about 160° F.

The gas-burner unit in a water heater is practically the same as the one in a gas clothes dryer (Figure 6). Furthermore, the same advice applies to gas-fired water heaters as applies to all other appliances which use gas:

If you experience a problem with the gas members of the unit, contact your local gas company and let them repair it, if possible. They will usually charge you only for new parts that have to be installed.

Gas and electric water heaters alike are protected by a pressure-relief valve usually located in the cold-water line directly above the tank (Figure 7). This device protects the tank (and home) if there is a thermostat failure.

Figure 7. The equipment on top of most water heaters resembles that shown here. Notice the pressure-relief valve located in the cold-water line at the right.

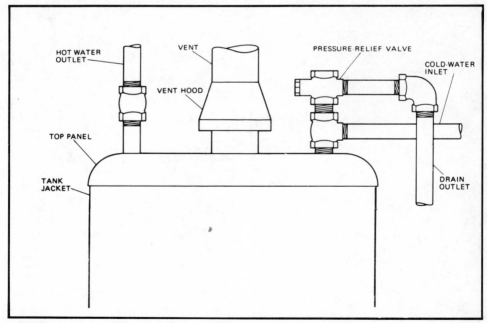

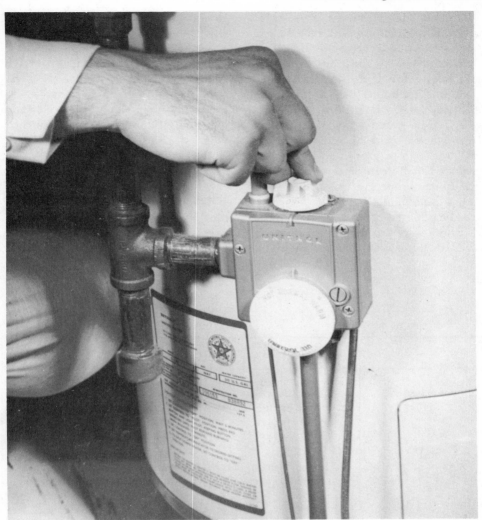

Figure 8. If you have a gas hot-water unit, learn how to light the pilot light. There should be instructions printed somewhere on the appliance.

Pressure-relief valves are set to give way at some point between 25 and 125 pounds per square inch of pressure above the tank's normal water pressure. If the thermostat fails and pressure builds, the valve's spring releases or its lead plug melts and the steam under pressure exits through the valve instead of causing the tank to rupture. Spring-loaded valves usually can be reset when the malfunction is corrected. In units using a lead plug that melts, the plug can be replaced.

There may be another component used in your water heater that you should know about. Some units possess a magnesium rod which acts as an anode. It attracts the corrosive agents in water so the corrosive agents don't attack the walls of the tank. When the rod becomes badly corroded, it should be replaced. You will know that this has happened when discolored water comes from the hot-water faucet.

what to do when water runs cold, becomes expensive, etc.

THE FOLLOWING CHART outlines the most common water-heater failures and how to handle them. Where an entry applies only to gas or electric components, it is so noted.

Problem	Causes	Procedure
No hot water	1. Blown fuse or tripped circuit breaker (electric)	1. Replace fuse or reset circuit breaker. If it happens again, there is a short circuit, probably in the water heater. Consult a serviceman.
	2. Heating element is burned out (electric)	2. Disconnect electricity and place a continuity tester across the heating-element terminals. Lack of continuity means the element has burned out. To replace an immersion-type element, close the cold-water valve and drain the tank past the element. Remove the old element and install the new one. Refill the tank and check for leaks. If a fitting leaks, seal it with a waterproof cement you can buy from a dealer of water tanks. Refill the tank and restore power. Induction heating elements are replaced by loosening the snap bolt and slipping the band off the tank. After the new element is in place, fasten the bolts, replace insulation and turn the power back on.

Problem	Causes	Procedure
	3. Calcium deposit buildup on immersion heating element (electric)	3. Shut off power and water and drain the tank. Remove the heating elements and soak them in a vinegar and water solution until clean. Reinstall them, fill the tank, check and seal leaks, and restore power.
	4. Defective thermocouple (gas)	4. Clean the pilot orifice. Then, turn the thermostat valve to "Pilot" position, press the pilot button and light the pilot (Figure 8). Hold the pilot button depressed for 45 seconds. Release. If the pilot doesn't stay lit, the thermocouple is bad. Replace it.
	5. Defective thermostat (gas)	5. Turn the thermostat valve to "On" and the temperature dial to "Hot." Run the hot water in a sink. If the burner doesn't light in two or three minutes, the thermostat is defective and should be replaced.
Hot water runs cold too soon (insufficient hot water)	1. Thermostat setting is too low	1. Turn setting up to "Normal" position.
	2. Lower heating element (immersion) is burned out (electric)	2. Check continuity and replace the element, if necessary, as explained above under "No hot water".
	3. Dip tube has developed holes	3. The dip tube in many units is made of plastic. It can develop holes and splits, causing cold water to spill into the top of the tank. To check, the power and water must be shut off and the tank drained. Disconnect the cold-water inlet and remove the dip tube. Replace with an exact-diameter copper tube.
	4. Tank is undersized	4. A tank can only supply so much hot water. If demand exceeds supply, the water will run cold.
Water beneath tank	1. Condensation	1. Examine other parts of a cold or damp basement. Condensation there would affirm condensation at the tank. Anyway, moisture as a result of condensation will not drip steadily as would a leak.

Problem	Causes	Procedure
	2. Leaky plumbing connections	2. Check all soldered (sweated) connections to see if they are leaking. If so, the connection will have to be resweated.
	3. Leaky immersion unit (electric) or thermostat (gas) projection into tank	3. Check flange and gasket. Replace a ruptured gasket and seal the opening with waterproof cement.
	4. Leaky tank	4. Replace the entire unit.
Cost of heating water suddenly soars	1. Leaking hot water faucet(s)	1. Replace washers in all leaking faucets.
	2. Thermostat is set too high	2. Keep the thermostat on "Normal".
	3. Scale deposits on immersion heating elements (electric)	3. Clean the elements as explained above under "No hot water".
Slow recovery (electric)	1. Top heating element of immersion unit is defective	1. Replace the element after taking a continuity test as explained above under "No hot water".
Hot water "steams"	1. Thermostat is set too high	1. Lower setting to "Normal".
	2. Thermostat contacts are burned (electric)	2. Examine terminals. If shorted and burned, replace the thermostat.
	3. Thermostat does not release (gas)	3. If the main burner fails to turn off when the temperature control is lowered, replace the thermostat.

Chapter 35

Electric and gas ranges

**Electric and gas ranges are actually simple appliances, consisting
essentially of heat sources and their controls. However, they are hazardous
and you should maintain a healthy respect for them.**

THIS CHAPTER is divided into two
segments. We begin with electric
ranges, and then discuss gas ranges.

The modern electric range utilizes
a 230-volt power supply. However,
the appliance is no more and no less
complicated than one of the cooking
appliances we discussed earlier in this
book which utilizes 115 volts.
Whether your electric range is a
built-in, free-standing, or countertop
model makes no never mind . . . the
troubleshooting information provided
here applies.

Caution: Immediately, let us again
warn you that you are dealing with
an appliance that draws a lethal dose
of electricity. Make sure the current
is turned off before you handle parts.
Make continuity tests with power *off*.
Become familiar with the wiring diagram provided by the manufacturer.
If replacement parts are needed, use
only those which meet manufacturer's
specifications. Any deviation constitutes a safety hazard.

Figure 1. Most electric ranges, like this
model, have two large cooking elements
and two smaller ones.

notes at random about electric ranges

GENERALLY, ELECTRIC RANGES have two large surface cooking elements and two smaller ones (Figure 1). The larger elements have wattages ranging from 2100 to 2600. Wattages of the smaller elements range from 1150 to 1500.

The modern range's surface elements are hermetically sealed units, consisting of nichrome resistance

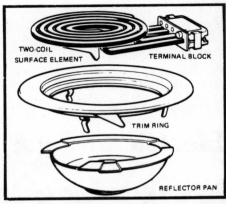

Figure 2. The heating element on top of the electric range is a sealed unit to insure maximum protection.

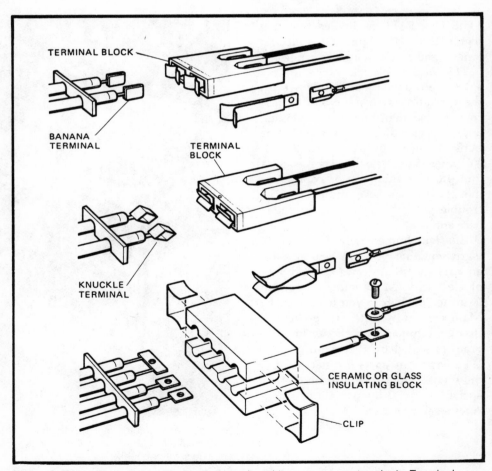

Figure 3. Elements are connected by banana, knuckle, or screw-on terminals. Terminal blocks are usually screwed onto the underside of the cooking top.

wire which is embedded in an insulation material (usually magnesium oxide) and housed in stainless-steel sheathing (Figure 2). The purpose of the insulation material is to keep the wire from touching the metal sheathing and causing a short or ground.

A single surface element possesses one or two resistance wires, and has two or four connectors, respectively. Connectors are made with one of three types of terminals. Terminals may be banana, knuckle, or screw-on (Figure 3). No matter—every surface element setup employs a terminal block which provides a positive connection between the element and its switching wires. In most ranges, terminal blocks are attached to the underside of the cooking top with screws.

The degree of heat which surface elements produce is controlled by switches. Two types of switches are in widest use. They are the step switch and the infinite-heat switch.

Step switches are rotary or pushbutton types that allow a choice of

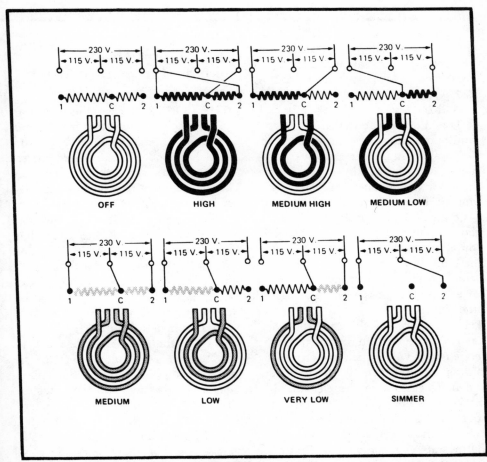

Figure 4. This wiring illustration depicts the operation of a seven-heat step system. Typical wattages would be 212 w, 287 w, 500 w, 850 w, 1150 w, 2000 w, and 2600 w.

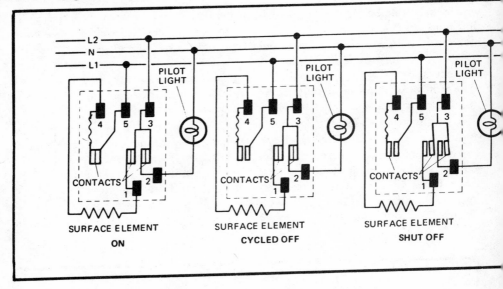

five to seven different heat settings (Figure 4). Typical wattages of a seven-setting step switch are 212 w, 287 w, 500 w, 850 w, 1150 w, 2000 w, and 2600 w.

The infinite-heat switch provides a continuous range of settings between "off" and "high." It employs a bi-metal strip which is, in reality, a thermostat like the ones discussed previously (Figure 5).

One end of the bimetal strip is anchored. The other end has a switch contact. As current passes through the bimetal and heats it up, the strip bends up and away from a cam follower strip that possesses the switch's other contact.

The position of the cam follower determines the length of time the surface element will remain on before the curling bimetal strip breaks contact and halts current to the element. In the "high" setting, the cam follower holds the contacts together without cycling. In all other positions, the thermostat-type component controls heat output by establishing the time that current is allowed to pass to the cooking element.

a word or two about electrically operated ovens

THE CONTROLS for the oven part of an electric range vary from manufacturer to manufacturer and from model to model. Some ovens possess only a thermostat, while others have in addition to a thermostat a selector switch and automatic timing clock.

A selection switch is included where an oven performs more than one function, such as broiling and baking, or if the range has more than one oven. Automatic timing clocks are connected to switches and can be tested for failure according to instructions provided in Figure 6.

As for thermostats—those generally used to regulate temperature in electric-range ovens are fluid-filled sensing bulbs similar to the bulbs on the ends of climatic thermometers (Figure 7). As the temperature increases, the fluid expands and activates a bellows that forces the contacts apart (Figure 8). This shuts off the current to the oven elements. As the temperature inside the oven de-

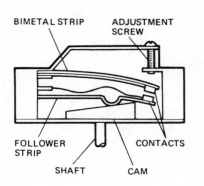

BIMETAL STRIP   ADJUSTMENT SCREW

FOLLOWER STRIP   CONTACTS

SHAFT   CAM

Figure 5. Cutaway depicts an infinite-heat switch, which provides a continuous range of settings. The bimetal strip acts like a thermostat. Current passing through the strip heats it, causing the strip to bend up and away from a cam follower strip containing the other contact of the switch. The higher the setting, the longer the surface element will remain on before the curling bimetal strip breaks contact and halts current to the element. The diagram at far left shows what happens at various stages of the process.

creases, the fluid contracts and contacts come together once again.

You can determine if the thermostat is calibrated accurately by placing a mercury thermometer in the oven and setting the thermostat for 400° F. Allow the oven to heat up, permitting the thermostat to cycle at least four times before checking temperature.

If the thermometer reads within 15° of 400°, the thermostat is properly calibrated. If not, recalibration is necessary.

Calibration instructions are normally stamped on the thermostat itself or are provided in the manual that accompanied the range. If instructions are not available, you can assume that each quarter of a turn of

Figure 6. Use this to test automatic timer. Voltage across 1 and 6 should be 115 v. If not, check for blown 15-amp fuse. If fuse is OK and motor drive doesn't turn, replace motor. Repair or replace timer if voltage is not 230 v. across terminals 1 and 4, and across 2 and 3 with timer set on manual and when timer has turned oven on in automatic mode.

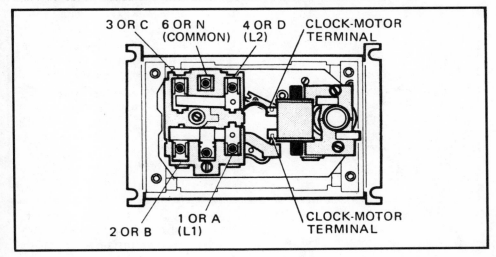

3 OR C   6 OR N (COMMON)   4 OR D (L2)   CLOCK-MOTOR TERMINAL

2 OR B   1 OR A (L1)   CLOCK-MOTOR TERMINAL

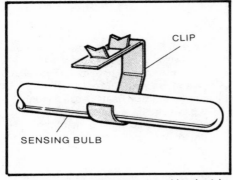

Figure 7. Most thermostats used in electric ovens have filled heat-sensing bulbs.

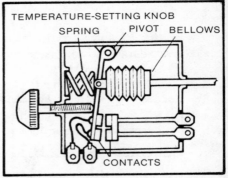

Figure 8. This cross-section shows the makeup of a bellows-type thermostat.

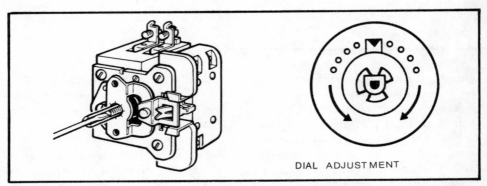

Figure 9. Thermostats are adjustable by turning either a screw or a dial. A general rule is that each quarter turn equals 25 degrees F.

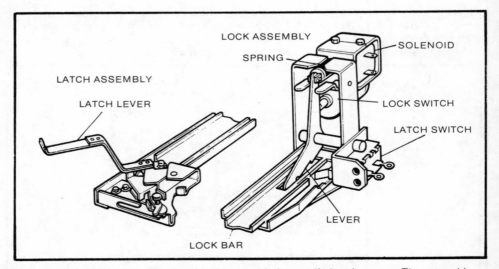

Figure 10. This is a typical latch and lock assembly for a self-cleaning oven. The assembly keeps the door locked when temperature exceeds 550 degrees F, as in the self-cleaning mode when opening the oven door could cause an explosion.

the calibration screw or dial equals 25° F (Figure 9).

Elements in the oven are similar in construction to surface elements. Broiler elements draw up to 3000 watts, while baking elements are rated at about 2500 watts.

Many modern electric ranges have self-cleaning ovens. These units possess more insulation, are made of heavier-gauge metal, have larger and more durable controls, and have a number of safety features not contained in regular ovens. They have to since they operate at temperatures in excess of 1000° F when in the self-cleaning mode.

The self-cleaning cycle utilizes the oven's thermostat, a bias circuit, and a special door-locking circuit. The bias circuit allows the thermostat to operate the oven at the higher temperatures needed for cleaning. The door-locking circuit keeps the oven door locked when oven temperature exceeds 550° F. The self-cleaning cycle will not start if the door is not locked.

The door-locking circuit is essential for safety (Figure 10). If the door is not held fast against someone trying to open it, an inrush of air mixing with carbonized soil at high temperature could cause an explosion.

Determining whether a self-cleaning oven is operating properly is a matter of observation following the cleaning process. If deposits that remain are brown and soft, cleaning did not take place. If deposits are dark brown, cleaning is incomplete. If a loose gray ash remains, cleaning has been completed.

troubleshooting an electric range

THE FOLLOWING CHARTS provide troubleshooting and repair information which will enable you to find and fix a malfunction or to be aware of what a serviceman is doing.

Problem	Causes	Procedure
Surface element doesn't heat	1. Blown fuse or tripped circuit breaker	1. Replace the fuse or reset the circuit breaker. If the same thing happens again, disconnect the power and check for shorts.
	2. Loose or shorted connection	2. Disconnect the power and tighten all connections. Replace any charred wiring.
	3. Defective switch	3. Place a voltmeter across the switch's input terminals, which are usually marked L1 and L2. You should get a reading of 230 volts. Turn the switch on and place the voltmeter across the output terminals. You should get a reading of 230 volts. Replace the switch if you don't get this reading.
	4. Defective terminal block	4. Disconnect the power and examine the inside of the terminal block. Replace if charred or broken. If the block is pitted or dirty, try to clean it with a small file. If this isn't possible, replace the block.

Problem	Causes	Procedure
	5. Defective heating element	5. If the element is a plug-in type, unplug and plug it into one of the sockets you know is working. If it doesn't get hot, replace the element. If the element is a screw-on type, pull it forward, place a voltmeter across the element's terminals and turn the element on. If you get 230 volts, but the element doesn't heat, replace the element. Make sure the replacement element is the exact size called for by the manufacturer.
Oven does not get hot	1. Blown fuse or tripped circuit breaker	1. You know what to do.
	2. Automatic timer not set correctly	2. Consult manufacturer's instructions in the owner's manual.
	3. Defective automatic timer	3. Check the timer as outlined in the text. If gears are broken or bind, replace or repair.
	4. Selector switch not set properly	4. Make sure the switch setting is correct.
	5. Defective thermostat	5. Place a voltmeter across the thermostat input terminals. You should get a reading of 230 volts. Loosen the bake or broil element and pull it toward you slightly until the terminals become accessible. Turn on the thermostat and check the voltage across the element's terminals. It should be 230 volts. Check the other element. If you don't get the correct readings, the thermostat is defective. Replace.
	6. Defective element	6. Inspect the elements for breaks or cracks. Check voltage at the terminals. If voltage is present but the element doesn't get hot, replace it.
	7. Loose or shorted wires	7. Check wires as you did above for the surface elements.
Uneven oven temperature	1. Thermostat out of calibration	1. Check and adjust as explained in the text.
	2. Defective door gaskets	2. Replace worn, flattened, or cracked door gaskets.
	3. Door out of alignment	3. Loosen door hinges and realign door. Retighten the hinges.

Problem	Causes	Procedure
Oven won't shut off	1. Defective thermostat	1. Turn off the power, pull out the bake element to reveal the terminals, set the thermostat in the "off" setting, hook up a voltmeter across the element's terminals and reconnect power. If the meter shows a reading of 230 volts, replace the thermostat.
	2. Defective automatic timer	2. Set the timer on "automatic" and turn the clock by hand until it clicks to the "off" position. There should be no voltage to the thermostat. If there is, repair or replace the timer.
Timer isn't operating properly	1. Timer not being used correctly	1. Refer to the instructions in the owner's manual.
	2. Loose connection	2. Disconnect power and tighten all connections.
	3. Defective timer motor	3. Disconnect power, remove the timer motor and test it directly with a 115-volt power source. If the drive gear doesn't turn, replace the motor.
	4. Blown fuse	4. Inspect the 15-amp fuse behind the control panel, and replace it if it's blown. If the new fuse blows, disconnect the power and check the timer for shorts as discussed in the text.
	5. Gears are shot	5. Inspect the gears for wear, breakage, and stripping. If the gears are jammed, try to free them by spraying with a silicone lubricant.
	6. Defective contacts	6. Check timer voltage as explained in the text.
Oven door drops down or won't stay shut	1. Door out of alignment	1. Realign.
	2. Worn or loose hinge pin	2. Disassemble the door, inspect the hinge pins and replace those that are worn or broken.
	3. Worn hinge	3. Replace.
	4. Broken spring	4. Replace.
	5. Broken roller bearing	5. Locate bearing. If it's possible to replace the assembly without replacing the door, do so. If not, replace the door.

electric and gas ranges

Problem	Causes	Procedure
Oven forms condensation	1. Oven is not being preheated correctly	1. Open the oven door to the first stop when preheating.
	2. Oven temperature is too high	2. Check the setting of the thermostat with a thermometer. Recalibrate the thermostat if necessary.
	3. Door is not sealing	3. Check door alignment and gaskets.
	4. Oven vent is clogged	4. Inspect the oven vents for obstructions and clean them. If the oven uses a filter, clean or replace it.
Oven lamp won't light	1. Loose or defective bulb	1. Tighten or replace with a new appliance bulb.
	2. Defective switch	2. Disconnect power, disconnect both leads going to the switch, place a continuity tester across the switch leads and turn on the switch. You should have continuity. If not, replace the switch.
	3. Bad socket	3. Disconnect power, remove the bulb, and bend the center socket outward a bit with your finger or a screwdriver. Replace the bulb and turn on power.
No heat for self-cleaning	1. Controls not set correctly	1. Consult the owner's manual.
	2. Fuse blown or circuit breaker tripped	2. You know what to do.
	3. Defective thermostat	3. See above under "oven does not get hot".
	4. Door not locked	4. Make sure door is latched. If it won't latch, check door and locking mechanism for alignment.
Cleaning is not complete (self-cleaning)	1. Controls not set correctly or cleaning time is too short	1. Consult the owner's manual.
	2. Low line voltage	2. Check voltage at the terminal block at the rear of the range. It should be within 10 percent of 230 volts. If not, call the power company.
	3. Defective smoke eliminator	3. Disconnect power and find the smoke eliminator. Disconnect its leads and place a continuity tester across the terminals. You should get a reading. If not, replace the part. Replace also if there are visible cracks in the mesh screen.

some thoughts about gas stoves

THE BEST ADVICE I can give you regarding a gas range is this: if you have trouble and your gas range operates on natural gas, call your local gas company. Most gas companies service and repair gas ranges free of charge, except for the cost of replacement parts. But if you want to tackle repairs yourself, or if your range operates on bottled gas, keep in mind that in principle a gas range works like an electric range.

The main difference, of course, is that a gas range uses a mixture of gas and air to create heat (Figure 11). Gas enters a burner from the main pipe through a small opening, called an orifice. The orifice meters out just the right amount of gas.

As gas enters the orifice, it mixes with a proportionate amount of air which enters the burner assembly through a shutter behind the orifice. In essence, the process is like the one which occurs inside an automobile carburetor.

The thoroughly mixed air/gas mixture flows to the burner, where a pilot light ignites it. When it is lit, the burner flame acts as the "ignition source" for the fuel mixture to come.

Just as an automobile carburetor must be adjusted properly to assure a correctly mixed fuel mixture and complete burning of the fuel charge, so must the burner of a gas range be properly adjusted to assure an odorless, soot-free flame. This can be done by adjusting the air shutter (Figure 12).

Shutters are held by screws. Loosen the screw to make the adjustment. With the burner turned on, open the air-shutter baffle until you get a soft blue flame. Now, slowly close the baffle, cutting off air, until the flame tips become tinged with yellow. In-

Figure 11. A gas range may seem like a simple appliance, but if possible let the gas company make the repairs.

crease the air once again until the yellow tips just disappear. Lock the baffle by tightening the set screw.

Controls of gas ranges and gas ovens are practically the same as those of an electric range. Problems that occur are also the same. Refresh your memory by going back in this chapter and re-reading the portion which applies.

Furthermore, self-cleaning ovens of gas-operated units operate exactly like self-cleaning ovens of electric ranges, with the only difference being that gas is used as the heating medium rather than electricity.

271

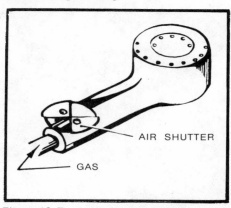

Figure 12. To obtain the proper gas-air mixture in a gas burner, simply adjust the air shutter.

troubleshooting a gas range

PRECAUTIONS you must follow to be safe are these—

1. Before you begin troubleshooting, pull out the electric plug which supplies devices such as electrically operated gas valves.

2. Turn off the gas supply. Probably you will find a shut-off valve on the main gas pipe.

3. Never use a match or any open flame to trace a leak. In fact, if you are not experienced in tracing gas leaks, you should not do it. Shut off the gas, get out of the house, and call a professional.

Problem	Causes	Procedure
Burners do not light	1. The gas supply is shut off	1. Turn on the gas.
	2. The pilot light has gone out	2. Relight the pilot.
	3. An electrical control has failed	3. Make sure you have electric power, check for a blown fuse or tripped circuit breaker, check the thermostat and timer (see the applicable data under electric ranges). Repair or replace faulty parts.
Sooty flame	1. Improperly adjusted shutter	1. Adjust the flame as described in the text.
	2. Air shutter is clogged	2. Clean and reset.

Chapter 36

Humidifiers

**Humidifiers are available in a multitude of shapes, sizes, and types.
However, from the least to the most expensive—from the smallest to the
largest—humidifiers have just one job; to dispense moisture into the air.**

ALTHOUGH IN THE WORLD of humidifier "fashion," there are innumerable varieties, each one can be placed into one of two general categories: furnace-type or room-type.

A furnace-type humidifier is incorporated right into a home's heating system. As the furnace goes on, the humidifier also goes on, discharging moisture as long as the furnace runs (Figure 1).

A room-type humidifier is a "piece of furniture," so to speak, which turns on when the humidity in the home falls below a level set by the operator and turns itself off again

Figure 1. This is a furnace-type humidifier. It turns on and off with the furnace and dispenses moisture into the air stream as long as the furnace runs.

Figure 2. Room humidifiers like this one have proven to be dependable and effective means of keeping the air moist. They are a "must" in northern homes heated by electricity.

when that level is reached (Figure 2).

The two general varieties of humidifiers vary considerably in makeup and the way in which they do their job. The problems that can affect the two, therefore, are different, too, so the approach to repairing a defective unit depends on its type.

does your home need a humidifier?

NOT EVERY HOME needs a humidifier. The need for humidification applies primarily to homes that are heated for a considerable period of time during the winter. If you live in the southern part of the country, therefore—Florida, southern California, Mississippi—you can probably do without humidification. In fact, in many parts, the need for a dehumidifier is of major importance.

But even if you live in North Dakota, Maine, Minnesota, or the like, your home's need for a humidifier depends in large measure on the type of heating system in the house. Some heating systems tend to reduce drastically the moisture content in the air to a point where it is not only uncom-

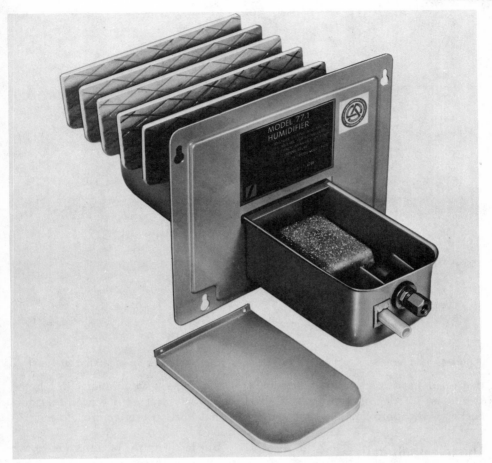

Figure 3. An evaporative-plate humidifier for installation in a furnace is, generally speaking, the least expensive of all models. Plates draw up water by capillary action.

fortable, but may be injurious to the health of the occupants.

The chief culprit is the forced-air heating system. Next in line is a home heated by electricity. The least humidity-robbing heating system of all is a hydronic system, but even a home heated by hot water or steam may need humidity added to the air.

Health experts have warned us for many years that dry air in a home during the winter is a major contributor to respiratory ailments, excessive colds, itching skin, and a "chilled" feeling most of the time.

The effects of dry air on a home itself are drastic. Cracked walls, squeaking hardwood floors, rattling doors, checkered and cracked paint, loosened furniture, peeling veneer—these and other problems affect homes and their furnishings, simply because heated air is too dry.

And there is more. It concerns the loss of energy and, consequently, of money. According to a government study, the comfort level in a home is increased one degree for every eight percent of humidity that is present in the air. Remember that for every *one*

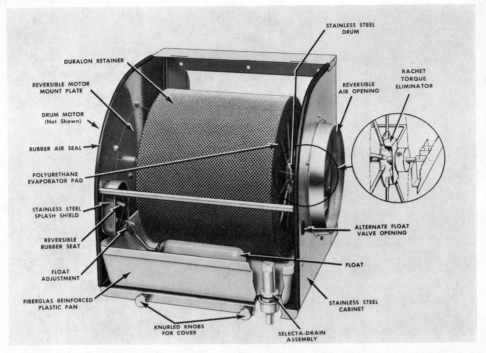

Figure 4. This furnace humidifier has a motorized drum that splashes water into air stream.

degree of heat you set your thermostat over 70 degrees, your heating cost rises by approximately three percent.

the role of air in the winter

HOW CAN ORDINARY HEATED AIR cause such damaging effects to health, property and pocketbook?

Air is like a sponge. It absorbs water. Cold air has less capacity for holding moisture than heated air. However, heated air acts like a large sponge with an insatiable appetite for moisture. In fact, heated air literally pulls moisture from everything it contacts.

Let's look at some numbers:

If the Relative Humidity Is—	Most People Feel Comfortable At—
50%	68° F
40%	70° F
30%	72° F
20%	74° F
10%	76° F

As the relative humidity in a home declines, therefore, the need for additional heat to feel comfortable is required.

But let's return for a minute to the more important aspect of dry air: health. The body is provided with a protective system in the form of mucus in the nasal passages. Germs, bacteria, and foreign matter (dust, say) entering the body as we inhale are trapped in this sticky substance. This ladened mucus moves from the nose to the throat where it can be discharged.

Under normal conditions, the system works great. But come the winter —on goes the heating system, and with it the amount of dry air. The mucus system literally can break down, because dry air absorbs moisture from the body, and mucus is moisture. Germs are left in the mucus passages to incubate and cause infection. There is now suspicion that dry

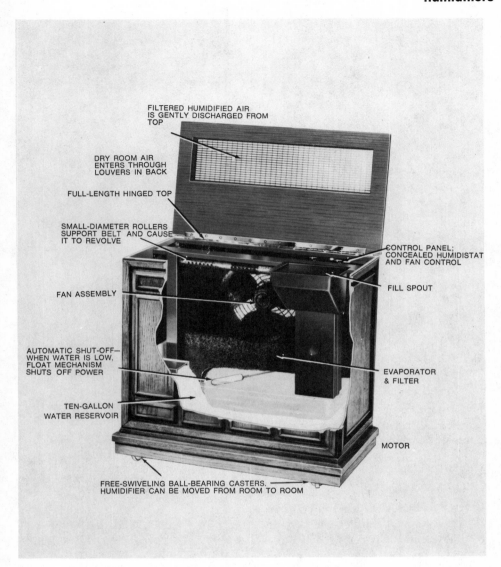

FILTERED HUMIDIFIED AIR
IS GENTLY DISCHARGED FROM
TOP

DRY ROOM AIR
ENTERS THROUGH
LOUVERS IN BACK

FULL-LENGTH HINGED TOP

SMALL-DIAMETER ROLLERS
SUPPORT BELT AND CAUSE
IT TO REVOLVE

CONTROL PANEL;
CONCEALED HUMIDISTAT
AND FAN CONTROL

FAN ASSEMBLY

FILL SPOUT

AUTOMATIC SHUT-OFF—
WHEN WATER IS LOW,
FLOAT MECHANISM
SHUTS OFF POWER

EVAPORATOR
& FILTER

TEN-GALLON
WATER RESERVOIR

MOTOR

FREE-SWIVELING BALL-BEARING CASTERS.
HUMIDIFIER CAN BE MOVED FROM ROOM TO ROOM

Figure 5. Room humidifiers are similar in design, with a large drum or belt that revolves to lift water from a reservoir into the airstream of a fan that blows air out into the room. The unit shown has a belt evaporator that is held by top and bottom rollers.

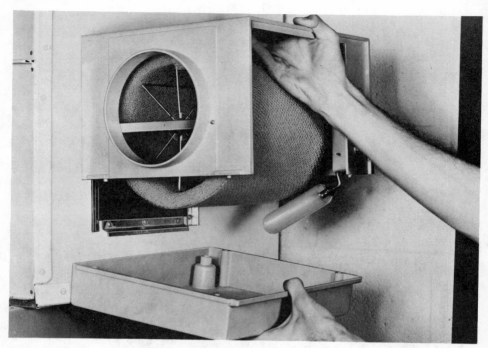

Figure 6. The most important thing to remember about furnace-type humidifiers is that they should be cleaned often. Otherwise they may clog up and become ineffective.

air, among other health difficulties, may cause infection that can lead to a loss of hearing.

the emphasis is on the term "relative"

WHAT WE HAVE JUST SAID may to some seem in conflict with one irrefutable fact: physicians often recommend that patients suffering from respiratory diseases, such as asthma, move their residences to a *drier* climate. Arizona is a favorite spot.

Right—but there is no conflict. The concern is not with humidity *per se*, but with *relative* humidity. Humidity doesn't make people comfortable or uncomfortable. Humidity doesn't make a house creak or creakless. Relative humidity is the key!

Relative humidity is defined as the amount of water vapor in the air as compared to the amount that the air can contain at a given temperature. Consider this:

The average relative humidity in the Sahara Desert is approximately 25 percent, and the average relative humidity in Death Valley is 23 percent.

The average relative humidity in many American homes not equipped with humidifiers during the winter is 13 percent! I don't have to point out that the temperature in these homes is nowhere near as high as the temperature in the Sahara or Death Valley.

what is an ideal relative humidity for a home?

WITH THE TEMPERATURE in your home at 68° F–70° F, the ideal relative humidity is 30 to 40 percent. The way to get this RH percentage, if you don't have it, is to install a humidifier.

It will put back into the air the moisture that heat steals.

Why not go ahead and increase the relative humidity to, say, 60 or 70 percent? Wouldn't this allow you to drop the thermostat further?

Yes, it would, but the consequences of too much moisture in the air aren't very pleasant either. You will create condensation problems, and with them mildew troubles. Plus other household damage, including peeling paint, and door and drawer swelling. The best balance is 30 to 40 percent RH at 68° F–70° F!

The next logical question, of course, is how can you tell if your home needs a humidifier. Forget fancy instruments. You don't need them.

If during the winter you feel chilled with the furnace thermostat set above 70° F, if everyone seems to get colds and other respiratory ailments too frequently, if you get a shock when you touch an item or another person, if your throat feels dry in the morning when you arise, and/or if you have blood in your nasal mucus—you need the services of a humidifier.

types and kinds—
one to suit every purpose

AS WE MENTIONED at the beginning of this chapter, there are two general kinds of humidifiers: furnace-installed and room. There are several variations of furnace-installed units that deserve discussion, so let's do that now.

The different kinds of furnace-installed humidifiers are the following:

1. **Evaporative plate.** These are the least expensive units. They consist of a chamber into which water enters by means of a copper line tapped off a main water line (Figure 3). Water level in the chamber (reservoir) is controlled by a float assembly which consists of a float and needle valve. When the float reaches a certain height, which is dictated by the level of water in the reservoir, the needle valve closes off the water inlet, shutting off flow. When the water level drops, and with it the float, the needle valve comes off its seat and more water is permitted to flow into the reservoir.

Another feature of a typical evaporative-plate humidifier are the evaporative plates. There are several of these, and usually they are placed one behind the other. Humidifier plates absorb water from the reservoir by means of capillary action, and moisture is "blown off" the plates by the movement of air through the furnace. The humidifier usually is mounted in the furnace plenum so moist air is circulated through the home as the furnace functions.

There are a number of disadvantages to the evaporative-plate type of humidifier, which many building contractors have installed in homes because of the units' comparative low cost. These disadvantages are (1) the output of the humidifier is not usually sufficient to accommodate the entire home; (2) the output of the unit cannot be regulated; and (3) the unit requires almost constant attention, especially in areas where hard water is a problem.

Calcium deposits which form in hard-water areas literally block up everything. Unless the unit is taken from the furnace plenum almost weekly and cleaned, which is no small task, it soon becomes clogged with crud and doesn't work.

Although there are no moving parts in a typical evaporative-plate humidifier, the water inlet becomes plugged up. When this becomes clogged, no water can enter the reservoir although the needle valve is off the seat.

2. **Vaporizer unit.** A vaporizer type of humidifier works like the portable vaporizer you use in a room where a patient with a cold or congestion is confined. Generally, the unit is mounted in the furnace plenum which contains an electric immersion element that heats the water to form steam. Steam is absorbed directly into the furnace duct and is circulated throughout the home as the furnace blower operates to circulate heated air.

3. **Atomizing unit.** An atomizing humidifier has controls that permit delivery of a desired number of gallons of moisture per day. It is installed either in the furnace plenum or in the cold-air return, depending on the model of unit that is being installed.

Water from the humidifier pan is atomized by a rotating mechanism and is thrown into the plenum or cold-air return where the moving air picks it up for circulation throughout the home.

There are variations of each of the different types of humidifiers we have just discussed. For example, one type of atomizing unit utilizes a motorized polyurethene drum that revolves and "splashes" water into the plenum or return (Figure 4). Another version has a nozzle which sprays a fine mist onto a fiberglass filter. The filter traps mineral impurities before water droplets pass into the circulating hot air.

facts about room humidifiers

ROOM HUMIDIFIERS range in size from very small units that you use in a room where someone has a head cold (small units may also be used to put humidity into a room filled with dry air—no one has to be ill) to large units that add humidity to a home.

A room humidifier (the term "room" is used here to designate large units) is designed to satisfy requirements of a home for humidity by using the principle of evaporation (Figure 5).

Inside a typical, large-size, attractive room unit is a large basin (reservoir) that is kept filled with water. This is done manually. There is no line extending from a main water line to the basin.

The second major component is a large drum to which is fitted a drum sleeve. This sleeve is made of a fibrous material which absorbs water.

The drum is positioned on two small rollers. One is a drive roller which is driven by the fan motor. The other is an idler (supporting) roller. As the drum revolves, the drum sleeve is continuously being dipped into and saturated by water in the basin.

Another important component of a room-type humidifier is the circulating fan, which is an ordinary kind with a standard motor that drives the fan blades.

The fan draws dry room air into the humidifier. The air passes through and around the saturated drum sleeve, and absorbs moisture. In addition, dust particles carried by the air are filtered out by the sleeve. This is one reason the sleeve gets dirty and begins to smell after a while. It requires cleaning, which we will discuss later. The moist, clean air passes out of the humidifier through a grille on top of the unit.

Most room humidifiers possess two controls: a humidistat and a fan control. The humidistat is a device that automatically shuts off the humidifier when the air attains the amount of moisture you have set the humidifier to provide.

The fan speed usually has two positions: low and high. The high speeds generally are used when you

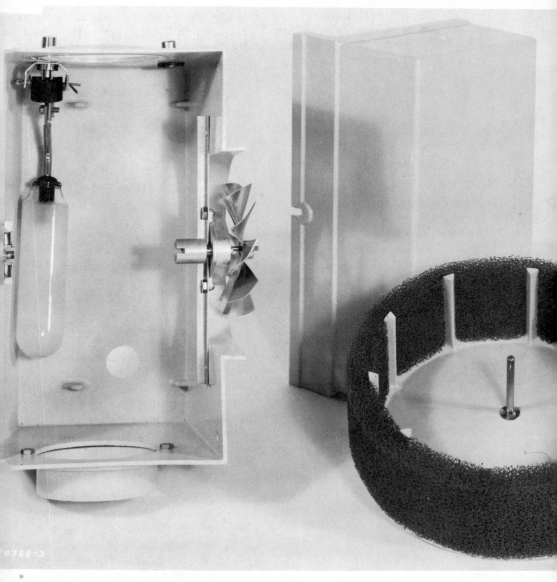

Figure 7. This shows the various parts of a typical atomizing type of humidifier, which is installed in either the furnace plenum or in the cold-air return. All of the parts require cleaning.

wish to fill your home with humid air as quickly as possible, such as when you first put a new humidifier into operation or you have had the unit turned off for a while, such as during the summer. In most parts of the country, it is not necessary to operate a humidifier during warm weather.

The low fan speed is used generally to maintain the level of desired humidity once that level has been reached.

all about buying and caring for furnace-type humidifiers

FOR A PRICE, you can have a humidifier "expert" come to your home and estimate the size of the furnace-type humidifier you should have. He does this by using a special instrument called a psychrometer, which estimates the amount of relative humidity in the home vis-à-vis temperature. His estimate also includes the size of the house and the output of moisture-producing appliances, such as washing machines and dishwashers.

You can make almost as accurate an estimate as he by using a very simple rule-of-thumb, which is this:

For effective humidification of your home during the heating season, your humidifier should be able to add one gallon of water per room per day. For example, if you live in a six-room house, the humidification unit you install in your furnace should be big enough to deliver six gallons of water per day.

As I mentioned before, it is helpful if the humidifier possesses a humidistat, as most expensive models do. This allows you to adjust the unit to deliver either more or less humidity.

One way to tell if the humidifier is producing too much moisture is to keep an eye on your windows. If the windows begin to form condensation, decrease the moisture output.

This is no problem if the unit has a humidistat. If it doesn't have a

humidistat, then you should simply turn off the flow of water to the unit by shutting off the valve controlling the water feed line.

Generally speaking, there is little that can go wrong mechanically with a furnace-type humidifier, because there are few mechanical parts. However, maintenance is all-important, because when a furnace-type humidifier fails, the cause more often than not is lack of a maintenance which has led to a buildup of calcium deposits.

Most furnace-type humidifiers should be cleaned out three times a year—more often in hard-water areas (Figures 6 and 7). The job is easily done, but since it varies somewhat from type of unit to type of unit, let us here provide you with the more important aspects of maintenance:

1. Usually to clean a furnace-type humidifier, you must remove it from the furnace. Shut off the valve on the water line feeding the reservoir and remove the humidifier from the plenum or cold-air (return) duct. Generally, the unit is held by sheet-metal screws.

2. Clean the reservoir. Sometimes this can be done just by washing the pan with a strong laundry detergent and rinsing. However, if calcium deposits have formed and do not come off, scrape them off with a wire brush or coarse steel wool. Rinse.

3. If the humidifier has a motor, as atomizing units do, consult your owner's manual, if it is available, regarding lubrication. If the owner's manual has been lost, examine the motor for lubrication points. They are often marked with the word "oil." Use an SAE 20 weight household oil, which is available in hardware stores, to lubricate the motor at each point. *Important:* Do not overlubricate.

One (or at most two) drop of oil is all that should be added.

4. If you are maintaining an atomizing unit, there may be a grille surrounding the base of the motor. Deposits that have settled on the grille usually can be cleaned off by scrubbing with an old toothbrush.

5. If you are dealing with an evaporator-plate furnace humidifier, one of the most important tasks you can perform in cleaning the unit is to make sure that the water nozzle is clear of clogging calcium. This can be done by reaming the nozzle out with a piece of wire. If that nozzle clogs up, no water will flow into the reservoir. The pan will dry out—so will the humidity in the home.

Inspect the plates of an evaporator-plate humidifier. If they are clean and intact, you can reuse them. If they are broken or covered with calcium, get new ones.

caring for a room-type humidifier

THE MAJOR FAILURE which can afflict a room-type humidifier is failure of the motor that drives the fan. This motor is similar to the ones we discuss in the chapter on small electric fans so I suggest that if the motor in your unit refuses to run that you consult this chapter.

However, motors of humidifiers which are not in operation most months of the year seldom fail.

Naturally, with a room-type humidifier you can experience a line-cord failure that would keep the unit from running. If you don't know how to handle this kind of problem this far back in this book, check back to Chapter 1.

In case of failure, also make sure the drum is properly placed on the drive and idler wheels. If the wheels become worn and fail to revolve, replace them.

There is an operational oversight to watch out for, too. Make sure the float is always in the water and not inadvertently "locked" up out of the way. A float in the "up" position will allow the humidifier to run although all the water has been dissipated. And it will cause the gauge to read "full" when it is empty.

As with furnace-type humidifiers, maintenance of a room-type humidifier is of more importance than repair, because it has to be done far more frequently. The majority of room-type humidifiers are cared for in much the same way. Here are some helpful tips:

1. Clean the drum sleeve often. If you don't, it will begin to smell.

Unplug the line cord, lift the top of the unit and lift the drum off its rollers. Allow water trapped in the drum recesses to drain back into the reservoir.

Remove the sleeve and place it in a mixture of lukewarm water and liquid dishwashing detergent for about 30 minutes. Agitate the solution every so often.

Remove and rinse the sleeve in clear lukewarm water so all detergent is removed. Shake excess water from the sleeve.

2. Empty the reservoir when excessive deposits accumulate or an odor appears. Wash the reservoir with a mild detergent and warm water.

3. Some fan motors are sealed and cannot be lubricated. Others require a few drops of SAE 20 weight household motor oil at the beginning of the season. Consult the owner's manual or look for lubrication points.

4. Apply a tiny dab of petroleum jelly (Vaseline) to the shaft of each roller before you start the humidifier for the season.

Chapter 37

Dehumidifiers

Are windows in your home hard to open and doors hard to shut? Do clothes have a musty odor? Are tools rusting? You probably need a dehumidifier. Here are important facts about this useful appliance, including how to care for it.

DEHUMIDIFICATION is, simply stated, the removal of excessive moisture from the air. Dehumidification is the opposite of humidification, which is the insertion of moisture into the air (see Chapter 36).

A home or part of a home may have to be serviced by a dehumidifier if the air is too moist, as it is in many parts of the country during warm weather. As the temperature rises, the ability of air to absorb and retain moisture increases. Air at 90° F, for example, will hold four times as much moisture as air at 50° F.

Moist air doesn't cause any known health problems as dry air might, but it can cause an infinite variety of damage to the home and its furnishings. The following summary lists some moist-air problems:
- Mildewed fabrics, luggage, and shoes.
- Sticking drawers and doors (wood absorbs moisture held by air).
- Peeling paint and wallpaper.
- Buckling wood floors.
- Sweating pipes.
- Moist basement walls.
- Deterioration of books.
- Rusting of metal items, such as tools and sports equipment.
- Swelling and warping of wood furniture and paneling.
- General mustiness.

how a dehumidifier works

DEHUMIDIFIERS designed for use in the home employ refrigeration systems that are similar to the refrigeration systems in refrigerators, freezers, and air conditioners (Figure 1). The essential parts are the same for all. They all have a compressor, evaporator coil, and condenser coil as well as other duplicating parts.

Dehumidification may also be accomplished by chemical means. A chemical with high moisture-absorption qualities, such as calcium chloride, lithium chloride, or silica gel, is placed so air will circulate over it. As air moves over the chemical, the chemical absorbs the moisture retained in the air, dehumidifying it.

Generally, though, the absorption method of dehumidification, which is also called the desiccant method, is used in commercial applications.

The principle behind the refrigeration method of dehumidification is that cool air does not hold as much moisture as warm air. Therefore, if warm air is cooled down, it must release moisture.

A simile may be drawn between the refrigeration method of dehumidification and what happens when warm air makes contact with a cold water pipe. As air meets the pipe, air cools down and releases its moisture. This action, which cools the air, produces condensation (water droplets) on the pipe.

In a dehumidifier, warm moisture-ladened air is drawn over coils through which a refrigerant is passing. The air is cooled, causing beads of moisture to form on the coil. This moisture drains off into a container, while the drier air flows through the dehumidifier and back into the room.

But let's get more specific. Dehumidification in the typical home-type dehumidifier is accomplished in the following manner:

We start at the compressor, the heart of the system. Like compressors employed in refrigerators and air con-

Figure 1. Many dehumidifiers are attractive and compact, blending into the decor. The appliance draws water from the air and prevents damage that excessive moisture can cause. The internal mechanism is similar to that of an air conditioner or refrigerator.

ditioners, the compressor in a dehumidifier is an enclosed shell that contains a pump which is powered by a sealed motor.

The compressors of the typical good-quality dehumidifiers are equipped with thermal overload protection switches that flip off if the unit overheats. This prevents the compressor from burning up. Once the compressor goes bad, you might as well buy a new dehumidifier. The cost of repair is almost the same.

The compressor pumps refrigerant through the sealed, circuitous system —that's its primary function. The refrigerant used in the typical dehumidifier is the same dichlorodifluoromethane (refrigerant 12) used in most refrigerators, freezer units, and air conditioners. It has excellent heat-transferring properties.

Refrigerant converts from liquid to vapor and back to liquid as the temperature which is brought to bear on it varies. Liquid refrigerant when put under pressure and metered through a relatively small opening in a tube will boil under relatively low temperature and convert to a gas. Vaporized refrigerant, when compressed, becomes very warm so that when it is cooled, it will more readily revert to a liquid.

• 1. During the first step of the dehumidification process, the refrigerant in vapor form is compressed by the compressor and becomes superheated. The superheated vapor is pumped through tubing into the condenser. The tubing in most dehumidifiers is made of copper and forms a connecting passageway between the compressor and other parts of the refrigeration system.

• 2. Next, the superheated vaporized refrigerant enters the condenser coil. The condenser, which in a typi-

cal dehumidifier is a steel serpentine-shaped tubing structure overlaid with fins, has the job of transferring heat from the refrigerant to the surrounding air, allowing the refrigerant to cool and revert to liquid form.

The cooling action is accomplished by an ordinary fan that blows over the condenser fins. Since the circulating air is cooler than the condenser, the air absorbs heat from the condenser.

• 3. The refrigerant, now in liquid form, enters a capillary tube as it leaves the condenser coil. The capillary tube is much narrower in diameter than the rest of the tubing used in the refrigeration system of a dehumidifier. This further drops the temperature of the refrigerant.

• 4. The liquid refrigerant, very cool now, flows into the evaporator coil where it absorbs heat from the moist, warm room air which is being drawn into the dehumidifier and over the surface of the evaporator. The evaporator of a typical dehumidifier is a circular configuration of high-thermal conductive aluminum tubing.

As the warm room air flows over the very cool evaporator, the air cools down and its ability to retain moisture is reduced. Water condenses on the evaporator tubing and drips down into a water container, which has to be emptied periodically.

Most dehumidifiers have a connection to which a length of garden hose may be attached. The hose may be extended to a drain. This setup permits detachment of the water container. It allows drainage from the dehumidifier to dissipate and eliminates the need for the homeowner to empty a receptacle (Figure 2).

• 5. As air imparts its warmth and moisture to the evaporator, it causes the refrigerant flowing through the

  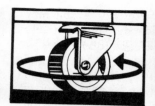 

Automatic humidity sensor keeps air at right dryness.

Signal light indicates when dehumidifier needs emptying. An **overflow switch** turns unit off automatically.

Swivel casters permit the dehumidifier to be moved about easily. This is important because unit is fairly heavy.

Drip tray catches water that drips off the coils. A hose may connect tray to drain.

Figure 2. Most dehumidifiers have one or more of the features shown on this General Electric model. Preventive maintenance of the unit is very simple.

equipment and tools, which would be ridiculous to purchase for the rare occasions when you will need them.

Your obligation, then, becomes one of doing what must be done to avert a failure. When it comes to a dehumidifier, preventive maintenance is very simple.

Every so often, with the line cord pulled from the wall, clean the dehumidifier, paying particular attention to the evaporator coil which you will see at the rear of the unit. Work a vacuum-cleaner nozzle into the cabinet as well.

However, more than anything else, the one way to protect a dehumidifier is to operate it under the temperature and humidity conditions at which it is designed to be operated. Operation under other conditions can cause serious damage.

When a dehumidifier is operated under adverse conditions, a thick layer of frost will build up on the evaporator coil. You should inspect the coil periodically to see if frost is developing. If it is, shut the dehumidifier off.

Generally, dehumidifiers should not be operated when the temperature in the area is under 65° F. However, a

evaporator to revert to vapor form. The moisture-free air returns to the room, and the vaporized refrigerant passes on to the compressor where the cycle is repeated.

how to care for a dehumidifier

AS WITH REFRIGERATORS, home freezers, and air conditioners, there is a limited number of actions you can take to repair a dehumidifier when a breakdown occurs. You are restricted primarily by a lack of proper more scientific method of establishing when you should (and shouldn't) use your dehumidifier is as follows:

1. Determine the temperature and relative humidity in the area being dehumidified using thermometers that show room temperature and humidity. These can be purchased in a department or hardware store.

2. Using the chart below, establish whether the dehumidifier should be operated. Continued operation of the appliance under the temperature and relative humidity conditions shown in the shaded areas of the chart can cause the unit to frost up.

Suppose the room temperature is 80° F and the relative humidity is 70 percent. It is safe to operate the dehumidifier. However, if the room temperature is 70° F and the relative humidity is 20 percent, operation of the appliance would cause frost on the evaporator coil and possible damage.

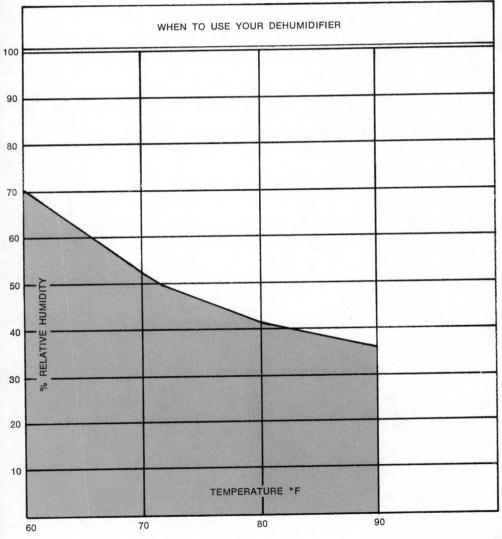

WHEN TO USE YOUR DEHUMIDIFIER

Too much humidity can, in some cases, particularly effect those who suffer from certain types of allergies.

If anyone in your family suffers from particular health problems affected by humidity, see your doctor.

The challenge is to maintain your home at the proper level of humidity by combining the effective work of both the humidifier and the dehumidifier.

In conclusion, it perhaps should be noted again that the humidity of your home can have a strong effect on your family's health (see preceding chapter on humidifiers), and that a dehumidifier can exert positive control on the quality of the air in the same sense that a humidifier can. Excess humidity can cause health problems in the same way that too little humidity can cause problems.

Chapter 38

A safety reminder

Safety precautions come first when you are working with electricity. If you forget to pull the line plug before working on an appliance, for example, your cost-saving repair may end up costing you your life.

SOME PEOPLE sneer at safety precautions. Many consider themselves rugged individuals, and sometimes they are lucky. However, many who consciously or unconsciously disregard sound safety practices suffer serious injury and death. Sooner or later the odds run out.

Safety first is nothing more than common sense. If a person, for example, doesn't know enough to disconnect an appliance from a wall outlet before probing with a screwdriver, he has no business working on any electrical device.

Common sense or not, however, it is our duty to outline here essential safety practices. It is in your best interest to follow them.

1. If you are not sure, don't do it! Refer to the section of this book that explains the procedure. If it is still not clear to you, forget it. Best call a qualified service technician.

In other words, know your limitations. If you lack tools or understanding, or if you just aren't comfortable performing an operation, leave it alone.

2. Before you even so much as lay a hand on an electric appliance, make sure the line cord is pulled from the wall outlet.

Some appliances that employ motors use capacitors that store up electricity. You should consult the unit's wiring diagram to determine if a capacitor is present.

Capacitors should be discharged before they are tested, or removed, to avoid damaging internal components and also to avoid possible shock. You can use a 20,000-ohm two-wire wire-wrapped resistor, which may be purchased in a TV supply store. Be sure the resistor part of the tool is insulated with tape. Touch the leads of the resistor across the terminals of the capacitor. This will discharge the capacitor, making it safe to handle.

Caution: Do not touch the resistor leads with your bare hands.

3. Never work on or even touch an electric appliance when it is in or around water. Be sure, too, that your hands are always dry.

4. Don't let anyone operate an appliance that is emitting a tickle or shock to the user. Unplug the unit. Test and repair.

5. Never operate an appliance that has a worn, frayed line cord or a damaged plug. Replace the cord.

6. It is best not to use an extension cord with an appliance. How-

ever, if you can't avoid temporary use of one, see that its wiring is at least as long as the appliance's line cord.

7. Never pull on a line cord. Grasp the plug to disconnect the cord from a wall outlet.

8. Ground all electric appliances. Ground all gas-operated appliances that also use electricity.

9. Before moving a gas-operated appliance, shut off the gas supply. If the appliance has to be moved beyond the limit of safety—the limit at which strain is put on the gas pipe—disconnect the pipe.

10. See that gas-operated appliances which require external venting are vented. Keep vents clean.

Chapter 39

Attic fans

The problems of an attic fan are few and easily handled. Here is what you need to know to keep it working for you during warm weather.

THE TYPICAL attic exhaust fan consists essentially of an electric motor and a large fan-blade assembly that is situated in front of louvered panels. A drive belt extends between a pulley on the electric motor and a pulley on the fan-blade assembly.

When current to the electric motor is switched on, causing the belt to rotate the pulleys and drive the fan assembly, a great volume of warm air is pulled from the home and exhausted through the louvers. The louvers are self-movable shutters that are blown open when struck by the air current created when the fan assembly begins rotating. When the fan is not operating, the louvers close, which helps to keep insects out of the attic.

Another essential part of a typical attic fan is the on-off switch. This switch is generally located in the home's living quarters, which permits the homeowner to operate the fan without going into the attic.

When a fan fails

WHEN AN ATTIC FAN malfunctions, it does so in one of two ways—

1. The unit operates when current is turned on, but the fan fails to cool the premises adequately.

2. The fan fails to operate when you switch on current.

In most instances of insufficient cooling, the cause of the trouble can be traced to an improperly adjusted drive belt or a belt that is damaged. Proceed as follows:

• Examine the belt closely on its inner surface for evidence of glaze. A glazed belt is one that slips on the pulleys, which curtails the rate of speed at which the fan-blade assembly is driven.

A glazed belt should be replaced. Furthermore, a drive belt that is frayed also should be replaced. A damaged belt is likely to snap. The electric motor will operate, but there will be no cooling.

In a typical setup, a damaged drive belt is removed by loosening the bolts which hold the electric motor. Loosening these hold-down bolts reduces tension on the drive belt, which permits you to slide the belt from the pulleys. Place a new belt on the pulleys, press back on the electric motor to tighten the belt, and secure hold-down bolts.

Caution: In obtaining replacement belts, be sure you get one that is the correct one for your unit. If you cannot establish the size of the belt, you should remove the old belt and take it with you to the appliance or hardware store which will supply a new belt.

• Determine whether the drive belt is tightened sufficiently by pressing in on the belt at a point which is midway between the electric-motor pulley and fan-assembly pulley. The drive belt should display between ¼ and ½-inch slack. If "play" exceeds ½ inch, tighten up on the belt by loosening the electric motor holddown bolts and pressing the motor back against the belt. Retighten holddown bolts securely.

In rare instances, a problem of insufficient cooling can result from the louvers failing to swing open when struck by the blast of exhausted air. This condition is easily determined by simply observing louvers with the fan turned on.

If some or all louvers fail to swing open, louver pivot points have probably rusted fast and need treatment. Turn off the fan and loosen stuck shutters by pushing them open with your hand. Apply a drop or two of SAE 20 oil (or heavyweight household machine oil) to each louver pivot point. Work oil into the pivot points by manually operating each louver by hand.

By the numbers

HERE, IN CHECKLIST order, is what you should do if your attic fan fails to operate when you turn on the switch:

1. Check the fuse or circuit-breaker box. Has the fuse or circuit-breaker protecting the attic fan circuit blown or tripped? Replace a blown fuse—reset a tripped circuit breaker. However, if the problem recurs, there is a short in the electric circuit that you should attempt to repair only if you are experienced in home electric repairs. If you are not, call a licensed electrician.

2. One electrical failure you can handle yourself is an on-off switch that goes bad. A sign of a failed on-off switch is sloppiness of the switch toggle as you activate the switch. Turn off circuit current, remove the faceplate over the switch, loosen screws and pull the switch from the switch box. Replace the switch by disconnecting it from wires.

3. If there is no trouble in the electric circuit, go into the attic and determine if the fan-assembly shaft bearings have frozen. With the fan turned off, rotate the fan assembly by hand. The blade should turn freely. There should be no binding and no noise. If the fan assembly fails to pass this test, it indicates that the bearings have probably failed. The fan assembly has to be overhauled.

Your fan assembly may require periodic lubrication of shaft bearings. The presence of a lubricating hole in or near the center of the assembly at the fan pulley would indicate this. To avert frozen bearings, be sure to lubricate the fan assembly with a drop or two of heavy household oil (equivalent to SAE 20) at the beginning and midway through the warm season.

If there is no lubricating hole, it means that the shaft bearings have been lubricated by the manufacturer and are sealed.

Caution: A fan assembly with damaged bearings may continue to rotate, but operation should not be permitted. Operation of the fan will place a undue strain on the electric motor, which may cause the motor to burn out.

4. Finally, an attic fan will fail to function if the electric motor becomes damaged internally. For information concerning how to approach this problem, refer to the chapter on Home Workshop Motors.

Chapter 40

Appliance surfaces

Many major appliances—refrigerators and freezers, clothes washers and dryers, and the like—have surfaces which are easily scratched. This chapter tells how to restore a marred surface to a like-new condition.

BEGIN YOUR REPAIR of a scratched appliance surface by going to an appliance dealer (preferably one selling the same brand of appliance as the one you are going to repair). Buy primer, finish paint, and a blending agent.

All three of these come in aerosol spray cans and are generally lacquer coatings. Get white primer if the appliance under repair is finished in a light color. Get gray primer if the appliance is finished in a dark color.

Hopefully, you will know the code number of the color which is now adorning your appliance. You may get this information from the dealer you purchased the appliance from or perhaps from the dealer who is supplying paint products. Lacking this information, you will have to select a color by eye.

In addition to the paint products, you will need Number 360 sandpaper, a sandpaper block, newspaper, masking tape, and rubbing compound (an automobile supply dealer can supply compound).

Now, to rid an appliance surface of scratches proceed in the following manner:

1. Mix kitchen liquid detergent and hot water. Wash the entire surface of the appliance. The purpose of washing is to remove wax and dirt, and restore the appliance's true finish. Follow washing with a clear-water rinsing.

2. Using a sanding block which you have outfitted with a piece of Number 360 sandpaper, sand the damaged area. It is imperative that you keep the sandpaper wet. Dip it frequently into a container of clear, cold water. Wet sandpaper keeps sandpaper grit from scratching the appliance surface.

Sand the scratch and a limited area around the scratch right down to bare metal. Then wipe away sanding dust with a clean, dry cloth.

3. Tape newspaper around the treated area to prevent spray-can overspray from getting on the finish. Chrome strips and decorative decals in the area of the damaged section should be covered over with masking tape.

4. Read the instructions-for-use on the can of spray primer. Then apply the primer. If you have never worked with primer and other spray-can paint products you should practice before applying paint to the appliance.

The spray nozzle should be held approximately 10 inches from the work surface. Do not maintain a constant spray. Rather, employ short bursts. Keep the spray can in motion at all times as spray is being applied with a smooth and moderately rapid back-and-forth stroke.

Your initial sprayburst should not be aimed directly at the work surface. Instead, aim it at a piece of masking to one side or the other, and bring the spray across the bare surface using a smooth sweep.

Apply only enough primer to cover the surface. Do not apply any more than necessary. Too much primer may run and sag, or may not provide a suitable surface to which the finish coat can take hold.

5. Allow the primer to dry to the touch. Now, with a piece of Number 360 sandpaper that you have dipped in water, lightly sand the surface. Do not sand heavily. You do not wish to remove primer. The idea is to just roughen the surface slightly.

6. Read instructions-for-use on the spray can of finish coat. Then, apply the finish. Work carefully.

To apply the finish coat successfully, make only one sweep across the surface and one sweep back. Then stop. Let the paint dry to the touch. When it has dried, make one more sweep. Stop. Wait. Follow this procedure until the freshly painted area matches the color of the surrounding surface when the fresh paint is dry.

7. The reason for applying a blending agent is to more precisely blend the fresh paint with the original finish. Read instructions-for-use on the spray can of the blending agent.

Apply the agent over the newly painted surface and also over an area which is approximately five inches on each side of the repainted surface. This extended coverage helps blend new and original finishes. Allow the blending agent to dry thoroughly.

8. Read instructions-for-use on the can of rubbing compound. Wet a clean cloth and apply a little rubbing compound to it. Using a gentle, circular motion, rub the freshly painted surface with the rubbing compound. Do not cut into the fresh paint. The purpose of the rubbing compound is to remove lint and dirt that may have embedded itself in fresh paint. Wipe off compound with a clean cloth.

Index